Available From the American Academy of Pediatrics

Achieving a Healthy Weight for Your Child

ADHD: What Every Parent Needs to Know

Allergies and Asthma: What Every Parent Needs to Know

Baby & Toddler Basics: Expert Answers to Parents' Top 150 Questions

The Big Book of Symptoms: A–Z Guide to Your Child's Health

Building Resilience in Children and Teens: Giving Kids Roots and Wings

Caring for Your Adopted Child: An Essential Guide for Parents

Caring for Your Baby and Young Child: Birth to Age 5*

Caring for Your School-Age Child: Ages 5–12

Dad to Dad: Parenting Like a Pro

Food Fights: Winning the Nutritional Challenges of Parenthood Armed With Insight, Humor, and a Bottle of Ketchup

Guide to Toilet Training

Heading Home With Your Newborn: From Birth to Reality

Mama Doc Medicine: Finding Calm and Confidence in Parenting, Child Health, and Work-Life Balance

My Child Is Sick! Expert Advice for Managing Common Illnesses and Injuries

Nutrition: What Every Parent Needs to Know

Parenting Through Puberty: Mood Swings, Acne, and Growing Pains

The Picky Eater Project: 6 Weeks to Happier, Healthier Family Mealtimes

Raising an Organized Child: 5 Steps to Boost Independence, Ease Frustration, and Promote Confidence

Raising Kids to Thrive: Balancing Love With Expectations and Protection With Trust

Retro Baby: Cut Back on All the Gear and Boost Your Baby's Development With More Than 100 Time-tested Activities

Retro Toddler: More Than 100 Old-School Activities to Boost Development

Sleep: What Every Parent Needs to Know

Waking Up Dry: A Guide to Help Children Overcome Bedwetting

Your Baby's First Year*

For additional parenting resources, visit the HealthyChildren bookstore at https://shop.aap.org/for-parents.

*This book is also available in Spanish.

healthychildren.org
Powered by pediatricians. Trusted by parents.
from the American Academy of Pediatrics

Autism
Spectrum Disorder

What Every Parent Needs to Know

2nd Edition

Alan I. Rosenblatt, MD, FAAP

Paul S. Carbone, MD, FAAP

American Academy of Pediatrics
DEDICATED TO THE HEALTH OF ALL CHILDREN®

American Academy of Pediatrics Publishing Staff

Mary Lou White, *Chief Product and Services Officer/SVP, Membership, Marketing, and Publishing*

Mark Grimes, *Vice President, Publishing*

Kathryn Sparks, *Manager, Consumer Publishing*

Shannan Martin, *Production Manager, Consumer Publications*

Amanda Helmholz, *Medical Copy Editor*

Peg Mulcahy, *Manager, Art Direction and Production*

Sara Hoerdeman, *Marketing Manager, Consumer Products*

Published by the American Academy of Pediatrics

345 Park Blvd

Itasca, IL 60143

Telephone: 630/626-6000

Facsimile: 847/434-8000

www.aap.org

The American Academy of Pediatrics is an organization of 67,000 primary care pediatricians, pediatric medical subspecialists, and pediatric surgical specialists dedicated to the health, safety, and well-being of infants, children, adolescents, and young adults.

The information contained in this publication should not be used as a substitute for the medical care and advice of your pediatrician. There may be variations in treatment that your pediatrician may recommend based on individual facts and circumstances.

Statements and opinions expressed are those of the author and not necessarily those of the American Academy of Pediatrics.

Products, Web sites, and brand names, including manufacturers and products, are mentioned for informational and identification purposes only and do not imply an endorsement of them by the American Academy of Pediatrics (AAP). The AAP is not responsible for the content of external resources. Information was current at the time of publication.

The persons whose photographs are depicted in this publication are professional models. They have no relation to the issues discussed. Any characters they are portraying are fictional.

The publishers have made every effort to trace the copyright holders for borrowed materials. If they have inadvertently overlooked any, they will be pleased to make the necessary arrangements at the first opportunity.

This publication has been developed by the American Academy of Pediatrics. The contributors are expert authorities in the field of pediatrics. No commercial involvement of any kind has been solicited or accepted in development of the content of this publication. Disclosures: The editors report no disclosures.

Every effort is made to keep *Autism Spectrum Disorder: What Every Parent Needs to Know* consistent with the most recent advice and information available from the American Academy of Pediatrics.

Special discounts are available for bulk purchases of this publication. E-mail Special Sales at aapsales@aap.org for more information.

Printed in the United States of America

9-411   2 3 4 5 6 7 8 9 10

CB0111

ISBN: 978-1-61002-269-9

eBook: 978-1-61002-270-5

EPUB: 978-1-61002-271-2

Kindle: 978-1-61002-272-9

PDF: 978-1-61002-273-6

Cover design by Daniel Rembert

Cover photograph by ESB Professional/Shutterstock.com

Book design by Peg Mulcahy

Library of Congress Control Number: 2018943108

What People Are Saying About the First Edition

Parents are craving knowledge and understanding of autism spectrum disorder and this guide is a wonderful resource to build that knowledge and encourage parents to advocate so that their child lives in a world where the dignity of every person is cherished, respected, and empowered.

> Timothy P. Shriver, PhD
> Chairman of the Board, Special Olympics

Covers a wide range of topics in a straightforward, commonsense manner, such as diagnosis, different behavioral therapies, family stress issues, and lots of other vital information. Essential reading for parents of young children with autism.

> Temple Grandin
> Author, *Thinking in Pictures: My Life With Autism*

Outstanding book and a tremendous resource for parents of children with autism spectrum disorder. It is also a must-read for anyone else working to help children with autism reach their full potential. The AAP and the book's editors, pediatricians Drs Alan Rosenblatt and Paul Carbone (who also happens to be the parent of a child with autism), know what they're talking about!

> Richard E. Besser, MD, FAAP
> Former Chief Health and Medical Editor,
> *ABC News*

Parents looking for a resource after an autism diagnosis will pull *Autism Spectrum Disorders: What Every Parent Needs to Know* off the shelf with great frequency. The AAP and Drs Carbone and Rosenblatt cover complex issues in an accessible manner. I will recommend this resource to families in need of quality information regarding services and supports for their children with autism.

> Patricia Wright, PhD, MPH
> National Director, Autism Services, Easter Seals

Autism Spectrum Disorders: What Every Parent Needs to Know is a must-read for every parent with a child on the autism spectrum. How you as a parent can help your child through play, language encouragement, structure, planning and partnering with professionals is outlined at each developmental stage from infancy through adulthood. Chapters on family relationships, your relationship with your pediatrician, and ways that you can become involved as an advocate, for both your own child and for systems change, guide and encourage. Stories from multiple families, told in their own words, describe personal experiences and coping strategies that provide hope and comfort throughout the book. Get this book—it's a complete gem!

Nora Wells, MEd
Director of Programs, Family Voices

Instead of reading like a book, going through the pages of *Autism Spectrum Disorders: What Every Parent Needs to Know* is like having a casual conversation in your living room with a guru on ASD. The chapters on family, advocacy, and resources are particularly unique and helpful. The information is accurate; comprehensive; well organized; written in a compassionate, reader-friendly style; and interlaced with inspiring stories and endearing humor. Most parents will resonate with some of the stories; many will resonate with all of them. Some stories will bring tears and smiles at the same time. It is a must-have book for parents, service providers, and advocates alike.

Chris Plauché Johnson, MEd, MA, MD, FAAP
Medical Director, Autism Community Network
Clinical Professor (Retired), University of Texas
    Health Science Center at San Antonio
Cochair, American Academy of Pediatrics
Autism Subcommittee (2003–2007)

From the Editors

We dedicate this book to the children and families who inspire, teach, and challenge us daily to seek better answers and solutions.

Dr Rosenblatt wishes to thank his parents, Roslyn and Harvey, of blessed memory, for teaching him from a young age that each child's needs are unique and for nurturing within him a curiosity about and a desire to maximize each child's fullest potential.

Dr Carbone thanks his wife, Katie, for her love, support, and understanding and also thanks Ben, for being the most wonderful son he could have ever hoped for.

On behalf of the Council on Children With Disabilities Autism Subcommittee, we honor the many contributions of our colleague and friend, Gregory Stephen Liptak, MD, MPH, FAAP (1947–2012), to the field of children with special needs.

Contents

Please Note xi

Acknowledgments xii

Chapter 1. What Is Autism Spectrum Disorder? 1

Chapter 2. What Causes Autism Spectrum Disorder? 19

Chapter 3. How Do I Know if My Child Has Autism
            Spectrum Disorder? 41

Chapter 4. Behavioral and Developmental Interventions to
            Support Children With Autism 69

Chapter 5. Tapping Educational Services 93

Chapter 6. When Other Therapies Aren't Enough: The Role
            of Medication 121

Chapter 7. The Role of Integrative, Complementary, and
            Alternative Medicine 143

Chapter 8. Partnering With Your Pediatrician 169

Chapter 9. Services in Your Community 187

Chapter 10. Accessing Care 203

Chapter 11. Adolescence and Beyond 215

Chapter 12. Putting It All Together: Everyday Strategies for
            Helping Your Child 239

Chapter 13. Autism Spectrum Disorder and Your Family 257

Chapter 14. The Future of Autism Spectrum Disorder 275

Chapter 15. Advocating for Children With Autism Spectrum
            Disorder 289

Afterword   Shana's Special Wish 297

Appendixes

A. Resources 303

B. Emergency Information Form for Children With
   Autism Spectrum Disorder 317

C. Early Intervention Program Referral Form 319

D. Medication Flowchart 321

Index 323

Please Note

Acknowledgments

Editors

Alan I. Rosenblatt, MD, FAAP

Paul S. Carbone, MD, FAAP

American Academy of Pediatrics Board of Directors Reviewer

David Bromberg, MD, FAAP

American Academy of Pediatrics Lead Staff

Kathryn Sparks
Manager, Consumer Publishing

Alex Kuznetsov
Manager, Children With Special Needs Initiatives

Medical Reviewers/Contributors

Alyssa R. Rosen, MD, FAAP

Lisa Shulman, MD, FAAP

Katharine Zuckerman, MD, FAAP

Parent Reviewers

Donna M. Johnson, MHS

Kelly King

Writer (First Edition)

Winnie Yu

CHAPTER 1

What Is Autism Spectrum Disorder?

As a PEDIATRICIAN whose son has autism spectrum disorder (ASD), I know all too well about the difficult emotions that often surround a diagnosis of ASD. My son was diagnosed as having ASD in 2004 at the age of 24 months. Before the diagnosis, we were concerned about his development, beginning in infancy. At times he seemed uncomfortable with symptoms of acid reflux, and at other times he was extremely quiet and hard to engage. While he has always made forward progress, he reached his developmental milestones later than other children. For example, as a young toddler, he had difficulty using gestures, such as pointing, to tell us what he wanted, and he didn't begin to talk until he was 24 months old.

While getting the diagnosis was painful, it ultimately helped me better understand him. It also began the process of knowing how to help him reach his potential.

Although his mother and I are pediatricians, it was difficult to adjust our expectations, just like any parents. At first, I thought about the things I did with my father that my son and I might not be able to do, such as playing sports. I later realized that although some things are challenging for him, there are many things we do together that bring us both much joy. I have learned during this journey that parenting a child on the autism spectrum is not "better" or "worse" than parenting any other child. It is simply different. My son has helped me appreciate and enjoy those differences.

We have always focused on what our son *can* do and not on what he can't. Along the way, we have tried to obtain the best therapies possible that allow him to reach even higher. As scientists, we had known that the best evidence-based therapy available for children with ASD is behavioral therapy, so we began his behavioral therapy program while he was very young. In addition to trying intensive behavioral therapy, we were open to trying complementary and alternative therapies as long as they were safe. After doing some research, we tried a few different nutritional supplements and the gluten-free/casein-free diet, understanding that there was limited evidence that these treatments would help reduce the symptoms of autism. After some time, we concluded that his progress with behavioral therapy was no better with these interventions than without them, so we discontinued them. We have continued to support him with ongoing behavioral therapy and have been delighted with his progress.

Now our son is an active participant in his community. With the support of family, friends, educators, therapists, and doctors, he enjoys many of the same activities as his peers: swimming, basketball, bowling, summer camp, reading, and discovering. All who take the time to get to know him are drawn in by his gentle demeanor, curious nature, and wonderful sense of humor.

—Paul Carbone, MD, FAAP

ə ə ə ə ə

ELLEN HAD ALWAYS TAKEN PRIDE in her son's intelligence, his expansive vocabulary, and his knowledge of dinosaurs. But at the age of 11, Brian was struggling socially. Classmates found his all-consuming obsession with dinosaurs annoying, and Brian grew impatient with them if they didn't know as much as he did about the prehistoric creatures. He had trouble understanding sarcasm from his peers. He couldn't tell when they were being mean but got overly sensitive when they weren't. He sometimes made rude, sarcastic comments during class while the teacher was talking.

Brian also behaved in unusual ways. He was always touching people when he was stuck waiting in lines, falling down at unexpected times, and making loud, inappropriate comments about people within earshot. What concerned Ellen the most was that Brian never seemed to look her in the eye while she was talking to him.

Over time, Ellen grew suspicious that something else was going on with her son, especially when she went back to college to get a degree in psychology and started doing more reading. Though he had already been diagnosed as having attention-deficit/hyperactivity disorder at age 7, she began to wonder if he also had ASD, a diagnosis that a teacher had once suggested but that Ellen had always dismissed. "He didn't fit the profile of what I thought was autism," she says. "I always thought children with autism were unattached, unresponsive, and in their own world."

Ellen had Brian evaluated by a psychologist. A screening test suggested that he had *ASD*. The more she learned about ASD, the more Ellen was convinced that Brian had it. Ellen considered whether to pursue a formal ASD diagnosis. On the one hand, she knew that with a diagnosis, Brian would be eligible for more therapy services. On the other hand, she was concerned the label would create stigma for her son. "And I'm afraid some people will look at me and think I'm a bad parent," she says.

᷃᷅ ᷃᷅ ᷃᷅ ᷃᷅ ᷃᷅

CHANCES ARE, YOU'RE FAMILIAR with some of the concerns that Ellen is facing or the difficult emotions that Dr Carbone has experienced while adjusting to his son's diagnosis. Like Ellen, you may be wondering whether you should have your child evaluated or what a diagnosis will mean for your child's life. Like Dr Carbone, you may be looking for information about where to find help for your child's social and communication challenges. Or maybe you suspect your child has ASD but haven't addressed your concern with your pediatrician yet.

We hope that reading this book will help provide you with the information you are seeking to make the best decisions for your child. In this book, you will learn how ASD is defined and diagnosed and the types of behavioral and developmental therapies available for treating it. You will learn when medications may be required and whether complementary and integrative medicine may be helpful. We also help you create a treatment team that includes your pediatrician, and we provide information to help you care for your child and get a handle on the types of services and assistance available to him. In addition, we help you understand the effect of ASD on you and the rest of your family. Stories from other parents help you understand that you are not alone on this journey. You will acquire an understanding of how ASD will affect your child as he grows older and the types of advocacy you can do as the most important member of the treatment team: the parent of a child with ASD.

≈≈ ≈≈ ≈≈ ≈≈ ≈≈

AUTISM SPECTRUM DISORDER is a biologically based neurodevelopmental disorder that affects a child's behavior and social and communication skills. For most children, this condition is chronic and requires lifelong management. The condition of some children—approximately 9%, according to studies—improves over time to a point at which it no longer meets diagnostic criteria for ASD. In general, these children are the ones who have typical learning abilities and have received early, intensive behavioral therapy (see Chapter 4). However, most children whose condition no longer meets criteria for ASD still have other developmental and behavioral symptoms.

No doubt, we certainly hear a great deal about ASD these days. A 2018 study by the Centers for Disease Control and Prevention estimated that 1 in 59 children is diagnosed as having ASD, about 1.7% of all children. Boys are 4 times more likely to be identified than girls, and white children are more often diagnosed than black and Hispanic children.

A major reason for the dramatic increase in the diagnosis of ASD has to do with changes in the way the condition is diagnosed. In 1994, the diagnosis was changed to include children with milder symptoms, including those whose language is closer to normal cognitive milestones. In addition, a growing body of research showing the importance of early, intensive behavioral treatment in helping children with ASD prompted the federal government to emphasize early detection, so more children could receive services at a younger age. The emphasis on importance of early diagnosis and intervention inspired several major public education campaigns to teach parents about ASD and the importance of early diagnosis. Because more children are now considered to have ASD, and diagnosis is occurring earlier in life, the prevalence of ASD has increased.

In spite of all the public interest in and attention on autism, figuring out whether your child has ASD is not easy. This condition is remarkably complex and difficult to diagnose. No 2 children exhibit the same symptoms, and severity varies widely. Some cases may be subtle, while others may be more straightforward. In most cases, the process of determining whether a child has ASD usually begins with parents who are concerned about their child's development. But in some cases, the early sign of ASD first comes to the attention of a pediatrician, teacher, or child care provider who observes something different in the way the child plays, learns, speaks, or acts.

> ### Can a child ever fully outgrow autism spectrum disorder?
>
> Symptoms of autism spectrum disorder vary greatly from one child to the next. While it's possible for the condition of some children—studies indicate approximately 9%—to improve to the point at which it no longer meets diagnostic criteria, most children continue to have some degree of developmental or behavioral symptoms.

We'll discuss more about diagnosis in Chapter 3. First, we'll go back in time to see how autism emerged as a major health concern.

A Brief History of Autism

Autism was first described in 1943 by Leo Kanner, MD, a child psychiatrist at Johns Hopkins University School of Medicine. It was Dr Kanner who first coined the term *autism*, borrowed from the Swiss psychiatrist Eugen Bleuler, who used the word to describe the idiosyncratic, self-centered thinking he saw in people who had schizophrenia. Dr Kanner used *autism* to describe 11 children in his practice who seemed to prefer isolation to social engagement. The children all displayed extreme aloofness and total indifference to other people. They made little eye contact and did not engage in imaginary play. Some displayed an amazing ability for rote memory.

Others were obsessed with routines, spinning toys, and mechanical objects. Dr Kanner believed that autism was an inborn disorder and that children with this condition entered the world without biological underpinnings for social interaction. These were children who lived in their own world. Even today, Dr Kanner's descriptions of autism are highly regarded and considered some of the best ever written.

In the 1950s, Freudian psychoanalysts put a new spin on autism, contending that the condition resulted from the emotional withdrawal of a baby born to a cold and emotionally distant parent. In particular, they focused on mothers and called these parents "refrigerator mothers." Bruno Bettelheim, PhD, then the director of the Orthogenic School in Chicago, became fascinated with children who had autism and advanced this theory. (Dr Bettelheim had a doctor of philosophy but was widely cited as a child psychologist. He lectured on psychology at the University of Chicago, despite the lack of any formal training.) Dr Bettelheim's most famous patient was a boy named Joey, whom he described in 1959 as a "mechanical boy" in the popular magazine *Scientific American*. At 18 months of age, Joey was unable to speak and was described by his grandparents as "remote and inaccessible." Joey became fascinated with mechanical objects and learned to take apart and reassemble an electric fan. By the age of 4, Joey was spending a great deal of his time rocking back and forth and becoming completely consumed with mechanical objects.

Like many of his colleagues at the time, Dr Bettelheim attributed Joey's unusual behaviors to his parents. Dr Bettelheim claimed that their "aloof" parenting style forced Joey to withdraw into his own world

Fascinating Fact

Donald Triplett, the first child cited in the now-famous report on autism by Leo Kanner, MD, was profiled in *The Atlantic* in October 2010. At the time, he was 77, living in Forest, MS. Although he faced many challenges throughout his life, he was embraced by his community and enjoyed doing activities such as playing golf. Read his story online at www.theatlantic.com/magazine/archive/2010/10/autisms-first-child/308227.

Early Signs of Autism Spectrum Disorder

Social Differences

- Resists snuggling when picked up; arches back instead
- May have temperament differences during infancy, such as being described as a "very quiet" or "very fussy" baby
- Makes little or no eye contact
- Shows no or less expression in response to parent's smile or other facial expressions
- May avoid following a parent's gaze or finger to see what parent is looking at or pointing to
- No or less pointing to objects or events to get parents to look at them
- Less likely to bring objects to show to parents just to share his interest
- Less likely to show appropriate facial expressions
- Difficulty in recognizing what others might be thinking or feeling by looking at their facial expressions
- Less likely to show concern (empathy) for others
- Difficulty in establishing and keeping friendships

Communication Differences

- Less likely to say single words by 15 months of age or 2-word phrases by 24 months of age
- May repeat exactly what others say without understanding its meaning (parroting, or echolalia)
- Responds to sounds (such as a car horn or a cat's meow) but less likely to respond to name being called
- May refer to self as "you" and others as "I" (pronoun reversal)
- Shows no or less interest in communicating
- Less likely to start or continue a conversation
- Less likely to use toys or other objects to represent people or real life in pretend play
- May have a good rote memory, especially for numbers, songs, television jingles, or a specific topic
- May lose language milestones, usually between the ages of 15 months and 24 months in some children (regression)

Early Signs of Autism Spectrum Disorder (*continued*)

Behavioral Differences (Stereotypic, Repetitive, and Restricted Patterns)

- May rock, spin, sway, twirl fingers, or flap hands (stereotypic behavior)
- May prefer routines, order, and rituals
- May be obsessed with a few activities, doing them repeatedly during the day
- More likely to play with parts of toys instead of the whole toy (for example, spinning wheels of a toy truck)
- May have splinter skills, such as the ability to read at an early age but often without understanding what it means
- May not cry if in pain or seem to have any fear
- May be very sensitive or not sensitive at all to smells, sounds, lights, textures, and touch (sensory processing differences)
- May have unusual use of vision or gaze (for example, looks at objects from unusual angles)
- May have unusual, or intense but narrow, interests

and marked the beginning of his descent into schizophrenia. In fact, autism was classified as a form of childhood schizophrenia in the first 2 editions of the *Diagnostic and Statistical Manual of Mental Disorders* (*DSM*), a manual published by the American Psychiatric Association to provide diagnostic criteria for behavioral conditions.

Dr Bettelheim's views persisted for years until experts began to consider autism from more biological perspectives. In 1964, a research psychologist named Bernard Rimland described infantile autism as a neurological disorder with a strong genetic component. Rimland and his wife were personally acquainted with autism—they were the parents of a child with autism, which they had diagnosed themselves.

Studies in the early 1970s showed that despite causing similar symptoms, autism was a disorder distinct from childhood schizophrenia. In 1977, the first study of twins and autism was published in the *Journal of Child Psychology and Psychiatry*. The study showed a strong genetic influence in

What Autism Spectrum Disorder Might Look Like

It isn't always easy for parents to know whether a child has autism spectrum disorder (ASD). Some of the symptoms of ASD may be seen in children with other types of developmental or behavioral problems or, to a lesser extent, in children with typical development. Also, not all the symptoms are seen in all children. Some children may display only a few of the symptoms. This is what makes the process of diagnosing ASD difficult. But here are some examples that may help distinguish a child with ASD from other children.

At 12 Months of Age

- A child with typical development will turn his head when he hears his name.
- A child with ASD might not turn to look, even after his name is repeated several times, but will respond to other sounds.

At 18 Months of Age

- A child with delayed speech skills will point, gesture, or use facial expressions to make up for her lack of talking.
- A child with ASD might make no attempt to compensate for delayed speech or might limit speech to parroting what is heard on television or what she just heard.

At 24 Months of Age

- A child with typical development brings a picture to show his mother and shares his joy from it with her.
- A child with ASD might bring her a bottle of bubbles to open but doesn't look at his mom's face when he does or share in the pleasure of playing together.

identical twins who had autism. If one twin had autism, the other twin was much more likely to have other cognitive differences too. Finding a genetic connection to autism meant that autism needed to be described more precisely so it could be properly studied and better understood. That became possible in 1980, when "infantile autism" finally received its own separate category in the third edition of *DSM*.

Defining Autism Spectrum Disorder Today

Even since the most recent edition of this book, the definition of ASD continues to evolve. The newest version of the diagnostic manual of behavioral disorders, the *DSM-5*, was published in 2013. We have therefore eliminated a more extensive discussion of the definition used in *DSM-IV* in order to focus on current standards. In short, the disorder remains essentially unchanged, but how it is classified and described is different.

> **My son is 20 months old and was developing typically until recently. Someone suggested he might be regressing developmentally, which may be a sign of autism spectrum disorder. What does that mean?**
>
> Regression occurs in about 33% of children with autism spectrum disorder (ASD). These children may appear to develop typically, then experience a gradual or sudden loss of social or communication skills without a change in their motor skills. Studies suggest that this is most likely to occur between 18 months and 24 months. They may stop talking if they've already started using words and may stop turning their heads when their names are called. They may withdraw into their own world and may appear more distant and less interested in their surroundings. They may become more irritable. For parents, the abrupt change is alarming.
>
> A close look at children's behavior before diagnosis shows that some of the delays in developmental milestones might have been present before regression, at least to a mild degree. When researchers looked at past home videos of these children at their first birthday parties, they saw subtle signs in some children before regression became obvious and ASD was detected. The most common sign they noticed was that these children did not consistently turn their heads when their names were called.

The New Definition of Autism

In the new *DSM*, the *DSM-5*, a single diagnostic category of ASD replaces the category of "pervasive developmental disorders" from *DSM-IV*, including autistic disorder, Asperger syndrome, pervasive developmental disorder–not otherwise specified, and childhood disintegrative disorder. The *DSM-5* provides a simplified way of defining autism.

To be diagnosed as having ASD per the *DSM-5*, a child must have problems in 2 main areas: social forms of communication, and restrictive or repetitive behaviors and interests. More specifically, these are

- Persistent struggles with social communication and social interactions in various situations that cannot be explained by other developmental delays. These may include problems with give-and-take in normal conversations, difficulties in making eye contact, a lack of facial expressions, and difficulties in adjusting behaviors to fit different social situations.

- Obsessive and repetitive patterns of behavior, interests, or activities. These may include unusual and constant movements, strong attachment to rituals and routines, and fixations on unusual objects and interests. These may also include sensory abnormalities, which have always been commonly seen in children with ASD but were not used previously to diagnose ASD. Children with sensory abnormalities may be hypersensitive to certain sounds, textures, or lights. They may also be unusually insensitive to things in the environment that usually cause pain, heat, or cold.

The new criteria note that symptoms must begin in early childhood and disrupt a child's day-to-day functioning. In addition, diagnosis must take into account an individual's age, stage of development, intellectual abilities, and language level.

If you have any concerns about the diagnosis your child receives or questions about *DSM* classification or terminology, talk with your child's pediatrician.

What We Know and Don't Know About Autism

We're a long way from the days when Dr Bettelheim pointed to parents for a child's autism. We now know that it is a neurodevelopmental disorder, something that occurs in the early formation of the brain. We also know the importance of early diagnosis and treatment and now have the tools to help us determine whether a child has or is at risk for ASD. To that end, organizations such as the Centers for Disease Control and Prevention and the American Academy of Pediatrics have waged successful public awareness campaigns such as "Learn the Signs. Act Early." (www.cdc.gov/actearly) to promote surveillance and screening that leads to early diagnosis. This has made early treatment possible for the benefit of millions of children. In addition, we know that certain therapies are more effective than others at treating symptoms.

For example, developmental and behavioral interventions are the mainstay of supporting individuals with ASD. Behavioral interventions focus on changing specific behaviors and symptoms. As these behaviors change, social relationships and mastery of basic developmental capacities improve. There are several different types of behavioral interventions (see Chapter 4). Studies have consistently shown that children with ASD who use intensive and systematic behavioral principles to reinforce developmentally appropriate skills from a young age have improved social communication, intelligence, language, behavior, and self-help skills when compared with children with ASD who do not.

Throughout this book, we discuss resources and services available today that did not exist just a few years ago and provide strategies on how to access them. People with special needs are more widely accepted in today's society, and the desire to include them in family and community life has opened doors and allowed them to participate in activities and go to venues that were previously inaccessible. It has been shown that reported quality of life for adults with ASD is determined more by the presence of family and community supports than by the characteristics of the disability. Children born with ASD today have greater hope for full and rewarding lives than they ever did in previous generations.

Even so, there are still many unknowns. Although it is now clear that ASD has many different causes, some of which can be identified, in many cases a precise cause is not determined. In addition, all children with ASD are unique, so no single treatment works for every child. While scientists do know that the rate of ASD diagnosis is rising rapidly, they have yet to figure out the rate at which ASD itself is increasing. The search for answers has led to unfounded theories and unproven remedies.

Take vaccines. Research shows that almost 20% of parents worry that vaccines are not safe for their children and might lead to health problems such as autism or diabetes. In particular, some people worry

My friend says her sister cured her son of autism with the gluten-free/casein-free diet. Should we try it?

Although the American Academy of Pediatrics does not endorse the gluten-free/casein-free (GFCF) diet, it does understand that some parents may want to consider trying it. Before doing so, it's important to discuss your child's nutritional needs with your pediatrician. For instance, a diet without casein restricts the amount of calcium and vitamin D a child gets and puts her at risk for osteoporosis later in life. Therefore, it's essential to find other ways to meet your child's needs for calcium, vitamin D, and iron. You also have to make sure your child meets her caloric needs. Your pediatrician might refer you to a registered dietitian.

Before your child goes on the GFCF diet, make sure to identify target behaviors and how you will measure changes in those behaviors. By doing so, you will be able to gauge whether the diet is working. Finally, make sure to keep your child's food preferences and routines in mind. Children with ASD are often resistant to change. And your child may not like the idea of eating foods that are different from what she's used to eating and what the rest of the family eats. You may need to use behavioral strategies to get her to eat new foods. If your child has improved irritability or intestinal symptoms but no change in symptoms of ASD, it may be that she has a common intestinal problem such as lactose intolerance.

about the measles-mumps-rubella (MMR) vaccine. Their belief is bolstered by the fact that regression in children who are later diagnosed as having ASD might occur weeks to months after the MMR vaccine is given. The timing has led many parents to mistakenly assume a cause-and-effect relationship between the MMR vaccine and ASD. Research has long since shown that vaccines do not cause ASD, but unfortunately, some parents still have vaccine concerns. (For more detailed information, see Chapter 2.)

Many people also worry about thimerosal, a mercury-based preservative used in vaccines to prevent bacterial contamination. That fear has also been proven false. Since 2001, most routine children's vaccines made in the United States have had no thimerosal, except for some flu vaccines. But the rate at which ASD has been diagnosed has continued to climb.

The search for a cause has also led to theories about abnormalities in the gastrointestinal (GI) tract that cause changes in the brain. The belief that ASD is a GI disorder has given rise to nutritional therapies that have limited scientific backing.

Of particular interest has been the gluten-free/casein-free diet. This diet is based on the belief that gluten (a molecule found in barley, rye, oats, and wheat) and casein (a molecule found in milk products) cause substances produced by these foods to enter the bloodstream and travel to the brain, triggering symptoms we see as ASD. You'll find more information on nutritional therapies and other alternative remedies in Chapter 7.

The Bottom Line for Parents of Children With Autism

As the parent of a child who has ASD—or a child whom you suspect has ASD—you probably want to learn more about ASD. In this book, we do our best to provide you with the most up-to-date facts and information about ASD. We also share stories from other parents, who are often the best sources of information as well as emotional support. Our goal is to empower you with the knowledge you need as you embark on this journey with your child. We encourage you to partner with your child's doctor, who can help you every step of the way. Armed with the appropriate facts and information, you will be able to make the best possible choices for your child given our current knowledge and understanding.

Autism Champion: Carmen Pingree

BACK IN 1979, when Carmen Pingree's son Brian was diagnosed as having autism, 95% of children with autism were institutionalized. The only program for children with autism near their home in Salt Lake City, UT, had 4 students in it, with 12 on a waiting list. And getting a diagnosis typically took years.

Even getting answers for Brian had been a struggle despite all the classic signs—Brian rocked for hours at a time, ignored the affection and attention of his family, and became fascinated with windshield wipers, heights, and lights. He had a penchant for unscrewing objects and undoing latches and locks. Experts labeled him "abused," "emotionally disturbed," and "mentally retarded."

When he was nearly 4 years old, he was finally diagnosed, much to Carmen's relief. "We finally had a name for what we were dealing with," she says. "We read books, attended conferences, met other parents, and found a small behavior therapy program with young dedicated professionals. The information lowered our frustration and gave us tools to work with Brian at home until we could find a way to expand the preschool program."

Together with other parents, Carmen obtained a school building that was being closed. Then she turned her energies toward getting funding from the Utah state legislature. She went back to college to get a master's degree in special education and political science, a perfect melding of the task that lay ahead. She invited legislators to visit the program, learn about autism, and hear budget requests over lunch.

Her husband and even her other 4 children got involved in the effort, which ultimately succeeded in securing funds for autism services in Utah, including the preschool program, an adolescent teaching home, and a residential treatment program.

Carmen didn't just lobby. She also began to pursue federal and community funding for autism research and helped create a 5-year joint epidemiological and genetic study between the University of Utah and the University of California, Los Angeles. Through the years, she became an autism research consultant for Stanford University and

Utah State University, the president of the Autism Society of Utah, and a frequent lecturer and researcher whose studies have appeared in numerous scientific journals.

When a new building was constructed in 2003 for the expanded preschool program (which by then included elementary-aged children with autism), it was named the Carmen B. Pingree Center for Children with Autism and recently renamed to the Carmen B. Pingree Autism Center of Learning. An active research site, the center also offers support for parents and siblings of children with autism spectrum disorder (ASD) and serves as a training ground for graduate students specializing in ASD, as well as pediatric and psychiatry residents.

Brian is in his forties now, but Carmen continues to advocate for families with children with ASD and serves on the advisory board of the center as well as the board of the program where her son resides. "Brian enjoys his role as uncle to the 20 Pingree grandchildren," Carmen says. "The whole family continues to involve Brian in their lives and to support programming for individuals with autism. They consider these opportunities for service a great blessing in their lives."

CHAPTER 2

What Causes Autism Spectrum Disorder?

CHANCES ARE, you had already known someone with autism spectrum disorder (ASD) before you learned or suspected that your child has ASD. Or maybe you had known someone who worked with children and adults who have ASD. The number of children identified with ASD has been rising steadily in recent decades. In the 1940s when Leo Kanner, MD, first described ASD, he thought it was a rare disorder that few doctors would encounter within the span of their careers. By 1990, it was still considered somewhat rare, identified in roughly 1 in 1,000 children. The modern realization that ASD is a more commonly occurring neurodevelopmental disorder was brought to light by a group of parents in Brick Township, NJ, in the 1990s. Believing they were seeing more cases of ASD in their community, they convinced a group from the Centers for Disease Control and Prevention (CDC) to investigate. The findings of the investigation identified an estimated 1 in 150 children in the Brick Township with ASD and led the CDC to establish a national network of sites to compare how common ASD was in other parts of the country. From data collected in 2000, this group of programs, known as the *Autism and Developmental Disabilities Monitoring (ADDM) Network*, found a similar estimate (1 in 150) after reviewing records of children in 14 communities across the United States. Since then, the ADDM Network has estimated how common ASD is in US children on 6 subsequent occasions and for the most part has reported a steady increase in cases of ASD. The most recent estimate from data collected in 2014 is that 1 in 59 children has ASD. While the CDC reviews medical and educational records to arrive at these estimates, parents across the United States have provided information through the National Survey of Children's Health, which was conducted by the Maternal and Child Health Bureau by interviewing parents in 2016. In that survey, parents reported that 2.5% of US children and adolescents aged 3 to 17 years had ASD. Clearly, ASD has become a major issue, one that prompted the CDC to declare it to be "an urgent public health concern."

The reasons for the 150% increase in cases of ASD since 2000 remain open to debate. Some of it can be traced to greater public awareness of the disorder and the development of screening tools that have helped parents and health care professionals alike to be more adept at identifying children with ASD. Changes in the diagnostic criteria that broadened the definition of ASD over the past 30-plus years have also contributed to the increase. Since 1980, when "infantile autism" first appeared in the third edition of the *Diagnostic and Statistical Manual of Mental Disorders (DSM)* as its own separate entity, criteria have been expanded to include milder cases of the condition such as pervasive development disorder–not otherwise specified (added in 1987) and Asperger syndrome (added in 1994). The current criteria for ASD, published in 2013 in the fifth edition of the *DSM*, seemed to narrow the criteria from that of the previous edition, although when the CDC compared how common ASD was in 2014 using both sets of criteria, the estimates were the same.

An increase in the availability of behavioral therapy and educational supports for children with ASD may also factor into the increase. For example, many insurance plans now cover a variety of ASD-specific therapies that were previously not covered, prompting more families and health care professionals to pursue ASD diagnosis to access these beneficial interventions. Something called *diagnostic substitution* has also been identified as another reason for the increase. This may have begun with the passage of the Individuals with Disabilities Education Act (IDEA) in 1990 when autism became recognized as one of the classifications that enabled children to access the special education program. Once autism was recognized as an educational classification by IDEA, the number of children within other categories such as "intellectual disability" or "emotional disturbance" decreased, while the number of children under the autism classification increased.

But some experts have concluded that these factors account for only some of the increase. Changes in how ASD is diagnosed, for instance, could explain only 25% of the rise in ASD cases in California between 1992 and 2005, according to a study from Columbia University. That would mean that 1 in 4 children diagnosed as having ASD today would not have been given that diagnosis in 1993. On the other hand, a recent study from England estimated the rate of ASD in adults to be like that of children. This would seem to indicate that the true risk for developing ASD is not increased for today's children. So while some recent events explain why ASD diagnosis is made more often, there is still vigorous debate as to whether the true risk of a child having ASD is increasing. For example, some experts point to changes in exposure to environmental toxins as possibly being linked to increases in the risk of ASD.

As part of this discussion, it's important to appreciate the difference between *an increased risk* for ASD (such as older age of parents) and what *causes* the condition (that is, certain medical and genetic syndromes). A *risk factor*, such as parental age, does not directly cause ASD but makes it more likely for the child to have ASD compared with those without the risk factor. The increased risk for ASD means that parental age is probably one factor among many that may contribute to the child's diagnosis but by itself may not be the cause. In children with congenital rubella syndrome (see the Other Environmental Exposures section on page 32 later in this chapter), an infection during the mother's pregnancy with the rubella virus causes the ASD, whereas in children with fragile X syndrome (see the "Fragile X Syndrome" on page 25 later in this chapter), the cause of the ASD is an expansion of a particular sequence of DNA on the X chromosome.

Challenges of Autism Spectrum Disorder

We are just beginning to learn about what causes ASD. In about 15% of children with ASD (according to studies using older genetic diagnostic technologies), the condition is associated with a clear underlying cause such as a chromosome abnormality, a genetic syndrome, or a known environmental exposure. In most children, however, the underlying cause of ASD is not obvious.

What we do know about ASD is that it is a biologically based neurodevelopmental disorder with strong genetic influences and a growing number of environmental risk factors. In short, ASD is the result of something that occurs during early development of the brain. Exactly what triggers the event (or events) in the brain is still not fully understood. Scientists are fairly certain that autism is the result of complex interactions between genetic risk and environmental exposure, which vary from child to child. Variations in genes that increase ASD risk are being identified at a rapid rate, along with the identification of environmental risk factors. One thing scientists are certain about: ASD comes in many forms and has multiple causes. Understanding the causes of ASD has been a major research challenge that is still only partially understood.

Genetics of Autism Spectrum Disorder

To understand hereditary influences on autism, it helps to have some basic knowledge of genetics. Genetics is the study of heredity, the passing on of cellular instructions from parents to their offspring, which determine traits of the offspring such as hair color, eye color, and height. All our body cells have 46 chromosomes—2 sex chromosomes and 22 pairs of nonsex, or autosomal, chromosomes. We inherit half our chromosomes from each of our parents. Chromosomes are made up of DNA, which is shaped like a double helix, or spiral ladder. Genes are the units of DNA that code instructions for making proteins that enable each cell to do what it's assigned to do. In other words, genes provide body cells with instruction manuals on what they need to do to make our bodies function. Changes in DNA can affect how genes work. A change or variation in an individual gene, called a *mutation*, can lead to certain diseases and disorders.

Scientists have known for decades that genetic makeup plays an important role in the development of ASD. Identical twins, who share the same genes, are significantly more likely to both have ASD than fraternal twins, who share fewer genes. Furthermore, the rate of ASD in siblings is much higher than the rate in the general population. According to a study published in 2011, about 19% of younger siblings of children with ASD were diagnosed as having ASD. Recent studies

Brain Structure Differences in Children With Autism Spectrum Disorder

Children with autism spectrum disorder (ASD) have distinct differences in their brain that are less likely to be seen in children without ASD. And while these differences don't explain the cause of ASD, they may help account for some of the differences in social communication, temperament, and motor skills that children with ASD often have.

Among the key differences are

- Larger than normal head size, also known as *macrocephaly*, seen in up to 16% of young children with ASD.
- Greater total brain volume.
- Fewer number of Purkinje cells in the cerebellum. Purkinje cells are large neurons in the brain that are responsible for coordinating motor skills. Recent studies have shown that they are also involved in language, attention, and mental imagery.
- Differences in maturation of the forebrain limbic system. The limbic system is made up of several brain structures, including the hippocampus, amygdala, thalamic nuclei, and limbic cortex. These structures are associated with emotion, behavior, long-term memory, and smell.
- Differences in the frontal and temporal lobes. The frontal lobes are involved in various aspects of higher cognitive functioning, control of emotions and behavioral impulses, and the ability to transform thoughts into words. The temporal lobes play an important role in auditory perception and processing, visual processing, and the formation of long-term memory. Sensations of touch and taste also seem to be integrated with memory in the temporal lobes.
- Brainstem differences. The brainstem connects the brain to the spinal cord. It carries sensory signals from the body to the brain and motor signals from the brain back to the rest of the body. The brainstem is also involved in regulating cardiac and respiratory functions, the sleep cycle, and consciousness.

Brain Structure Differences in Children With Autism Spectrum Disorder (*continued*)

- Differences in the neocortex. The neocortex is the thin outer layer of the brain involved in higher functions such as sensory perception, generation of motor commands, spatial reasoning, conscious thought, and language. Differences in formation of this region of the brain are also associated with intellectual disability and seizures.

Scientists know that many of these brain structures are formed during the first 2 trimesters of pregnancy. As a result, experts suspect that environmental influences that may contribute to the development of ASD are most likely those that occur to the mother early in her pregnancy. Furthermore, newer brain imaging techniques suggest that there are differences in the connections between different parts of the brain of individuals with ASD. Future research will help us understand the nature of these connections and how they affect the function of the brain in a manner that leads to symptoms of ASD.

suggest that between 64% and 91% of the risk of a child developing ASD is related to inheritance. And biological sex plays an important role too, as boys are more likely to have ASD than girls. In the 2011 study, approximately 1 in 4 younger male siblings developed ASD, whereas 1 in 11 younger female siblings were diagnosed as having ASD by the age of 3 years. In its 2018 report, the CDC estimated that boys were 4 times more likely to be identified with ASD compared with girls.

Experts know, too, that many variations in genes are linked to ASD, not just a single change (as there is in, say, children with sickle cell anemia); none of these are in all children with ASD. Some children with ASD have genetic variants that are inherited from their parents, and other changes occur from spontaneous mutations that are not inherited from either parent. These variations most often involve small deletions and duplications of genetic material, called *copy number variants*. Other changes involve a small change to the genetic code rather than a duplication or deletion. Other genetic causes of ASD are part of other types of chromosomal changes that are primarily linked to underlying genetic syndromes. For example, fragile X syndrome is caused by small changes to the X chromosome (one of the sex chromosomes) and about half of children with this condition have ASD. To demonstrate how many different genetic causes there are for ASD, any one genetic change that has been currently described accounts for no more than about 1% of all cases of ASD. Using today's genetic testing technology, the American College of Medical Genetics and Genomics estimates that a genetic evaluation would be expected to demonstrate the cause of ASD in 30% to 40% of children with ASD.

Genetic Disorders and Autism Spectrum Disorder

Some people diagnosed as having ASD have known genetic changes in a single gene that result in a specific genetic syndrome. Not every child with one of these disorders has ASD, but having one of these genetic syndromes raises the likelihood that a child also has ASD. A partial list of the many genetic syndromes associated with ASD follows.

Fragile X Syndrome

Fragile X syndrome (FXS) is a genetic condition that affects the X chromosome and is passed down on the mother's side. It is the most common genetic cause of intellectual disability in boys. Because boys have only one X chromosome, they are affected more severely than girls. Boys with FXS may have distinctive physical features that may include having an unusually large head, unusually large ears, and unusually large testicles (after puberty). Children with FXS may also have weak muscles and loose joints. As many as 50% of people with FXS will have ASD.

If your child has ASD and either intellectual disability or global developmental delays (meaning your child isn't reaching all the developmental milestones that are expected at different ages), if your child has the physical features of FXS, or if there is a history of intellectual disability in the family, testing for FXS should be done.

Rett Syndrome

Rett syndrome occurs primarily in girls and usually appears sometime in the first 24 months after birth after a period of normal development. Girls with Rett syndrome typically lose control of hand skills and develop hand-wringing movements. They also develop difficulties in walking, slowed head growth, seizures, and trouble with social skills.

Thanks to DNA sequencing, Rett syndrome can be diagnosed in more than 90% of cases. Girls with ASD, especially those who have the characteristic hand movements, can be considered for Rett Syndrome testing.

Tuberous Sclerosis Complex

Children who have tuberous sclerosis complex (TSC) have benign tumors in the brain, the skin, and other organs. The condition is often associated with recurrent seizures and developmental delay. The link between ASD and TSC is strong—as many as 25% of children with this condition have ASD.

Angelman Syndrome

Angelman syndrome affects 1 in 15,000 children. Children who have this disorder have intellectual disability, an unsteady gait, atypical laughter, seizures, and distinctive facial features. The condition is often overlooked as a cause of ASD, intellectual disability, or cerebral palsy. Certain genetic tests can identify more than 80% of cases.

Phenylketonuria

Universal newborn screening has almost eliminated this once common cause of intellectual disability and ASD. Phenylketonuria is a metabolic disorder that affects the body's ability to process a specific chemical called *phenylalanine*, which is found in many foods. When the chemical builds up in the body, it can become toxic to the developing brain. Restricting the foods that contain phenylalanine in early infancy can prevent disabilities.

16p11.2 Deletion Syndrome

This disorder may be present in approximately 1 in 300 children with ASD. Children with this condition may have ASD, developmental delay or intellectual disability, language delay, and large head size and overweight.

16p11.2 Duplication Syndrome

This disorder may be present in approximately 1 in 400 children with ASD. Children with this condition often have ASD, mental health conditions, and small head size and underweight.

15q Duplication Syndromes

This group of conditions may be present in approximately 1 in 500 children with ASD. Children with these conditions often have ASD, developmental delay or intellectual disability, seizures, and low muscle tone.

New Genetic Tests to Understand Autism

A new genetic test called *chromosome microarray analysis* allows geneticists to see extremely tiny changes in small chunks of DNA. Today, testing that is even more sensitive includes *whole exome sequencing*, which is combined with the chromosome microarray analysis to determine the entire sequence of protein-producing DNA molecules in a child's chromosomes. These tests are starting to give us a better understanding of how changes in DNA cause autism spectrum disorder. These new, specific tests can be expensive, so you should get preapproval from your insurance company to make sure they are covered.

Benefits and Limitations of Genetic Testing to Understand Autism

Benefits

- Establish a precise cause of your child's autism spectrum disorder (ASD).
- Enable carrier status identification in other family members.
- Improve the accuracy of risk counseling for having another child with ASD.
- May allow for more-informed reproductive decision-making, including the use of artificial reproductive technologies.
- May limit additional diagnostic testing in search for a cause of the ASD.
- Even if no specific treatment is available for an identified genetic diagnosis, there are benefits in being able to identify associated conditions and in minimizing the impact of frequent complications encountered with a specific genetic diagnosis.
- Once a genetic diagnosis is established, it may enable participation in ongoing research studies to expand present knowledge of the condition and to test treatments as they become available.
- Joining a registry for the specific genetic condition may enable families from around the globe with the same diagnosis to be in contact with and serve as supports for one another.

Limitations

- In most cases, will not identify an underlying cause.
- Expensive and may not be fully covered by insurance.
- Even if a diagnosis is established, it may not change treatment recommendations.
- Results may be inconclusive, if a mutation or copy number variant (deletion or duplication of DNA) of unknown significance is identified.

Epigenetics as Possibly Having the Answer

Epigenetics merges nature and nurture. It is the study of how the environment changes the way genes work. Epigenetic changes occur on the surface of genes and may be caused by exposure to environmental factors such as pollution in the air you breathe and stress you experience. Scientists believe it's possible that these epigenetic changes are passed on from one generation to the next.

Most often, these epigenetic changes result from methyl groups, chemical entities that latch on to DNA and then silence or activate the gene. Some experts believe that epigenetics may eventually help researchers pinpoint potential environmental contributors to ASD, as well as many other diseases (for example, cancer, Alzheimer disease, obesity), leading to the development of new therapies for treatment. Epigenetic factors are already known to cause certain genetic disorders such as Angelman syndrome (see the Angelman Syndrome section"Angelman Syndrome" on page 26 earlier in this chapter).

Among recent findings using epigenetics is a study of oxytocin. Experts have long suspected that people with ASD do not have as much oxytocin (the bonding hormone responsible for social behavior such as recognizing loved ones, building trust in others, and alleviating anxiety) as those without ASD. Recent research from scientists at Duke University has shown that the problem may actually lie with oxytocin receptors, which allow the hormone to bind to neurons (nerve cells) and take effect. The researchers found that people with ASD have more methyl groups on the oxytocin receptor gene than people without ASD. When these methyl groups become part of the genetic code, it is believed that the gene is "turned off," which could explain some of the social difficulties in people with ASD. Controlling methylation of these genes may possibly lead to new treatments, but more research is still needed before that can occur.

Environmental Exposures and the Risk for Autism

Researchers are actively investigating what it is in our environment that may increase the risk for ASD, and over the years there have been no shortage of theories as to probable causes. Some parents, for instance, point to vaccines, especially if their child displayed no signs of ASD until after he or she received the vaccine. There is a natural tendency to wonder whether ASD is linked to an event, such as vaccination, that occurred just before the symptoms of ASD became noticeable. After many studies, however, scientists have found that no link between vaccines and ASD exists.

Three main theories that have been raised about vaccines and ASD are

1. The measles-mumps-rubella (MMR) vaccine causes autism by damaging the lining of the intestines.
2. Thimerosal, a mercury-containing preservative in some vaccines, causes autism by damaging the nervous system.
3. Receiving too many vaccines at once or too early in life leads to autism by affecting the immune system.

Let's review the science that has been done to study each of these concerns.

Measles-Mumps-Rubella Vaccine

Many studies have looked at the measles-mumps-rubella (MMR) vaccine and ASD. These have concluded that there is no link between the MMR vaccine and autism. For example, one study published in the *New England Journal of Medicine* compared the rate of ASD between a large group of children in Denmark (440,655) who received the MMR vaccine and a large group of children who didn't receive the MMR vaccine (96,648). If there was a link between ASD and MMR, we would have expected that the MMR group would have had a higher rate of ASD. But researchers found no difference in the rate of ASD between the 2 groups.

Thimerosal

Thimerosal is an organic mercury-containing antibacterial compound that was in US vaccines until 1999. Many studies since 1998 have looked at thimerosal and ASD and concluded that children who receive vaccines with thimerosal have no greater risk of ASD compared to children who do not receive thimerosal-containing vaccines. For example, researchers compared the receipt of thimerosal in 256 children with ASD to 700 children without ASD who had similar age and biological sex as the children with ASD. They found that exposure to thimerosal-containing vaccines was not related to an increased risk of ASD. Researchers of another study evaluated the performance on a large battery of psychological tests of 1,047 children between the ages of 7 years and 10 years. After comparing the performance of children who were exposed to different amounts of thimerosal-containing vaccines, they found no link between thimerosal exposure and deficits in intelligence or psychological functioning.

Too Many Vaccines

These days, a common concern is that getting a number of vaccines at the same time might somehow weaken the immune system, triggering the development of ASD. Because of this belief, some have suggested that parents should space out vaccines by using a nonstandard vaccine schedule. There are a number of reasons why this is not recommended. First, receiving multiple vaccines at the same time is safe. Today's more refined vaccines even when given together cause *less* stress to the immune system than vaccines of the past. This means that even though children receive more vaccines at the same time, the challenge to the immune system is less than in years past. Second, there is evidence that delaying vaccines does not make a difference in development. A recent study comparing school-aged children who received their vaccines on time with those who did not showed that timely vaccination was associated with better performance on numerous tests of language and intelligence. Less-vaccinated children did not perform better on any of the tests. Another recent study showed that children with higher exposure to vaccines that stimulate the immune system were no more likely to develop ASD compared to those who had less exposure. For parents who are concerned that children receive too many vaccines too soon or who believe delaying immunizations is beneficial, these studies provide reassurance that timely vaccination during infancy is safe. Last, it's important to understand that the vaccination schedule created by the CDC was designed to protect children when they are most vulnerable to disease. Delaying vaccines or not vaccinating your child puts him or her at risk for vaccine-preventable diseases. Even those who are fully vaccinated increase their chances of contracting a vaccine-preventable disease if they live in a community where many people are on nonstandard vaccine schedules. One study showed that for every 1% increase in proportion of school-aged children who were on these schedules, the risk of pertussis (whooping cough) infection among fully vaccinated children doubled.

Skipping or delaying vaccines also increases the risk for other children in your neighborhood. For example, many communities in the United States recently have or are currently experiencing outbreaks of measles and pertussis because there are too many unvaccinated children. Unvaccinated children help the virus or bacteria move more easily from person to person. These diseases can lead to serious illnesses or even death. Newer studies suggest that younger siblings of children with ASD are less likely to be immunized because of parental concerns about vaccines. Because of the overwhelming evidence, we strongly feel that vaccines are safe for children with ASD and would like to see them protected from potentially serious diseases, some of which have the potential to harm them more than they would children without ASD. If you have any concerns about vaccines, be sure to talk with your child's pediatrician. More information on the evidence for vaccine safety, including information about the studies we have reviewed, can be found at www.HealthyChildren.org/vaccinestudies.

Other Environmental Exposures

What scientists do know is that ASD may often result from complex interactions between environmental exposures and a person's genes. So while you may be born with a genetic predisposition for ASD, in some cases an environmental exposure or event—which may even occur in the womb—may be required for that gene to be expressed in a way that leads to ASD.

Some experts suspect that certain chemical toxins or other agents in our environment may be contributing to the causes of ASD. For example, several recent studies have shown that pregnant women living in areas with more air pollutants (such as ozone) have a higher risk of having children with ASD. Toxins such as inorganic mercury have been touted as likely suspects, as have many other heavy metals (such as lead), pesticides, and substances in plastics. The human-created class of chemicals known as *polychlorinated biphenyls* is also suspected as a culprit that may adversely affect the neurodevelopment of young children. There is ongoing research to further investigate these concerns. It is important to note, however, that while these environmental studies done of large populations help researchers better understand the potential causes of autism and where to focus more research efforts, they are not intended to be used to make decisions about individuals with ASD. For example, it is not recommended to perform tests from blood or hair to quantify environmental agents such as heavy metals. This is because there is inadequate evidence on how to know whether these substances were the cause of an individual's ASD, the results are difficult to interpret (since we all will have these substances in our bodies), and the proposed treatments, such as chelation therapy, can be dangerous.

Experts do know that exposure to certain drugs during pregnancy can contribute to the development of ASD. Two drugs in particular deserve mention. One of them is valproate, an anticonvulsant used to treat bipolar disorder and epilepsy. The other is thalidomide, a drug now used to treat multiple myeloma, a type of bone marrow and blood cancer. Thalidomide had been used to treat morning sickness in pregnant women in the late 1950s and early 1960s but was subsequently banned for causing birth defects. These medications are believed to affect the development of the fetus's brain in the early trimesters of pregnancy, a time when developmental abnormalities in the brain are most likely to occur.

Several infections during pregnancy have been investigated for their possible links with ASD. But so far, only one infection—rubella—has been definitely associated with autism. Rubella, also known as *German measles*, causes a rash, a fever, and muscle and joint pain. Congenital rubella develops in a fetus when a mother is exposed to the rubella virus early in her pregnancy. Babies born with this disorder often have many birth defects in addition to severe developmental delays. They may also have symptoms of ASD. In recent years, the disorder has become less of a concern since the rubella vaccine was introduced, which is ironically a component of the MMR vaccine.

Of note, more-recent studies have investigated a proposed link between taking a group of common medications that treat depression during pregnancy, called *selective serotonin reuptake inhibitors* (SSRIs), and ASD. Three large studies have been published since 2013. The first reviewed more than one-half million births in Denmark and showed that women taking SSRIs during pregnancy was not linked to an increased risk of ASD in their children. The second examined nearly 1,000 mother-child pairs in California whose children had ASD, developmental delay, or typical development. It was concluded that among boys, the use of SSRI medication during the first trimester of pregnancy might increase the risk for ASD and developmental delay. The last study examined more than 100,000 births in Quebec and showed that SSRI use in the second and third trimesters of pregnancy increased the risk of ASD. Making recommendations for women with depression in light of these conflicting results is challenging. It is important to first note that untreated depression during pregnancy has been linked with an increased risk for preterm birth, low birth weight, and developmental delay. Thus, there may be significant benefits to treating depression during pregnancy. In addition, while the use of SSRIs during pregnancy may increase the risk of ASD, the risk is still relatively low. For these reasons, pregnant women with depression should discuss the risks and benefits of all treatment options with their doctors.

Recent studies suggest that babies exposed to large amounts of alcohol in the womb can develop ASD as well as a spectrum of other neurodevelopmental disorders. These babies have fetal alcohol syndrome or alcohol-related neurodevelopmental disorder. They often have growth deficiencies that lead to short stature, small head circumference, decreased muscle tone, facial abnormalities, cardiac defects, and delayed development. Children with fetal alcohol syndrome may also be diagnosed as having ASD, though the link between autism and prenatal exposure to alcohol requires further research.

Family Health Factors and the Risk for Autism

The health of Mom and Dad always plays a major role in a child's health, so it's no surprise that experts have probed for links between family health and ASD. In particular, scientists have zeroed in on the mother's history of autoimmune diseases, illnesses that cause the body's immune system to attack itself. In particular, research has shown that children whose mothers have rheumatoid arthritis, celiac disease, systemic lupus erythematosus, or a family history of type 1 diabetes are more likely to have ASD. Recent studies suggest that the presence of anti-brain antibodies in the blood of mothers with autoimmune disease may play a role.

The likelihood of ASD is increased in children of older fathers and mothers. This may have to do with the increased risk in men for passing on DNA with mutations as the body ages. No one knows exactly why older women and men are more likely to have children with ASD, but experts suspect that a woman's hormonal changes at an older age could affect fetal brain development. More research is needed to know exactly how advanced maternal and paternal ages affect risk for ASD. Studies have shown that each 10-year increase in maternal age and paternal age from the age of 20 raises the risk of having a child with ASD by 18% and 21%, respectively. In addition, several studies have looked at the risk of ASD in children conceived by assisted reproductive technology with somewhat conflicting results, requiring more study to definitively answer this question.

The amount of time between pregnancies—also known as the *inter-pregnancy interval*—is also a risk factor. One study that examined birth records of second-born children showed that those who were conceived within 12 months of the birth of their older sibling were 3 times more likely to be diagnosed as having ASD. Children conceived 12 to 23 months after an older sibling were almost 2 times more likely to have been diagnosed as having ASD.

Effect of Pregnancy Complications and Newborn's Health at Birth on Risk for Autism Spectrum Disorder

Data from several studies indicate that mothers who have gestational diabetes are more likely to have babies with autism spectrum disorder (ASD). Gestational diabetes occurs when pregnant women develop high blood sugar (also called *blood glucose*) levels. The condition is usually detected with an oral glucose tolerance test in the 24th to 28th week of pregnancy. Glucose levels usually return to normal after delivery. More recently, researchers have also found that related conditions during pregnancy such as obesity and high blood pressure may also raise the risk of ASD.

In fact, a number of prenatal and perinatal risk factors are associated with ASD. Some of these include preterm birth, fetal distress, low birth weight, and birth trauma. But just because there is an association does not mean that these factors *cause* ASD. These are just conditions that may elevate risk, and the contribution of each risk to an individual's overall risk may be relatively low.

A baby born with encephalopathy, for example, has an elevated risk of developing ASD. *Encephalopathy* is a term used to describe any type of brain disease that alters the brain's function or structure. One study showed that 5% of survivors of newborn encephalopathy were later diagnosed as having ASD. It's possible that these children were genetically predisposed to encephalopathy or ASD.

In addition, babies who had jaundice at birth may be more likely to develop ASD. Jaundice is the yellow color seen in the skin of many newborns. It occurs when a newborn's liver can't break down bilirubin, a substance in bile produced by the breakdown of red blood cells. A study showed that babies who had jaundice were at greater risk for ASD, especially if they were born to mothers who previously had children and if they were born between October and March (fewer hours of daily sunlight). While the study does not say that jaundice causes autism, it does suggest that jaundice may be among the factors that elevate risk.

Ongoing Research Into What Causes Autism

Solving the mystery of what causes ASD has spawned intense research efforts around the world. Some of the major research projects now underway are

- The Centers for Autism and Developmental Disabilities Research and Epidemiology is being directed by the CDC in Colorado, Missouri, Wisconsin, North Carolina, Maryland, and Georgia. Each center is working on aspects of a project called *Study to Explore Early Development* and looking to identify factors that might put children at risk for ASD. For more information, see www.cdc.gov/ncbddd/autism/seed.html.

- Early Autism Risk Longitudinal Investigation (EARLI) is following more than 1,200 mothers from pregnancy through the first 3 years of their babies' lives to examine potential environmental risk factors that may be involved in causing ASD. The EARLI study will look at the DNA profiles of all family members and test the hypothesis that ASD has a genetic and epigenetic basis. Research is being done at multiple sites including Johns Hopkins University; Drexel University; Children's Hospital of Philadelphia/University of Pennsylvania; University of California, Davis; and Kaiser Permanente in northern California. For more information, see www.earlistudy.org.

- CHARGE (Childhood Autism Risks from Genetics and the Environment) was launched in 2003 as the first comprehensive study of environmental causes and risk factors for autism and developmental delay. The CHARGE study recognizes that no single factor accounts for all autism cases, nor is there one event or exposure that can be responsible for the rapid increase in diagnoses over the past few decades. This study is being conducted at the University of California, Davis, MIND Institute and involves children born in California who are between the ages of 24 months and 54 months. For more information, visit http://beincharge.ucdavis.edu/newsupdates.php.

● The Environmental Influences on Child Health Outcomes program was recently launched by the National Institutes of Health and is a new 7-year initiative to investigate environmental exposures—including physical, chemical, biological, social, behavioral, natural, and built environments—on child health and development. More information can be found at www.nih.gov/echo.

● The SPARK Study, funded by the Simon's Foundation Autism Research Initiative, seeks to collect genetic, behavioral, and medical information on more than 50,000 children and families affected by autism. The project, with sites at 20 different medical schools and autism research centers, hopes to better understand which genetic and environmental factors underlie autism risk. More information can be found at www.sparkforautism.org.

I have a daughter who has autism spectrum disorder and a son who does not. Could my son carry a gene for autism spectrum disorder that he will pass on to his offspring?

Experts know that if one child in the family has autism spectrum disorder (ASD), that child's siblings are at greater risk for developing ASD too. If your son does not have ASD, the odds that he will pass on a gene for ASD is low. However, his odds may be slightly higher than someone else who does not have a sibling with ASD, especially if he has some ASD traits (something called *broad autism phenotype*). If your daughter undergoes genetic testing for children with ASD and a genetic cause (a gene variant consistent with the diagnosis of ASD) is found, it is likely that a genetic test will be recommended for your son. If he carries the same gene variant, it may increase the risk of ASD for his children. The genetics underlying ASD are complex, and it may be helpful for parents to seek counseling from a geneticist or genetic counselor to better understand recurrence risk.

❧ ❧ ❧ ❧ ❧

Autism Champion: Alison Singer

ALISON SINGER was a successful television executive at NBC when her daughter Jodie was diagnosed as having autism in 2000. The diagnosis changed Alison's life forever. She left television and became acting CEO of Autism Speaks when it was launched in 2005.

In 2009, she founded her own organization, the Autism Science Foundation. The group raises money to support autism spectrum disorder (ASD) research, brings together parents and scientists to share information, and trains scientists to work with the media. It also brings the latest science to people at the forefront of ASD— parents and educators.

Getting the science out is Alison's way of combating the myths that continue to linger about vaccines and the unproven remedies that are often touted as treatments. Even now, Alison gets frequent e-mails offering an alleged cure. "These opportunists prey on the desperation of parents who are willing to try anything they think might possibly help their child," she says. "Believe me, I get it. We love our children so much and want them to improve and so we are willing to try anything. That's why it's so important to do the science to test interventions. We need to know what works and what doesn't. These are not quick fixes; they take time and lots of effort, but they really do help."

Jodie is now 21 years old. Time has taught Alison that with the right therapies, children with ASD can make significant improvement. "The day they're diagnosed is the bottom," says Alison, who also has a younger daughter who does not have ASD. "It's the worst day. From then on, the kids will continue to gain skills. They will make gains that astonish you, even if it's sometimes 2 steps forward and 1 step back. Those steps back are frustrating, but I have learned to appreciate the steps forward more than I ever imagined was possible."

Her advice to parents? Talk to other parents in your community. "Services are always delivered locally," she says. "Your best source of information will often be other parents in your school district."

CHAPTER 3

How Do I Know if My Child Has Autism Spectrum Disorder?

CARLY WAS CONCERNED. At 17 months, her son Asher wasn't talking yet, and when she called his name, he would rarely respond. At the 18-month visit, Asher's pediatrician listened to her concerns and performed an autism screening test. He informed her that he also shared her concerns about Asher's behavior and development. Asher was referred to a specialty clinic and subsequently diagnosed as having autism spectrum disorder (ASD). While the diagnosis was a shock to his family, they were ultimately thankful to have their concerns validated. The diagnostic evaluation also allowed them to learn more about Asher and how to help him. Today, at the age of 7, Asher still faces challenges with social skills and communication but is making steady progress, much to the delight of his family.

🐢 🐢 🐢 🐢 🐢

GETTING A DIAGNOSIS for a child with ASD often isn't easy. Unlike some conditions, such as diabetes or celiac disease, ASD is not diagnosed with a blood test. Currently, no x-rays (also called *radiographs*) or scans can detect ASD. Instead, the diagnosis is made on the basis of caregivers' descriptions of the child's development and by careful observations of characteristic behaviors by providers who have expertise with ASD. In some cases, the path to a diagnosis begins with something as simple as a parent's hunch or a sense that something is a bit different.

Diagnosing ASD is sometimes difficult for many reasons. For one, every single case is different. While children on the autism spectrum share similar characteristics, exactly how those traits play out will vary from one child to the next. The severity of autism varies considerably too. For example, some people with ASD have very mild forms, display virtually no speech problems, and are capable of independently meeting their needs as adults. Some may even be considered gifted and exceptionally bright. Others have severe forms of the condition, with significant disability, and may have a lifelong dependence on others to meet their needs. Still others have genetic disorders or medically complex conditions requiring medical stabilization before a child's developmental status can be accurately determined.

One thing experts do know now is that early diagnosis and treatment of ASD is very important in determining how well a child lives with it. Herein lies the challenge. While most signs of ASD are apparent by the time a child is 24 months old, many children are not diagnosed until they are older.

The age of diagnosis may depend on where a child falls on the spectrum as well as other socioeconomic factors. One study showed that the average age of diagnosis of children having more severe forms of ASD was 3.1 years, while for those with less severe forms, it was 7.2 years.

The study also uncovered some possible explanations as to why some children are diagnosed sooner and others are diagnosed later. Children were typically diagnosed later if they lived in a rural setting, came from households with lower incomes, and had consulted 4 or more different primary care physicians. Symptoms make a difference too; children who had severe language delays were diagnosed an average of 1.2 years earlier than those who did not. Those who demonstrated hand flapping, toe walking, and unusual play were diagnosed at a younger age, while those who were oversensitive to pain or had a hearing impairment tended to be diagnosed later.

Children with ASD who have intellectual disability or global developmental delay are usually diagnosed earlier than those who do not. Those who have regressive autism, that is, whose signs of ASD appear after a period of seemingly normal development, are also more likely to be diagnosed early. Boys are generally diagnosed at a younger age than girls. It's possible that certain traits in girls with ASD, such as shyness, may be more socially acceptable and therefore more easily overlooked. Also, it has been suggested that girls with ASD, compared with boys with ASD, may have a better ability to "camouflage" or hide their social skill difficulties in social situations.

Although diagnosing a child at a young age is important for getting the early intervention that is so critical to children with ASD, in 2009 a national study showed that the median age of diagnosis was 6 years, and more than a quarter of children were not diagnosed until age 8. The good news is that the age of earliest diagnosed cases is dropping. According to the Centers for Disease Control and Prevention, the earliest cases were diagnosed between 49 months and 66 months in 2002; by 2014, the age of earliest case identification was between 32 months and 55 months.

Early diagnosis requires a partnership between parents and pediatricians. Within this partnership you, as the parent, should feel comfortable bringing up any concerns you have about your child's behavior or development—the way she plays, learns, speaks, and acts. Likewise, the role of your child's pediatrician is to listen and act on your concerns. During your child's visits, the pediatrician may ask specific questions or ask you to complete a questionnaire about your child's development. Pediatricians take these steps because they understand the value of early diagnosis and intervention and know where to refer you if concerns are identified. This chapter helps you recognize the early signs of ASD so you can better partner with your child's pediatrician to get your child the help she needs. The importance of this partnership cannot be stressed enough.

Beginning Autism Monitoring Early in Infancy

Like adults, all babies are unique. Some start babbling early on, while others are late talkers. Some start crawling at a young age; others seem to take longer to start moving about. Even within families, parents often marvel at how differently their children grow and develop. But experts are increasingly convinced that early signs of ASD are evident even during the first few years after birth.

While it may be challenging to diagnose ASD in a child younger than 24 months, it is important for you, as a parent, to monitor your child's development carefully so you can identify any concerns as soon as possible. For instance, by the end of their third month of age, most infants have started to smile and show pleasure in playing with others and are gradually becoming more communicative with their expressions and body movement. They're usually able to raise both head and chest when they're on their tummies and stretch out their legs and kick. Place their tiny feet on a firm surface and they will push down. Most can open and shut their hands and bring their hand to their mouth. They can usually reach for dangling objects and are starting to take hold of toys.

Meanwhile, they may be watching you intently and following moving objects. They can often recognize familiar objects and people from a distance. Your infant may smile at the sound of your voice and turn his or her head in the direction of sound. Some may be cooing (making vowel sounds) and imitating the sounds you make.

In babies who may have developmental disabilities such as ASD, some of these milestones may be delayed or absent. Babies with ASD may only rarely respond to loud noises, smile at others, or reach for objects. Some may seldom take note of their hands or follow moving objects. They may only occasionally vocalize, pay attention to new faces, or support their head well.

Of course, even perfectly healthy babies may not achieve these milestones by the end of 3 months of age either. Some babies simply develop a little more slowly. If your baby does not meet all these milestones on time, it does not necessarily mean she has ASD or another developmental disability. While ASD and other developmental disabilities are not typically diagnosed during infancy, children who are late in achieving developmental milestones benefit from treatment. If your child does display signs of a developmental delay, you can contact an early intervention or Part C services program, which is geared to help babies and toddlers from birth through age 3 who may be at risk for a developmental disorder. We discuss this in greater detail in Chapter 4. Most important of all, watching for these signs will make you aware of a potential problem, so you can bring it to your pediatrician's attention. If these delays persist or new ones develop, you and your child's pediatrician can intervene at an earlier age to help your child reach her full potential.

Early Signs of Autism Spectrum Disorder

When your child has a cold, you expect a runny nose, some coughing, and perhaps a low-grade fever. When your child has eczema, you know his skin will itch and develop a rash. But when your child has ASD, it's a lot harder to know what to expect, especially given how different the condition reveals itself in each child. But some signs are common in most children with ASD.

Unusual Language Development

Language development varies widely among children with ASD. Some are early talkers and never seem to run out of things to say. Others are naturally quiet and start speaking much later. Speech typically begins with producing vowel sounds, or cooing, in the first few months after birth. By 6 months of age, infants can combine consonants and vowels, called *babbling*, making simple sounds such as "da" or "ba." Babbling gradually evolves as your infant starts to link these sounds ("da da") and introduce new ones such as "pa."

Between 4 months and 6 months, a typically developing infant will display a back-and-forth pattern of speaking that alternates between cooing, or babbling, and silence. For instance, babies often vocalize to themselves when they first wake up, only to fall silent when Mom enters the room, as if waiting to hear what she has to say. When Mom leaves to retrieve diapers, they may start vocalizing again. When babies vocalize in this manner, it is possible for caregivers to sustain a "conversation" with them in which turn taking occurs, that is, adults speaking in regular sentences and babies cooing and babbling. These back-and-forth vocalizations, together with eye contact and shared emotions (elements of nonverbal or body language), set the stage for later conversations using real words. Over time, a baby's sounds become more distinct and start to sound like words. Eventually, a typical child will begin to form short sentences.

Most parents are eager to hear their children utter their first words. A child's first utterances often inspire awe and excitement. So it's not surprising that when these events do not occur, parents are apt to take notice and bring it up with their child's pediatrician. Language delays are often the first signs noticed by parents and doctors that raise concern that a child may have ASD. They're often the first indication to a pediatrician that a child needs evaluation.

Language differences characterize all forms of ASD, to varying degrees. In some children with ASD, language skills may be absent or delayed. Other children, such as those who may be referred to as having autism with "typical" or "advanced verbal" skills, may possess advanced speaking skills but struggle having a back-and-forth conversation because they have the need to speak only about a preferred topic. This type of language challenge common to children with autism and typical or advanced verbal skills reflects qualitative differences in language development that distinguish their language skills from those of typically developing peers. Specifically, these differences are in the area of pragmatic language—using language for social communication.

Pragmatic language involves skills such as picking up on body language, maintaining eye contact, understanding implied meaning, using normal voice inflection and volume when speaking, maintaining the topic of conversation, and recognizing the interest level of others in what is being discussed. Such differences may not be obvious until preschool when interacting with peers. Whereas many children with ASD have language delays, all children on the autism spectrum have challenges with pragmatic language.

Most language delays are evident by the time a child is 18 months old. It is most apparent if you notice that your child is not showing the desire to communicate or express himself with gestures such as pointing. Children who have milder forms of autism will usually develop speech, but their language may be odd and lack purpose. For example, they may say words that seem to have no intent and that may be taken from television programs or movies. The early speech patterns of children with ASD may have some distinctly unusual patterns.

Echolalia

Echolalia is the repetition of another person's speech. It may be *immediate*, meaning the child will repeat what he hears right after he hears it, or *delayed*, meaning the repeated phrase will pop up hours, days, or even weeks later.

Keep in mind, though, that echolalia can occur in children who do not have ASD too. The difference, however, is that in children who do not have ASD, echolalia tends to be of the immediate kind and then completely disappears from the child's vocabulary. In children who have ASD, echolalia may last throughout their lives. And the degree of echolalia significantly affects their ability to communicate effectively with others.

They also tend to display a mix of immediate echolalia and delayed echolalia and are more likely to repeat larger chunks of material. For example, rather than repeat the slogan of a television commercial, they may recite the entire commercial and do so for long periods, even while others are trying to communicate with them.

At first, echolalia may create the impression that a child with ASD is verbally gifted. His vocabulary, grammar, and syntax may make him sound sophisticated for his age. Some kids may even display remarkable skills at labeling colors, shapes, letters, and numbers. But in a child with ASD, the voice may be delivered in a monotone fashion or another type of peculiar intonation. A closer listen often reveals delayed or absent receptive language, which means difficulty in understanding what is spoken to him. Most children with typical development are able to follow simple one-step commands by the time they are 12 to 15 months old. If you ask a child with ASD to get a toy, he is less likely to respond. If you ask him to identify a familiar object, such as a sippy cup or shoe, from among several items, he is often unable.

Pop-up Words

Some children with ASD will say a word without any provocation and for seemingly no reason. Delivery is entirely spontaneous and often inconsistent. For instance, a child may be playing with a ball when he starts saying, "Dog," when there is no dog—real, stuffed, or in pictures—nearby, nor has a dog been recently seen. In some children, the pop-up word will be spoken during times of stress, such as a child in the dentist's office who says, "Bye-bye," when the dentist attempts to place him into the procedure chair. Pop-up words can last for days or weeks and then disappear.

Giant Words

Children with ASD sometimes say phrases that link together several words, such as "Whatisit? Idontknow." These phrases are spoken without true meaning, and the children are unable to combine words into sentences that have any real meaning.

Some children appear to master all the language skills appropriate for their age, only to have them diminish between 15 months of age and 24 months of age, often at 18 to 21 months. These children may have regressive autism. When a child has regression, he may lose verbal skills as well as communicative gestures. The loss may be sudden or gradual. Loss of language skills may be accompanied by social withdrawal and activity that is more self-directed. For many parents, the loss of language skills is often a red flag that something is amiss.

For more information about how your baby and young toddler should be communicating with you, see the "Milestones During the First 24 Months After Birth" box on the next page in this chapter.

Social Skill Deficits

Human beings are hardwired for socializing. We want to share our lives with other people, so we gather for meals, throw parties, and meet for coffee. The drive to be social starts in the newborn and infancy periods when babies gaze adoringly at their parents, coo at the sound of their voices, and later point at objects they want them to see. In children with ASD, that desire for connectedness is diminished or absent. Children with ASD may be content to be left alone and are less likely to seek out others for interaction. The lack of social reciprocity may seem to emerge in toddlerhood, but experts now know that more-basic social skill deficits can be apparent even earlier. Crucial building blocks of more advanced social skills include joint attention, social orienting, and pretend play.

Milestones During the First 24 Months After Birth

Long before your baby utters her first word, she has already started communicating with you, using smiles, looks, movements, and sounds. Children develop at different rates, but they are usually able to do certain things at certain ages. Following are general developmental milestones. Keep in mind that they are only guidelines. If you have *any* questions about your child's development, ask your child's pediatrician—the sooner the better. Even when there are delays, early intervention can make a significant difference.

By 12 months, most toddlers will

- Look for and be able to find where a sound is coming from.
- Respond to their name most of the time when you call it.
- Wave goodbye.
- Look where you point when you say, "Look at the _____."
- Babble with intonation (voice rises and falls as if they are speaking in sentences).
- Take turns "talking" with you—listen and pay attention to you when you speak and then resume babbling when you stop.
- Say "da da" to Dad and "ma ma" to Mom.
- Say at least one word.
- Point to items they want that are out of reach or make sounds while pointing.

Between 12 months and 24 months, most toddlers will

- Follow simple commands, first when the adult speaks and gestures and then later with words alone.
- Get objects from another room when asked.
- Point to a few body parts when asked.
- Point to interesting objects or events to get you to look at them too.
- Bring things to you to show you.
- Point to objects so you will name them.
- Name a few common objects and pictures when asked.
- Enjoy pretending (for example, pretend cooking). They will use gestures and words with you or with a favorite stuffed animal or doll.

Milestones During the First 24 Months After Birth (*continued*)

- Learn about one new word per week between 18 months and 24 months.

By 24 months of age, most toddlers will

- Point to many body parts and common objects.
- Point to some pictures in books.
- Follow one-step commands without a gesture such as "Put your cup on the table."
- Be able to say about 50 to 100 words.
- Say several 2-word sentences and phrases such as "Daddy go," "Doll mine," and "All gone."
- Be understood by others (or by adults) about half the time.

Joint Attention

A toddler does not look at Elmo on the television despite his father pointing and saying, "Look!" A young child finishes a drawing of his mother but does not bring it over to show her. A school-aged child rarely shares what happens at school with his parents despite their repeated requests. These children with ASD all demonstrate deficits in joint attention. Joint attention is engaging another's attention to objects, events, or other people simply for the enjoyment of sharing an experience. Like all developmental milestones, it is mastered in steps that occur at predictable ages throughout childhood.

Joint attention starts early when a typically developing baby recognizes a parent or familiar caregiver's voice, smiles, and reacts with happy smiles of his own. At about 8 months of age, an infant will follow your gaze when it shifts away to see what you are looking at. Sometime between 10 months of age and 12 months of age, when you point in the direction of an interesting object or event and say, "Look!" your infant will respond by turning his head to see what's intriguing you. Your infant will then turn his gaze back to you to affirm that he saw what you were indicating.

In children who have ASD, this type of experience sharing may not develop at the same rate. Babies with ASD are less likely to look in your direction or show interest in engaging you. Saying the baby's name loudly or touching him on the shoulder may not get his attention as easily as it would with typically developing babies. Even if it does, a child with ASD is not as likely to look back at you to share in what you've both just looked at.

The difficulty with social engagement continues into toddlerhood. At about 12 months, a typically developing child will begin trying to assert himself socially by asking for an object that is out of reach. He may do this by making simple sounds such as "uh" or pointing with an index finger. This is called *imperative pointing*, or pointing to request. By about 14 to 16 months of age, a child with typical development will point at an object he likes simply to comment to you that it is pleasing to him and to share that experience with you. This is called *declarative pointing*, or pointing to show. He will alternate between looking at you and looking at the object or event that has captured his interest. This is the full expression of joint attention. Consistently demonstrating joint attention, experts say, reliably predicts whether a child will develop functional language within a year.

Delayed or lack of joint attention is one of the most specific early signs of ASD. Compared with children with typical development, children with ASD are less likely to point to or comment about objects or events. When they do point, they may show little enthusiasm and make little effort to connect with you while pointing. Although some children with ASD may point to shapes, objects, and colors they have learned, it is more often to label than to share an experience. Despite these challenges, numerous studies have shown that with early intervention, children with ASD can improve their joint attention.

Social Orienting, or Response to Name

The first time a baby turns her head at the sound of her name is an exciting moment for most parents. Developmentally, it's also an important social skill milestone, known as *social orienting*. This milestone is usually achieved by the time an infant is 8 to 10 months old.

Children who have ASD may not acknowledge a caregiver's attempt to get their attention. It may take calling a child's name louder and louder to finally get her attention. Failure to respond to their name is one of the most common early signs of ASD in young children but is sometimes overlooked. While it is important to consider the possibility of a hearing problem, most children with ASD hear and respond to environmental sounds (for example, the doorbell) but seem to respond less to the human voice. In a 2017 study, researchers found that children aged 6 to 24 months who were later diagnosed as having ASD were less likely to respond to their name compared with children who were not diagnosed as having ASD. It is important to note, however, that many children diagnosed later as having ASD in the study did respond to their name, indicating that while this is one important sign of ASD, it is not always present. With time and intervention, most children with ASD will improve their ability to respond to their name.

Pretend Play Skills, and Friendships

As you might imagine, you will notice differences in the way children with ASD play with toys and with other children. Typically developing children will begin playing by grasping objects, a skill that develops around 4 months of age. They may start mouthing objects, and at 8 to 10 months of age, they may start banging toys together or against the floor or table, or tossing them around. This stage of play is known as the *sensory-motor stage*. Around 12 months, they become more aware of how toys are meant to be handled and may start playing with them more appropriately. For instance, instead of banging blocks on the floor, they may now stack the blocks. Soon after, pretend play emerges, and they may use toy bottles to feed a baby doll or a toy telephone to chat with Grandma. Pretend play gradually becomes more sophisticated, and simple objects may be used to represent other, more complex ones. Bananas, for instance, may become telephones, and wooden blocks may be used as cars.

Compared with typical children, children with ASD engage in significantly less pretend play before the age of 24 months. They may have very little interest in toys, preferring instead to play with everyday objects such as string, pens, and rocks. If they do develop an interest in toys, they may tend to play with parts of the toy and not the whole toy itself. So rather than push a toy truck along the floor, a boy with ASD might pick it up and focus on spinning the wheels or opening and closing the doors. Children with ASD who have normal nonverbal intelligence may be especially skilled at putting things together, such as stacking cups and assembling puzzles, and may later on become masterful at computer games, or what is called *constructive play*. Some children with ASD may also insist on repeatedly lining up objects, which is known as *ritualistic play*. These types of play do not involve imitation, observation, or other people and are better suited for children who do better at play that involves trial-and-error problem-solving skills.

What can be deceiving is that some children with ASD enjoy rough-housing. They may like it when Dad tosses them in the air or tickles them on the floor. Many children who have ASD enjoy the sensory-motor aspects of this type of play. Though it may appear to be typical behavior, it is often the sensory aspect of this kind of play that a child with ASD prefers as opposed to the social engagement. In other words, he is seeking out the sensory stimulation that occurs when he is tossed or tickled, not necessarily the companionship of the other person.

To an unsuspecting parent, the behavior of a child with ASD may appear easy to manage because he is content to play by himself for hours without seeking out Mom or Dad. But a closer look at the child's style of play will reveal that the play is sensory motor, constructive, and ritualistic, and it does not involve other people. Later on in life, a child with ASD often may have difficulty interacting with peers and cooperating in groups with social rules. As a result, children with ASD are more at risk for being bullied and left out of social circles.

Repetitive and Unusual Behaviors

Children who have ASD may display different behaviors and peculiar mannerisms. They may flap their hands, rock their bodies, or twirl their fingers, especially when they become excited. Some children walk on their toes, nod their heads, or sniff and lick nonfood items. These behaviors are called *stereotypies*, that is, repetitive behaviors that outwardly serve no apparent purpose and yet are performed compulsively. Stereotypies are generally harmless but can, in some cases, interfere with the child doing something else or prevent the child from learning a new skill. Stereotypies may not be obvious until after the age of 24 months.

Although stereotypies are common in children with ASD, they don't occur just with autism. Children who have intellectual disabilities or global developmental delays may also demonstrate stereotypies. Even young children with typical development may sometimes flap their hands when they're excited or go through periods of walking on their toes.

Restricted Interests

Most children don't escape childhood without developing a strong bond to a beloved teddy bear, special blanket, or treasured doll. Children with ASD, on the other hand, may not, preferring instead to latch on to a hard object such as a pen, a flashlight, or an action figure. The attachment to that object is also more persistent, and they may insist more intensely on holding the object at all times.

Children who have autism with typical or advanced verbal skills may be less consumed with objects and more enamored with topics and facts. But the fierce interest in these topics is often stronger than it is in children with typical development. In some cases, a child with autism and typical or advanced verbal skills may have an encyclopedic storehouse of facts and information about the topic. Topics of interest are not necessarily unusual for small children. For instance, Ellen's son Brian developed a strong interest in dinosaurs, which was no surprise because his father is a paleo-artist who has several paleontologists as friends. Besides, many young children are fascinated with dinosaurs. But Brian's interest in dinosaurs has been all-consuming. He is often more than willing to discuss dinosaurs with others, to the exclusion of other subjects, even when his classmates show no interest. The intensity of his interest is common in children with autism and normal or advanced verbal skills.

Other Common Features of Autism Spectrum Disorder

Language differences and deficits in social skills are the most prominent and defining characteristics of children with ASD. But many children also have other difficulties.

Cognitive Challenges

Although cognitive deficits aren't considered a core feature of ASD, they are common among children who have this disorder. At one time, experts estimated that *intellectual disability*—the term varies depending on age and different assessment tools—applied to 90% of all children with ASD. The 2018 data from the Centers for Disease Control and Prevention indicate that these problems affect about 31% of children with ASD.

What many children with ASD do have is unevenness in their skills and development. A child with ASD may, for instance, be an exceptional math whiz but may struggle to read. Some children may also have incredible focus, memory, and mathematic skills, while others display notable musical and artistic talents. In rare instances, a child with ASD may have highly developed skills and talents that earn him the label of "savant." A savant—as performed by Dustin Hoffman in the movie *Rain Man*—is a person with exceptional skills in a narrow area. For example, some savants may be capable of doing rapid calculations, memorizing large amounts of information, and mastering complex pieces of music with little practice. Savant abilities are somewhat rare (ranging from less than 1% up to 10%) in children and adults with ASD.

Sensory-Motor Symptoms

For children with ASD, the sounds, sights, and textures that we experience daily can often be a challenging minefield to navigate. Some are hypersensitive, or overly bothered, by things in their environment. Others are hyposensitive, or completely insensitive, to sensations that others consider bothersome. But a child's sensitivity to sights and sounds may not be consistent across the senses. For example, loud noises at a party may put a child with ASD on edge, even though she's totally oblivious to the sound of her mother's voice calling her name. A child with ASD might excessively inspect toys or other objects by gazing at them for a particularly long time or from different angles while remaining uninterested in the rest of her surroundings.

Some children have tactile defensiveness—they're overly sensitive to certain textures and surfaces, such as the elastic in socks or labels in shirts. Some may resist hugs because they don't like to be touched. They may also have oral aversions to certain textures in food. Children with ASD may also show unusual sensory-seeking behaviors, such as a tendency to walk on their toes (even though they have full range of motion at their ankles), flap their hands, spin, rock back and forth, jump, or chew on objects.

Some children with ASD have unusual motor skills. Some may appear to have advanced fine motor skills such as stringing beads, but most have trouble with gross motor skills such as running, climbing, and jumping. Many also have trouble with coordination and motor planning, which involve thinking through a task and then doing the movements in the proper sequence. Some children with ASD may be clumsy. Some children may appear hyperactive and show symptoms of attention-deficit/hyperactivity disorder (ADHD). Others may be withdrawn and less active, making little movement.

Common Health Problems Associated With Autism

Children with ASD often have other health and psychiatric conditions. These associated conditions may have profound effects on them. They can often affect children's behavior, their ability to learn, and their overall health and well-being. Treating these conditions may help a child's overall functioning, which is why talking with your child's pediatrician about them is critical. In fact, a child may have one or several of these problems. Medications to help control some of these conditions are discussed in Chapter 6. Here are some common medical, behavioral, and mental health conditions in children with ASD.

Seizures and Epilepsy

Children with ASD are more likely than children with typical development to experience a seizure—sudden and excessive electrical discharges in the brain that can produce a variety of symptoms from unconsciousness and contractions of the muscles to undirected, uncontrolled, and unorganized movements. Seizures are more common in children with ASD who have global developmental delay, intellectual disability, severe motor deficits, or a family history of epilepsy. During a seizure, a child may make jerky movements with his limbs, lose consciousness, or stare off into space. Seizures in children with ASD are most common when the child is younger than 5 years and again during adolescence. Children with ASD who are suspected to have seizures may require additional tests, including an electroencephalogram or an imaging test of the brain, to confirm seizures and look for potential causes.

Gastrointestinal Disorders

Children with ASD may be more likely to have gastrointestinal (GI) issues than typically developing children. Many children with ASD experience chronic symptoms such as constipation, diarrhea, vomiting, and abdominal pain. Most GI disorders in children with or without ASD are functional, meaning that there is not a specific cause within the GI tract that can be identified. This is especially true for some GI disorders such as constipation, which may result from a child's selective eating habits and pickiness about food. Some GI disorders are caused by a specific problem in the GI tract that is causing symptoms. This is true for GI disorders such as celiac disease, an autoimmune condition triggered by gluten and related proteins. It is especially important to tell your child's pediatrician about any weight loss, blood in the stools, black or tarry stools, prolonged or persistent vomiting, prolonged diarrhea, abdominal pain that is in only a small area of the abdomen, or frequent fever because these may be symptoms of a more serious GI disorder.

Children with GI issues and ASD may have difficulty informing their caregivers that they have abdominal pain. Instead, you may notice behaviors such as frequent clearing of the throat, screaming, whining, groaning, and sobbing for no apparent reason. Some children may display delayed echolalia and repeat a phrase they've heard in the past about their stomach or pain, such as "Does your tummy hurt?"

Other children may grimace, grit their teeth, or wince. Some may mouth their clothing, lean their abdomen against furniture, or tap their fingers on their throat. Some children may eat, drink, and swallow more or may have less interest in the foods they previously enjoyed. Unusual postures such as the arching of the back, self-injurious behaviors, or an increase in repetitive behaviors may also be signs of GI distress.

Abdominal pain or discomfort can result in changes in a child's overall well-being too. You may notice your child becomes irritable or may develop sleep problems. It is important to tell your child's pediatrician about these symptoms or any of the other nonverbal behaviors common with GI conditions. After listening to you and examining your child, the pediatrician might choose to try a medicine to treat the most likely GI disorder (such as constipation or gastroesophageal reflux) or test further for some of these conditions.

While ongoing research is exploring whether some children with ASD have unique problems within the GI tract, the current way to treat GI disorders in children with ASD is the same as for children without ASD. This is because it is assumed that the problems within the GI tract are the same for both sets of children. There is no evidence at this point that children with ASD have unique microscopic abnormalities in their intestines or overgrowth of yeast or other organisms that worsen behavior.

As of this printing, there is also no evidence that GI problems directly cause ASD. One such theory was put forward in the 1990s. It claimed that changes in the GI tract (a "leaky gut") caused by the measles-mumps-rubella vaccine given to 12-month-olds actually caused ASD. This study was later found to be significantly flawed and was retracted from the medical literature. Despite many theories of a GI basis for autism, there hasn't been any proof of a specific link between a disordered GI system and symptoms of ASD. (See Chapter 7 for more information on this issue.)

Tics

Some children with ASD have tics—brief, mostly involuntary movements or sounds that are also the defining symptoms of a neurological condition called *Tourette syndrome*. The 2 conditions have a lot in common, including echolalia, obsessive-compulsive behaviors, and abnormal motor behaviors. Some evidence suggests that some of the same brain abnormalities in people with ASD also exist in people with Tourette syndrome. In moderate to severe cases, medical treatment can be quite helpful.

Sleep Disorders

Studies show that between 40% and 80% of children with ASD experience sleep problems. They may have trouble falling asleep, staying asleep, or waking up early. Severe sleep problems may affect a child's quality of life, may worsen his ability to pay attention, and may cause him to be irritable and display more repetitive behaviors. Likewise, caregivers of children with sleep problems will likely have sleep interruptions as well, adding to a family's overall stress level. Some children with ASD appear to need less sleep than their typical peers. It is important to discuss sleep problems with your child's pediatrician because they may be caused by other medical conditions (such as gastroesophageal reflux) that cause pain and lead to night awakenings. (See Chapter 6.)

Obesity

Children and youths with ASD have at least as great, if not greater, a risk of obesity as the general population. People with ASD have fewer opportunities and perhaps less interest for active leisure or organized sports, have repetitive eating patterns that may include high calorie foods, are more likely to be prescribed medications that have increased weight gain as side effects, and/or may be rewarded with unhealthy food for good behavior. You should monitor your child's diet and activity level at least as much as you would for a typically developing child. Work with your pediatrician to come up with a healthy eating plan and an appropriate physical activity regimen. Programs that address healthy weight for typically developing children and youths may need to be modified for successful use in those with ASD.

Attention-deficit/hyperactivity Disorder

Many children with ASD have difficulty staying on task and focusing and may be impulsive and hyperactive. Some children on the autism spectrum wind up being diagnosed as having attention-deficit/hyperactivity disorder (ADHD) as well. Attention-deficit/hyperactivity disorder is a biological, brain-based condition that, left untreated, can lead to difficulties in school, low self-esteem, and problems in making and keeping friends. The condition is quite common and affects an estimated 6% to 9% of all school-aged children.

Children with ADHD have trouble filtering out irrelevant information. They struggle with prioritizing, with organizing, and with delaying gratification. In children who have ASD, however, inattention may be related to self-directed thoughts or activities, such as the persistent repetition of a word, a gesture, or an act, rather than to minor distractions in the environment. Some children with ASD and ADHD may be treated with medication.

Aggression and Self-injury

Many children with ASD have difficulty moderating the intensity of their emotions and controlling their impulses. Combined with the frustration of not being able to easily communicate their wants and needs, children with ASD may exhibit aggressive behaviors and self-injury. On the other hand, a painful ear infection may cause a child to bang her head against the wall. Acting aggressively may also stem from stomach cramps caused by constipation. Aggressive behavior may be caused by an underlying psychiatric condition such as anxiety. With so many different causes, if your child is becoming aggressive toward others or herself, you should talk with your child's pediatrician. Often it will be necessary for a number of professionals to work together to find out the cause of the aggression. Once the cause is known, there are many potential therapies that help. Some children with ASD may benefit from medication that treats the underlying cause of the aggressive or self-injurious behaviors.

Anxiety Disorders

Children with ASD are prone to anxiety, which may show up as anything from feelings of nervousness to hyperactivity and other inappropriate behaviors such as screaming or aggressive acts. Because many children with ASD are extremely rigid in their routines, unexpected changes can lead to an increase in anxiety and inappropriate behaviors. Anxiety may be more common in children whose families have a history of this condition. Children with ASD who have challenges communicating may become anxious if they do not know how to respond or cope appropriately.

Children with ASD who have anxiety can sometimes become obsessive in their behaviors. Many children become extremely rigid in their routines. They may want to move through their mornings in the exact same order every day and insist, for example, that their stuffed animals be laid out in the same precise arrangement every day. When those rituals and routines are disrupted, they may have trouble adapting or have more intense or prolonged tantrums when caregivers try to transition them from one activity to another. Anxiety in children with ASD can be treated with specific behavioral therapy directed toward recognizing and managing anxiety symptoms or with medications (or with both).

Depression

Children who have ASD are more vulnerable to depression, a mood disorder that in children with typical development may lead to sadness, inactivity, and lack of interest in favorite activities. It may be more challenging to recognize depression in children with ASD and other developmental disabilities. When considering depression, it may help to compare your child's current state with how she typically acts, paying particular attention to crying spells, enjoyment of activities, interest in being around others, sleep patterns, appetite, and energy level. In children with ASD and depression, the intensity, frequency, and duration of behaviors such as aggression and irritability may increase from typical levels. Often, there is a family history of depression. Depression in children with ASD can be treated with specific behavioral therapy directed toward depressive symptoms or with medications (or with both).

What to Do if You Have Concerns About Autism

The best thing you can do if you think your child might have ASD is to bring up your concerns with your child's pediatrician. By listening to your concerns and observing your child, your pediatrician can work with you to decide on the next step. If your pediatrician shares your concerns and recommends a more complete ASD evaluation, the process will help you learn more about how you can help your child reach his full potential. While your child getting an ASD diagnosis may be difficult for you and your family, your child receiving the diagnosis at a young age means you can start early with intervention therapies that will, in the long run, be the best for your child.

Carly, for instance, knew for months that something wasn't right with her son Asher. She was distressed to get the diagnosis but immediately had help from an early intervention therapist who had been in the room when Asher was diagnosed. Carly took a couple of weeks to let the diagnosis sink in and to start figuring out what she needed to do. In the meantime, the therapist registered Asher for early intervention services, which Asher attended a few times before starting at a school for children with special needs 2 months later.

During every one of your child's health supervision visits, your pediatrician may ask about any concerns you may have about your child's behavior or development. Be sure to take these opportunities to talk about any concerns that you or other caregivers may have. Also, inform your pediatrician about any other family members who have ASD or symptoms of ASD. Your pediatrician will carefully observe your child and perform an examination. The frequent visits you have with your child's pediatrician will allow for a complete view of your child's overall development.

At your child's 9-, 18-, and 24- or 30-month visits, your pediatrician may ask you to fill out screening questionnaires about your child's development. Some of these questionnaires will ask about all aspects of your child's development. Others may ask about signs of ASD. It's important to know that these tools assist your pediatrician in identifying children at risk for developmental disabilities but are not used to diagnose any specific condition. If your child is found to be at risk, he will be referred for a comprehensive evaluation. It is during this evaluation that a specific developmental disorder may be diagnosed.

A comprehensive evaluation for ASD may involve assessments by several professionals who ideally work as a team. Team members might include your child's pediatrician, a developmental pediatrician, a psychologist, a psychiatrist, a neurologist, a speech-language pathologist, an occupational therapist, a social worker, an audiologist, and others. Each of these professionals has a unique role in the evaluation of a child with suspected ASD (**Table 3-1**).

Words to Know About Development

Developmental surveillance: The process your pediatrician uses to identify children who may be at risk for developmental disorders such as autism spectrum disorder (ASD). This involves listening to your concerns about your child's development and behavior, making careful observations of your child during visits, and asking about other family members with developmental disabilities.

Developmental screening: A process your pediatrician uses that involves parental questionnaires (standardized tools) about your child's behavior and development to further clarify whether your child is at risk for a developmental disability.

Comprehensive evaluation: A multistep assessment of children who, through surveillance and screening, are found to be at risk for ASD. It involves asking caregivers questions, observing the child, performing a physical examination, and administering any tests that may assist in arriving at a specific diagnosis. Ideally, this is done by a team of professionals.

A Patient's Story: Jacob

A case study in the October 2010 issue of the *Journal of Developmental and Behavioral Pediatrics* recounts the story of Jacob, a 22-month-old boy with no family history of autism. But his parents' answers to 3 questions on a screening test raised concerns. They revealed to their pediatrician that Jacob did not pretend play, such as talking on the phone or taking care of a doll; did not respond to his name when they called; and sometimes stared at nothing or wandered for no purpose. On a different screening test of general development, the parents expressed concerns about Jacob's limited speech. At almost 24 months of age, Jacob spoke only 2 words in Hebrew and one in English. Given the results on these 2 screening instruments, Jacob was referred for a diagnostic evaluation to look for developmental problems, autism being just one of them.

Regardless of exactly who is involved, your child's evaluation should include a health history, a physical examination, careful observation, and a hearing test. In addition, other team members might do more-formal evaluations of your child's language and cognition as well as administer other ASD-specific tests. Still other tests may be recommended if it seems that your child's autism is associated with a medical condition such as those listed in Chapter 2. (**Table 3-2** lists screening tools that pediatricians may use to help refer children for ASD evaluation.)

Even with so many experts and diagnostic tools available, accurately diagnosing a child as having ASD remains a challenge. Because there is not yet a clear biological marker that can be detected in the blood or seen on digital imaging to identify children with ASD, a lot of factors may complicate an accurate diagnosis. Some of the criteria used to diagnose ASD are not easily applied to very young children, especially those younger than 24 months. Also, it is not uncommon for families to receive different diagnoses from different evaluators. In addition, it is difficult in some parts of the country to have access to a team of health care professionals with the skills and expertise to diagnose ASD.

Table 3-1. Interdisciplinary Assessment[a] Team for Children With Autism Spectrum Disorder

Team Member	Role
Audiologist	Evaluates for hearing loss as cause of developmental delay
Developmental pediatrician, child neurologist, and/or pediatric health care professional	Performs medical evaluation Identifies and treats associated conditions
Geneticist and genetic counselor	Performs evaluation when an underlying medical condition or genetic syndrome is suggested by family history, examination, or clinical course Counsels family on recurrence risk
Occupational therapist	Evaluates for fine and gross motor differences Evaluates for sensory processing differences Develops plan for treatment
Psychiatrist	Evaluates and treats associated psychiatric conditions and maladaptive behaviors
Psychologist	Administers cognitive or developmental testing Administers diagnostic tools Identifies associated psychiatric conditions and develops behavioral treatment plan
Social worker	Identifies family needs Refers family to formal and informal support agencies and organizations
Speech-language pathologist	Evaluates for expressive, receptive, and pragmatic language differences Develops plan for treatment

[a] To facilitate recollection of developmental milestones and behavior, parents should review baby books, records, and video recordings of their child's early years before attending a diagnostic evaluation.

Table 3-2. Selected Autism Spectrum Disorder Screening Questionnaires by Age	
Screening Tool	**Ages**
Communication and Symbolic Behavior Scales Developmental Profile Infant-Toddler Checklist (CSBS DP ITC)	6–24 months
Brief Infant-Toddler Social Emotional Assessment (BITSEA)	11–48 months
Modified Checklist for Autism in Toddlers, Revised, with Follow-Up (M-CHAT-R/F)	16–30 months
Parent's Observations of Social Interactions (POSI)	16–35 months
Social Communication Questionnaire (SCQ)	For child 4 years or older (who has developmental skills more advanced than or the same as a 24-month-old)
Childhood Autism Syndrome Test (CAST)	4–11 years
Krug Asperger's Disorder Index (KADI) (for people who have autism with typical or advanced verbal skills)	6–21 years
Autism Spectrum Screening Questionnaire (ASSQ)	7–16 years
Autism Spectrum Quotient (AQ)—Adolescent Version	11–16 years

When the Diagnosis Is Autism Spectrum Disorder

It can be difficult to learn that your child has a lifelong developmental disability. Naturally, you, as a parent; other caregivers; and extended family need time to adjust your expectations. You will undoubtedly worry about what the future holds. Keep in mind during these difficult times that most children with ASD will make significant progress in overall function. Many children with ASD can do exceptionally well and may be able to participate in a regular education classroom. Many will have meaningful relationships with family and peers and achieve independence as adults.

It is important to remember that while an ASD diagnosis for your child may change what you thought your parenting experience would be, we now know that children with ASD and other developmental disabilities can achieve so much more in life than it may seem at the time of diagnosis as long as they are given appropriate support and opportunities. Even parents like Carly, who was initially devastated to learn her son had autism, realize now that getting a diagnosis will help them better understand their children and allow them to move forward with finding the right services for them. In the coming chapters, we describe how you can help your child access the support and opportunities that will allow her to reach her full potential.

> **Until recently, our 20-month-old son was always chatty and seemed to be on his way to saying some words. But my husband and I have noticed lately that he isn't speaking as much or doing as much pointing or gesturing as he did just weeks ago. We recently moved to a new house and my husband started a new job with different hours, so he sees less of our son. Could the changes in environment be affecting our son's communication skills? We're worried.**
>
> It's tempting to attribute the slowdown in your son's language skills to the move or not seeing as much of his father. But if your child is experiencing noticeable changes in his ability to communicate, you need to bring this to your pediatrician's attention. Your son is at an age when setbacks in language skills may be a sign of autism. Approximately 33% of children with autism spectrum disorder appear to be developing normally and then lose some or all of their language and social skills. Discuss your concerns with your child's pediatrician. Getting prompt attention, even without a definitive diagnosis, will allow you to learn how to help your son and gain access to early intervention, which will help him reach his full potential.

❧ ❧ ❧ ❧ ❧

Autism Champion: Catherine Lord, PhD

CATHERINE LORD, PHD, was an undergraduate when she took a psychology class at the University of California, Los Angeles, with O. Ivar Lovaas, PhD, the psychologist who helped develop the applied behavior analysis therapy for autism spectrum disorder (ASD). "It was just at the time when he was taking on the challenge of autism as a way to test a theory that operant conditioning could teach anyone anything," Dr Lord recalls.

Dr Lord participated in a project involving teaching children with ASD to speak. "I worked with 2 children who were so different from each other who also had amazing similarities," she says. "I think that is what captivated me originally. I was also fascinated by the links that people with autism make between ideas and the things they see, even when they cannot easily communicate about them."

Today, Dr Lord is the distinguished professor, School of Medicine, University of California, Los Angeles. She is credited with devising the Autism Diagnostic Observation Schedule (ADOS), a standardized assessment of communication, social interaction, and play for diagnosing individuals as having ASD. She is also a coauthor of the Autism Diagnostic Interview, Revised (ADI-R), for clinicians to use in interviews with caregivers about a child's early development, communication, social interaction, and patterns of behavior.

The goal, she says, was to create a way to compare children from one center with the next. "We realized that the process by which clinicians were making diagnoses was quite different at each center," Dr Lord says. "Even the criteria for diagnosis were different. We wanted to have information about various symptoms of autism so that we could describe participants in a way that anyone could interpret."

The ADI-R and ADOS have been important in providing standardized methods for research on the genetics and neurobiology of ASD. Both instruments have allowed clinicians all over the world to have valid and reliable tools for identifying and specifying the behaviors that we now know as ASD.

CHAPTER 4

Behavioral and Developmental Interventions to Support Children With Autism

YOU'VE JUST LEARNED that your child has autism spectrum disorder (ASD). While this can be an emotional time for you and your family, the next step is to find the right interventions or treatments for your child, a process that can be challenging yet rewarding. A solid intervention plan can help your child reach his full potential. Any therapy you consider should be individualized to your child's strengths and challenges, have specific goals, have a way to monitor progress toward those goals, and have scientific evidence of effectiveness. In this chapter, we look at several different behavioral and developmental approaches for treating ASD, including comprehensive interventions geared to addressing multiple areas of development and more-targeted interventions to address specific challenges. Keep in mind that there is no single prescription for all children, and at first you may feel overwhelmed by all the options available to you. You'll also get a lot of advice from various experts, family members, and other families of children with ASD. In the end, choosing the right mix of therapies for your child will take careful thought and consideration. It may also depend on your child's age and developmental needs, resources in your community, insurance coverage, and what best suits your family, which we discuss in later chapters. For now, it's important to know exactly what your options are.

Developing Goals and a Treatment Plan

The process of identifying treatment goals starts with the diagnostic evaluation discussed in the previous chapter. Ideally, the provider or team of professionals who performed your child's diagnostic evaluation administered tests that describe your child's level of functioning in areas such as communication, social skills, and self-help, or adaptive skills. In addition, they may have identified challenging or maladaptive behaviors (such as tantrums or physical aggression) that may interfere with future learning. These results will help you and your child's treatment team develop goals for intervention. The main goal of any ASD treatment is to help your child learn the skills he'll need to function in this world. For a child with ASD, that means helping him gain essential communication and social skills and eliminating behaviors that are disruptive or unhelpful. It's also important to teach your child how to apply those skills in different situations in ways that are socially appropriate, a process known as *generalization*. In other words, these interventions will help him get along with other children, learn the most he can at school, and master basic daily life skills. The process won't be easy, and it may take months, even years, for you to see progress, depending on your child's specific challenges. But the end goal is this: you want to maximize your child's independence and quality of life and at the same time alleviate stress on your family. To accomplish this, it is helpful to meet with your child's pediatrician to assemble a team of professionals who work together to develop and implement a management plan that addresses the needs of your child and family.

It is also important to remember, however, that long-term studies following children with ASD into adulthood indicate that ASD is generally considered a lifelong condition. While some parents focus on "curing" ASD as a treatment goal, there are a growing number of individuals with ASD who appropriately point out that they should be celebrated for who they are, be accepted and included in their communities, and have the right to make decisions about their lives. We agree. In our own practices when counseling families about treatment plans, we encourage active participation of the child in every decision as is developmentally appropriate. A recent study showed that

The Autistic Self Advocacy Network

In their own words, the Autistic Self Advocacy Network (ASAN) mission is "to advance the principles of the disability rights movement with regard to autism. ASAN believes that the goal of autism advocacy should be a world in which autistic people enjoy equal access, rights, and opportunities. We work to empower autistic people across the world to take control of our own lives and the future of our common community, and seek to organize the autistic community to ensure our voices are heard in the national conversation about us."

Many individuals consider their ASD a characteristic that is not a disorder or disability but something they celebrate, a concept and a movement called *neurodiversity*.

They have also championed the concept of self-advocacy—the right to make their own decisions about their lives—and have adopted the phrase "Nothing About Us, Without Us!"

They also point out that a key component of intervention is the concept of community inclusion. They work for "inclusion and respect for all, and to advocate for the rights of autistic people to equal opportunity at school and at work, and to improve funding for community services and supports along with research into how they can best be provided."

Derived from Autistic Self Advocacy Network Web site. http://autisticadvocacy.org. Accessed November 2, 2018.

the strongest factor linked to quality of life in adults with ASD is having a feeling of acceptance from their family and community, regardless of their level of functioning. So no matter where your journey leads you and your family, we hope that you stop to celebrate every victory, no matter how small, along the way.

When Intervention Should Begin

It was once believed that children who have ASD couldn't be diagnosed until they were toddlers or beyond. In recent years, it's become apparent that signs of ASD usually appear in the first 24 months after a child's birth. In 2007, the American Academy of Pediatrics began recommending universal screening of all children at their 18- and 24-month well-child visits (also called *health supervision visits*). Looking for signs of ASD at this young age meant that it was important for parents to have options for therapy and to have this therapy start as soon as possible.

The Components of a Good Plan

Every plan is different, just as every child is unique. And how a child responds to a particular intervention will vary too. Each plan has its own philosophy, practice, and approach. Some are comprehensive behavioral approaches that focus on teaching your child new skills while minimizing maladaptive behavior. There are approaches that are developmental and use interactions with caregivers and others to help children learn to socially interact, communicate, and regulate their emotions, while others are relational and use relationship-building skills to improve a child's social functioning. Some have been designed to be used in educational settings and emphasize the organization of the classroom as well as structure and predictability of the teaching style in order to help a child with ASD learn in school. Still others are more focused on developing specific skills such as speech, self-care, and socializing. Others may merge different approaches. You may find it helpful to do more than one program and to change treatments as the needs of your child change. You can observe therapies in action by registering and viewing videos within the Treatment section of the ASD Video Glossary (http://resources.autismnavigator.com).

Experts agree that some principles and elements are key to making a young child's intervention program successful. For starters, placing the child into an intervention program is best done as soon as you and your pediatrician suspect he has ASD, rather than waiting for a definitive diagnosis. Children who receive therapy early generally do better than those who wait. Most young children with ASD will benefit from a comprehensive treatment model that uses a behavioral, developmental, or blended approach; is intensive (meaning around 20 or more hours per week); and works on a variety of goals over a prolonged period of time. The intervention may be given in different settings, such as your home, a community center, or a classroom, and may occur one-on-one with a therapist or within a group of peers.

A good intervention program should also involve other people besides the therapist to reinforce new skills in the routine settings of your child's daily life (known as *generalizing new skills*). Parents, for instance, should always be part of the process and may even undergo rigorous training to learn how to help their child. Siblings often become part of the process, as well as grandparents, babysitters, and others involved in the child's care. With school-aged children, teachers may be involved too. In addition, to the extent possible, your child should have opportunities to interact with peers with typical development. (For more information, see Chapter 9.)

An intervention program often provides structure by incorporating predictable routines, a visual schedule of activities, and well-defined physical boundaries that minimize distractions. The child should have the opportunity to apply the skills he learns in the program to new environments and situations and have the chance to practice functional skills for daily living. At the same time, it's important that whoever is doing the therapy is measuring and documenting your child's progress. Only by knowing how well your child is doing will you be able to gauge a therapy's effectiveness.

Because ASD is a complex condition that affects several developmental areas, it's important to put together an intervention program that addresses multiple areas of concern, including social skills and communication. In addition to teaching skills you want your child to acquire, it's important to help him or her minimize behaviors that are not helpful. Ultimately, you are preparing your child for greater independence and responsibility, be it in the home, at school, or in the community. For example, a recent study showed that about half of parents of children with ASD reported that their child was physically aggressive toward them, and about one-third were aggressive toward others outside the home. Because aggression has been found to be the factor most strongly linked to parental stress, it is important to address it as early as possible within an intervention program.

It's important to understand that not all children require the same amount of treatment. Just as the condition varies among children, so, too, does the therapy. Children with typical to advanced intellectual ability, for instance, may need less intervention. Children with ASD who have more-prominent symptoms or challenges that interfere with their daily functioning may require several types of treatment at a higher intensity (that is, number of times and hours per week). Some children will need therapies for only a few years, while others may benefit from more-prolonged treatment. Older children, in particular, may need more-targeted therapies for specific problem behaviors. Most children with ASD will benefit from support with independent living, jobs, social relationships, and mental health well into adulthood. Familiarizing yourself with the various options available is key to finding therapies that will work for your child. Your pediatrician can help familiarize you with the different professionals that offer services as part of your child's overall intervention program.

Approaches to Intervention: Applied Behavior Analysis

Some of the more well-known ASD therapies use a method known as *applied behavior analysis* (ABA). The principles of ABA are based on the work of B.F. Skinner, a behavioral psychologist in the 1930s who said behavior was manipulated and controlled by events in the physical world. These principles were refined and later used in the 1960s by psychologists and researchers to teach children with autism. Applied behavior analysis has also been used to teach and modify behaviors in children and adults with other behavioral and developmental challenges. Applied behavior analysis has the most evidence-based support in the scientific literature and is currently regarded as one of the most effective interventions for children with ASD.

In short, ABA is a method of teaching that uses reinforcement to motivate and shape desired behavior. It begins with a basic understanding of the ABCs of behavior (*antecedent*, *behavior*, and *consequence*).

- *Antecedent* is the verbal or physical drive, such as a direct request from Mom, that precedes the behavior.

- *Behavior* is the child's response to the antecedent. If Mom asks him to point to an apple and he does, he is demonstrating an appropriate behavioral response to the antecedent.

- *Consequence* is what happens after the child performs the behavior. The type of consequence determines whether the behavior will occur again in the future or gradually diminish. Positive reinforcement—praise and a mother's smile, for example—is more likely to ensure that the child will point to the apple the next time Mom asks.

Traditional ABA, sometimes called the *Lovaas Model,* grew out of research in the early 1970s by O. Ivar Lovaas, PhD. By the mid-1980s, Dr Lovaas was able to demonstrate in his research that using ABA in intensive and early interventions for children with ASD enabled almost half of them to succeed in regular education classrooms. However, even children who do not participate in regular education classrooms can benefit from ABA, and parents can also use ABA methods to teach and manage their child's behavior. Studies have shown that children who receive intensive ABA therapies may be able to make significant and sustained gains in intelligence, language, academic performance, and self-care behaviors. They can also make notable strides in social skills.

The goal of ABA is simple: increase the behaviors and skills that help your child make forward progress and decrease those that are undesirable, that are troublesome, or that may limit her access to her community. To achieve this, it's important that your child work with a skilled therapist who will break down the skills and behaviors into small, measurable steps. Desired behavior is then taught using repeated trials, with desired behaviors reinforced with positive rewards that your child finds highly motivating. Your child should also have the opportunity to practice these behaviors in a variety of settings, such as the home, the school, and the community.

Applied behavior analysis has been used in many settings for different purposes and can be used for people with ASD in teaching communication, play, self-care, work, social, academic, and community living skills. The original therapy by Dr Lovaas delivered 40 hours a week of one-on-one work with a trained professional. However, many experts now believe that ABA therapy used fewer hours per week can still be effective. Your child's treatment team will recommend the most appropriate intensity, based on your child's needs.

If there are challenging behaviors such as prolonged or intense tantrums or aggression, your therapist may recommend doing a *functional behavior analysis* (FBA). An FBA identifies antecedents and consequences surrounding the specific behavior. The FBA can suggest strategies for intervening that will alter the behavior and ways to gauge whether the intervention is working. Although you may hear more about this assessment tool in the context of a school setting, an FBA can also be used as part of an ABA intervention program.

Applied behavior analysis programs are typically led by professionals certified in behavior analysis, known as *board certified behavior analysts* (BCBAs). Oftentimes, registered behavior technicians administer much of the therapy with supervision performed by the BCBA. Generally, the BCBA will meet with you regularly to review your child's progress and to involve you in any decisions to be made. Applied behavior analysis interventions include many different approaches that are used on the basis of the needs of the child. Let's examine a few.

Discrete Trial Training

One of the most widely used ABA therapies is known as *discrete trial training* (DTT). Discrete trial training is often used to teach basic skills such as paying attention, following directions, and imitating instructions. A trained instructor works one-on-one with a child, who is given an instruction or a request, which is technically known as a *discriminative stimulus*. If the child performs the request, the instructor praises him for what he did and may even give him a reward that he finds immensely enjoyable.

Here's how DTT works: Let's say you want to teach your child to say hello when he sees other people. The instructor would explain and demonstrate to your child that he needs to say hello when the instructor enters the room. Walking into the room is the antecedent, and your child saying hello is the behavior. Each time your child says hello, he is praised by the instructor and given a reward, such as a sticker, which is the consequence. If your child does not say hello, the therapist may help your child by having him repeat a hello that the therapist says. This extra help in demonstrating correct behavior is called a *prompt*. The scenario is then repeated until your child masters this skill. Learning is successful when the child follows the request independently, consistently, in multiple settings, and without prompts.

Keep in mind that the instruction may be delivered verbally, in a visual such as a picture, or with a gesture, such as pointing. However it's given, it should be done so clearly, concisely, and in a way that is easily understood by your child.

Formal DTT is often done in sessions that last 2 or 3 hours, with sessions for young children being done at a small desk or in a therapy room with a therapist. Each session consists of short periods of structured time that are devoted to a single task, with short breaks throughout the session.

Critics of DTT say that the method does not teach children spontaneity and that the behaviors learned in such a highly structured setting aren't easily transferred to a child's natural environment. To address these concerns, there are other methods using ABA that are considered more naturalistic, meaning they take place in settings that are more familiar to the child.

Incidental Teaching

Shaping a child's behavior can sometimes involve placing her into a situation that compels her to do something. For instance, you might seat a child at a table with paper and no crayons, which would compel her to ask you for the crayons. If you hold a child's favorite toy without offering it to her, you will compel her to ask you to give it to her. The lessons the child acquires are taught incidentally, without formal instruction.

Pivotal Response Training

Instead of targeting a specific skill, pivotal response training (PRT) (previously called *natural language paradigm*) focuses on developing overarching, or pivotal, behaviors that affect other behaviors such as motivation, initiating communication with others, and self-management. By improving these broad behaviors, PRT indirectly improves play skills, social behaviors, and the ability to control one's own behavior.

Unlike DTT, which uses a more specific curriculum, PRT is child directed and taps into the child's natural instinct and desire to interact with adults. It uses rewards and reinforcements tailored specifically to the individual child and involves parents regularly in the child's most natural setting: her home.

Verbal Behavior

Using the same principles of ABA, verbal behavior (VB) works by encouraging the child to use language to get what he wants. Treatment is based on a book by the same title written by B.F. Skinner in 1957. The treatment breaks down language into 4 units—Skinner called them *operants*—each with its own function and purpose. Children who have ASD often use words as labels, or *tacts*. When a word is used to request something, it is called a *mand*. If the word is being used in a discussion when the object is not there, it's said to be *intra-verbal language*. When a word is repeated, it is called an *echoic*.

The goals of VB are to teach different ways to use language and encourage the child to make greater use of language to make requests and have discussions. The theory behind VB is that knowing language is different from using language.

Developmental Relationship Interventions

Through interactions with others, children learn to communicate and show appropriate emotions. The developmental approach is to use these interactions with parents to improve social skills by imitating, adding onto, or joining in activities started by the child.

Because social communication challenges are one of the core features of ASD, experts believe that improving a child's relationships with his caregivers, including parents, teachers, and therapists, is key to overcoming many challenges of ASD. Among the most common treatments are the Developmental, Individual Difference, Relationship-based (DIR) approach and Relationship Development Intervention (RDI).

Developmental, Individual Difference, Relationship-based Approach

The Developmental, Individual Difference, Relationship-based (DIR) approach works on the principle that a child's emotional development is the basis of her capacity for learning. Healthy emotional development leads to the ability to engage with others, communicate with purpose, and play in a meaningful way.

The DIR approach describes an intervention and philosophy created by Stanley Greenspan, MD, and Serena Wieder, PhD. Drs Greenspan and Wieder said children must achieve 6 developmental milestones, which form the foundation for all learning and development, for proper emotional and intellectual growth. These milestones are the abilities to

- Regulate their response to the sensory world and stay calm.
- Engage and relate to others in an intimate and loving way.
- Participate in 2-way communication.
- Communicate in more-complex ways, using gestures first and later words to express desires.
- Create emotional ideas.
- Develop emotional and logical thinking.

In children who do not have ASD, these milestones unfold naturally. But children with ASD often need an intervention to help spur these processes along. Dr Greenspan referred to his model as "floortime" (also called *Greenspan Floortime* or *DIRFloortime*) because as the name implies, it brings the therapist or parent down to the floor to meet the child at her level. Floortime was the first model that used the DIR intervention approach. Therapy follows a child's natural interests, affect, and emotions.

Treatment is individually tailored to the child's developmental level—socially, emotionally, and intellectually—and takes into account how the child experiences the sensory world. The idea is to play with the child by following her lead and at the same time engage her in a way that is warm and inviting.

Like with ABA, the goal of the DIR approach is to help your child learn to regulate her own behavior, engage with other people, and communicate effectively. Greenspan Floortime sessions typically last 20 to 30 minutes at a time and may be combined with and applied to other forms of therapy. Over time, activities become more complex as children learn more skills.

The DIR approach is used within the Play and Language for Autistic Youngsters (PLAY) Project. The PLAY Project is administered by parents who receive coaching, modeling, and video feedback from trained therapists. One recent study of the PLAY Project in young children with ASD (ages 2–6 years) showed improvements in language, development, and parent-child interactions.

Relationship Development Intervention

Relationship Development Intervention (RDI) was created by Steven Gutstein, PhD, and Rachelle Sheely, PhD. It focuses on activities that encourage social interaction and motivate the child to become more interested in interpersonal exchanges. According to Dr Gutstein, people who have ASD tend to withdraw because they are overwhelmed with sensory information. As a result, they prefer what is called *static systems*, such as memorizing facts and rigid rituals and routines, to dynamic systems, such as social relationships and complex thinking, which are characterized by unpredictability.

The RDI program targets what the creators of the program describe as the 6 main deficits of ASD.

- *Emotional referencing:* The ability to learn from the experiences of others.
- *Social coordination:* The ability to observe and continually regulate one's behavior to engage in meaningful relationships with others.

- *Declarative language:* The ability to use verbal and nonverbal language to interact with other people.

- *Flexible thinking:* The ability to quickly adapt strategies in the face of changing circumstances.

- *Relational information processing:* The ability to obtain meaning from information in the context of something larger. This skill includes solving problems with no right-and-wrong solutions.

- *Foresight and hindsight:* The ability to reflect on the past and anticipate potential future scenarios in a way that is productive and helpful.

Relationship Development Intervention is administered primarily by parents but also by teachers and other professionals. Parents learn the program through training seminars, books, and other materials and work with an RDI-certified consultant. It begins with family-guided participation, in which the child works one-on-one with the parent. Everyday tasks such as preparing rice, watering flowers, and cleaning a sink can be used in RDI. The program relies less on verbal instructions and more on visuals, including facial expressions, to encourage eye contact and nonverbal communication to engage the child in joint tasks.

In the second phase, known as the *dynamic education program,* lessons become more challenging and complex. The curriculum combines developing mental processes with traditional academic training and real-world problem-solving. As children progress through the program, they are encouraged to use these skills in settings that are increasingly unfamiliar and distracting. The child may learn from making mistakes as well as how to evaluate contradicting information and handle misunderstandings.

So far, studies of the effectiveness of RDI are encouraging. More-rigorous evaluations, however, in which outcomes of children receiving RDI are compared with those who do not receive RDI, have not yet been published.

Naturalistic Developmental Behavioral Interventions

Naturalistic developmental behavioral interventions (NDBIs) blend aspects of developmental and behavioral approaches. For example, they may take advantage of the play that children naturally do on their own in order to teach skills such as turn taking. The ABA approach added to this activity might be having a measurable goal around turn taking and the use of prompts to help the child make progress toward the goal. Naturalistic developmental behavioral interventions are also frequently based on manuals that give practitioners specific training and instructions so that the therapy is administered in a similar way among different children.

The most thoroughly studied NDBI is the Early Start Denver Model (ESDM), which uses play with a teacher or parent to teach a host of developmental skills. These skills cover all areas of early development: cognitive skills, language, social behavior, imitation, fine and gross motor skills, self-help skills, and adaptive behavior. The ESDM may be used for children as young as 12 months (and is now being tested on even younger children, including infants, with ASD-like features) with the overall goal of promoting the child's social and communication development. Though ESDM encompasses several areas of skill development, it is especially focused on teaching the child imitation, nonverbal communication (including joint attention), verbal communication, social behaviors, and play.

During an ESDM session, a child will be engaged in a joint activity with a therapist or parent in which there is constant give-and-take and turn taking between the therapist and the child. Activities are designed around what interests the child and use objects found in the child's natural environment. That might mean playing patty-cake with the child or rolling a ball back and forth. The ESDM is considered an intense intervention and may involve up to 20 to 25 hours of intervention a week (which may include time working with the parents and child together), but the number of hours per week is based on the needs of the child. The interaction is intended to be emotionally positive, even fun, and is designed to encourage the child to become more social. Instead of keeping a child in a classroom or a therapist's office, these playful lessons can be delivered by therapists and parents alike so the child is engaged with a responsive caregiver throughout her day.

In a recent study, researchers compared the outcomes of 48 young children with ASD (ages 18–30 months) who were split into 2 groups:

those who received ESDM and those who received other therapies available in their communities. Children in both groups were tested before the therapies began as well as 1 to 2 years after the start of the therapies. Compared with children who received other therapies, those who received ESDM performed better on tests of intelligence and self-help skills and their ASD symptoms were less severe. In a follow-up study, children in both groups had their brain waves evaluated with an electroencephalogram while looking at faces and objects. While viewing faces (a social activity), children in the ESDM group had brain waves that were more like that of typically developing children compared with children who received other therapies. So there was not only improved symptoms of ASD in the ESDM group but a corresponding change detected in the brain!

Focused Interventions to Develop Specific Skills

The comprehensive treatment models highlighted earlier in this chapter address multiple goals across different areas of development. Often they are used in younger children with ASD, especially during toddlerhood and the preschool years. Other more focused interventions are used to target more narrow and specific areas of development. Examples might include children with ASD who continue to need extra help with speech, self-care, motor skills, and sensory processing issues. Children may also benefit from group and individual social skills training.

Speech-Language Therapy

Because social communication differences are core features of ASD, many children with ASD will benefit from some form of speech-language therapy to enhance their communication skills. As stated earlier, some children with ASD encounter challenges in communicating their wants and needs, while others may inadvertently be one-sided in their conversations and benefit by working on 2-way communication. Teaching children with ASD to converse with others in social situations (also called *pragmatic communication*) involves comprehension and expression. The extent of speech-language therapy varies from one child to the next and depends on the needs of the individual.

The exact services your child requires are determined after evaluation by a speech-language pathologist, often called a *speech-language therapist*. Therapy itself may be done individually, in a small-group setting, or in a classroom. However, therapy is most effective when it involves everyone—teachers, support staff, families, and even the child's peers—to encourage the child to practice speech and language skills in a natural setting throughout the day.

It's important to think of communication as being more than speech, especially because recent studies show that about 30% of individuals with ASD do not gain the skill of verbal speech. Because some children with ASD become frustrated about not being able to verbally communicate their wants and needs, they may benefit from augmentative communication—using gestures, sign language, or picture communication programs. For example, your child may benefit from the Picture Exchange Communication System, a method that uses ABA principles to teach children with less-developed verbal abilities to communicate with pictures. With guidance from a therapist, teacher, or parent, the child learns how to exchange a picture for an object and eventually learns to use pictures to express thoughts and desires. Eventually, the child learns to create sentences using more than one picture and to answer questions.

Introducing augmentative communication to children with ASD who are not yet using verbal communication does not keep them from learning to talk, and there is some evidence that they may be more stimulated to learn speech if they already understand something about symbolic communication. Augmentative communication may also include the use of electronic devices or applications, some of which have synthesized speech output.

Social Skills
Socially interacting with other people is a key challenge for children with ASD, often because they may have difficulty understanding the point of view of their conversational partner. Without these important social skills, they may have

- Challenges starting, maintaining, and ending an interaction
- Difficulty understanding nonverbal and verbal social cues, such as eye contact, facial expressions, and gestures
- Difficulty understanding the unwritten social rules for a particular situation
- Difficulty compromising, negotiating, and resolving conflicts
- Difficulty maintaining focus and attention during play or leisure activities

Therefore, teaching social skills can be a critical part of any intervention program. Of particular benefit is joint attention training, which may be especially important in children who are not yet speaking. Joint attention, that is, the sharing of experiences, forms the foundation for the development of later social language abilities and can predict how well a child develops those skills. In fact, studies show that functional speech and language typically starts about a year after a child masters joint attention. Joint attention is often a skill that is targeted within behavioral, developmental, and NDBI approaches in young children with ASD.

Symbolic (or Pretend) Play Skills

Symbolic play skills, or pretend play, are another important early and necessary component of the later development of social skills. A 2006 study showed that children who were in a joint attention or symbolic play intervention group had better social play interactions afterward than children who did not receive these interventions.

A good social skills intervention teaches children how to respond to friendly overtures from other children and adults, teaches them how to initiate social interactions, and helps them access the activities in their communities that are important for them. It also teaches them how to use and manage a broad variety of social skills. A typical training session may teach children something as basic as how to make eye contact or something more challenging such as how to invite a friend over to play. Social skills training can take many different forms. Lessons are usually taught by social workers, speech-language therapists, or psychologists, using a variety of methods such as storytelling, visual cueing, games, video modeling, and role-playing. Many social skill interventions incorporate typically developing peers, and they have demonstrated improved interactions between children with ASD and children without ASD and improved friendships between a child with ASD and typically developing peers.

Social skill interventions may take place within groups or individually and within classrooms or in behavioral health settings. A recent study that examined the evidence of many different types of social skill interventions showed that children with ASD improved their social interactions with peers and friendship quality but did not demonstrate that participants improved their ability to recognize different emotions.

Formal social skills curricula do exist; one such program that has been studied is the Program for the Education and Enrichment of Relational Skills. This program is a parent-assisted social skill intervention for high-functioning teens with ASD. The program consists of 14 weekly 90-minute sessions that parents and teens attend separately. Examples of session topics include conversational skills, electronic communication, humor, sportsmanship, teasing, arguments, disagreements, rumors, and gossip. Teens who participated in the program, compared with those who did not participate, had better awareness and demonstration of social skills and had increased interactions with their peers. If you have a school-aged child or adolescent with ASD, you might consider asking your child's educational or behavioral team about creating goals around social skills. In addition, the family plays a critical role in daily interactions that can teach and model social skills. These interactions can be easily woven into the child and family's daily activities. It's also important for the child to have a wealth of opportunities to engage with peers with typical development. For more information on how parents can encourage social skills, see Chapter 12.

Occupational Therapy

Children with ASD often have deficits in the areas of fine motor skills, sensory processing, and motor planning. These can show up as difficulties with basic self-care skills, such as getting dressed, using a spoon, or brushing teeth. Some have trouble with fine motor skills, such as building puzzles, handwriting, or using scissors, and basic life skills, such as sitting still in a classroom. Occupational therapists (OTs) can often help with these issues. An OT evaluates the child's fine motor skills and sensory processing development and prepares strategies for learning tasks of daily living. These interventions may be delivered in sessions with a therapist and then practiced at home and school. Goals will depend on the needs of the individual child, but occupational therapy strives to help children gain more independence and live a higher quality of life.

Sensory Integration Therapy

As reviewed in Chapter 1, the latest diagnostic criteria for ASD in the fifth edition of the *Diagnostic and Statistical Manual of Mental Disorders* includes recognition that children with ASD may have sensory challenges. *Sensory integration* is a term that has been used to describe processes in the brain that allow us to take information we receive from our 5 senses, organize it, and respond appropriately. We also have a vestibular sense (balance) that tells us how to position our bodies and heads and a proprioceptive sense (awareness of body in space) that helps us know what we do with our joints, muscles, and ligaments. In children who have ASD, sensory processing deficits have been theorized to cause difficulties that affect behavior and life skills. As a result, some children may be overly sensitive or under-responsive to stimuli in the surroundings. Loud music, for instance, may cause intense discomfort, while bright fluorescent lights that bother others may be riveting to some children with ASD. Children with sensory processing deficits may have difficulty with motor skills, balance, and coordination. Some children will look for ways to seek out certain sensations and engage in behaviors such as rocking back and forth, playing overly rough, head banging, and oral exploration of nonedible objects.

Sensory integration therapy, which was developed in the 1970s by an OT, A. Jean Ayres, is designed to help children with sensory processing problems (including possibly those with ASD) cope with the difficulties they have processing sensory input. Therapy sessions are play oriented and may include using equipment such as swings, trampolines, and slides.

Sensory integration also uses therapies such as deep pressure, body brushing, weighted vests, and swinging. These therapies appear to sometimes be able to calm an anxious child. In addition, sensory integration therapy is believed to increase a child's threshold for tolerating sensory-rich environments, to make transitions less disturbing, and to assist a child in maintaining attention and focus without getting overly tired or hyperactive.

Although there are scientific studies to show that children with ASD are more likely to have sensory processing problems, the effectiveness of sensory integration therapy as a therapy for ASD is somewhat limited. While this finding may still allow for the therapy possibly being helpful in some children, effectiveness might be more objectively judged in an individual child by identifying specific goals and tracking progress. Talk with your child's pediatrician if you suspect that your child has difficulties with sensory processing; there may be resources in the community for further evaluation.

You may also learn about auditory integration training or behavioral optometry as methods for controlling sensory input. Both treatments aim to alter the child's response to sensory stimuli, but neither method has proved to be scientifically valid. Also, there is no evidence that any problems seen in children with ASD are related to these auditory or visual problems. (See Chapter 7.)

How to Access Autism Interventions

Now that you have at least some understanding of the many treatments of ASD, you may be wondering where to go for help. The answer varies, depending on the age of your child and services available in your community. A good place to start is with your child's pediatrician. You can also find information through local chapters of national organizations such as Autism Speaks, Family Voices, and others listed in Appendix A. Another good resource is other parents who have already begun this journey.

In general, if your child is younger than 3 years, you can access many of these services through the Early Intervention (EI) Program. The EI Program is a federal grant program run by individual states under

Part C of the Individuals with Disabilities Education Act (IDEA) that works with children from birth until their third birthday. It is also called the *Program for Infants and Toddlers with Disabilities*. Although the program exists in all 50 states, eligibility for the program and types of services varies by state. The program targets children who show a delay in cognitive, social, or communication skills. They may also have a delay in physical or motor abilities or self-care skills. Anyone can refer a child to EI, including a pediatrician, parent, grandparent, or child care provider. The child doesn't even need a diagnosis.

The EI program's team of specialists will test and evaluate your child to see whether he qualifies for the program. If, after the initial evaluation, your child is eligible for the program, you will help develop an Individualized Family Service Plan (IFSP), which explains the services recommended for your child and how EI will help you and your family support your child. The IFSP will describe your child's current developmental levels, ways to improve your child's development, and the outcomes you can expect. It will also outline the specific services that you and your family will receive and the goal dates for starting and ending those services. In addition, the IFSP will assign service providers in an EI program, which include many types of professionals such as social workers, speech-language therapists, OTs, physical therapists, registered dietitians, developmental therapists, behavioral therapists, and psychologists. Services may be provided in your home or in the community. Individual states may have more-intensive services available for children diagnosed as having ASD or at high risk for ASD, such as ABA or ESDM or another NDBI, so check with your local EI program for the most up-to-date information. For a quick overview of what is covered in your state, visit http://ectacenter.org/~pdfs/topics/earlyid/partc_elig_table.pdf.

Children and youths aged 3 to 21 years access services through the special education program (Part B of IDEA). A call to the special education department of the local school district, starting with the special education coordinator at your home school, is a good place to start. You can access special education services for your child even if she is not in public school. We review a lot more about educational services in the next chapter.

Medical insurance, either through the Medicaid program or through private health insurance, is another way that many families are increasingly able to access ASD interventions. For example, almost every state in the United States has passed ASD insurance reform legislation that mandates insurance coverage for at least some ASD interventions. These reforms were made possible by dedicated parents and advocates who worked hard for change. More recently, many state Medicaid plans have followed suit and are now covering ASD interventions as well. Many of these mandates specifically cite comprehensive treatment models, such as ABA, as ones that are covered. While there is variability on the basis of where you live and the plan you have, it may be that your insurance plan can help your child access needed services. We'll get into more specifics about insurance in Chapter 10.

Autism Champion: Kirsten Sneid

WHEN KIRSTEN SNEID learned her son Evan had severe autism, she was devastated. But she was determined to find a way to connect with him. "I never asked why, why him, or why us," she says. "If I went down that road, I don't think I'd ever get out of there. Instead, I prayed. What now? Where now? Who now?"

She started by abandoning her nursing career to raise Evan and his older brother, Ian, who had been diagnosed as having pervasive developmental disorder–not otherwise specified, which has since been reclassified as autism spectrum disorder (ASD). She began hosting wine parties and coffee hours at her home, where she brought together other parents of children with ASD. In 2001, she became the founding president of the Autism Society in her county to help improve services for children with ASD. "It started as a support group," she says. "We were constantly knocking on the doors of community service providers. We realized that this was a community health care crisis that required a community response." The group is now called the *Autism Society of the Heartland*.

Obstacles arose at every turn. When Evan hit preschool, Kirsten realized there were no good preschool programs for kids like him. So she created an applied behavior analysis program in her home and hired college students who were studying occupational therapy and speech-language pathology. The program was so successful that the local school district used it to create its own. Kirsten also joined the Kansas Coalition for Autism Legislation and lobbied legislators for insurance coverage for ASD services. She helped organize think tanks such as the Greater Kansas City Autism Initiative and served on numerous advisory boards, including the Thompson Center for Autism and Neurodevelopmental Disabilities at the University of Missouri and the Kansas Center for Autism Research and Training (K-CART) at the University of Kansas.

These days, Evan is 22 years old with limited verbal skills. At 24, Ian graduated community college with an associate's degree in arts and sciences, went on to university, and graduated cum laude in political science and international relations and he graduated from the police academy and is currently interviewing with area police departments. He no longer meets the criteria for ASD. Kirsten returned to her nursing career and served on the board of the Expanding College for Exceptional Learners, or EXCEL, until 2017. The group helps provide funding to bistate colleges willing to create educational opportunities for postsecondary students with intellectual disabilities. "It's up to the university to put it together, but we help them succeed," she says. Currently, she serves as a community council member with her local Developmental Supports agency to assess the needs, safety, and well-being of those aging into community services, as well as on the advisory board for K-CART at the University of Kansas.

Kirsten says all she ever wanted was to help families of children with ASD know they are not alone. "I am really just a worker ant who has had the pleasure and the privilege to surround myself with brilliant, motivated people wanting to create change," she says. "And we have."

CHAPTER 5

Tapping Educational Services

PARTICIPATING IN a traditional school setting can be challenging for children who have autism spectrum disorder (ASD). Anxiety, fixation on routines, difficulties with sensory input, and the need to perform repetitive behaviors make it a challenge for many children with ASD to absorb what they're taught or sit still through a lesson. Compounding the difficulties are the social challenges that many children with ASD experience. But with the right accommodations, going to school can be fun, rewarding, and worthwhile for children with ASD. In fact, under federal law, all children, including those with disabilities such as autism, are entitled to a free and appropriate education. That means your child may be able to receive special education, that is, a program of instruction that is tailored to your child's special needs and places him in a setting that will help him make progress.

Special education services begin once a child turns 3 years old with the move from early intervention (EI) programs (reviewed in Chapter 4) into early childhood special education (ECSE) programs (developmental preschools) and then into grade school. Special education continues to be available until an eligible individual is 21 years old. You already learned about the many kinds of behavioral and developmental services that your child may receive, in Chapter 4. Those same services may also be provided in school, as part of your child's special education services. In most cases, your child will receive a mix of these services.

In this chapter, we look at what you can expect when your child transitions from EI to ECSE and then to grade school. We also help you understand some of the teaching strategies that might work best for children who have ASD. While the teachers, administrators, and staff at your school will play an important role in how well your child does there, you are an important part of the team as well. As is true with children with typical development, parents play an important role in their child's academic success. That is especially true in the case of children with disabilities such as autism, in which parental input, guidance, and oversight are essential to a child's progress.

Knowing Your Rights: A Word About the Individuals with Disabilities Education Act

First enacted in 1975 and most recently amended in 2015 (as of this writing), the Individuals with Disabilities Education Act (IDEA) is a law that ensures that all children with disabilities have access to "free and appropriate education in the least restrictive environment." The act governs how states and public agencies provide EI, special education, and related services to more than 6.5 million eligible babies, toddlers, children, and youths with disabilities, including those with ASD. Babies and toddlers between the ages of birth and 3 years receive EI services under IDEA Part C. Children and youths between the ages of 3 years and 21 years receive special education and related services under IDEA Part B.

Federal law greatly emphasizes parental involvement and stresses the importance of including parents in decisions about their children's education. Before a school district identifies the need for highly specialized and individual instruction as part of a child's education program, it must provide prior written notice to, and obtain consent from, the child's parents. The district must also provide parents with information about their rights under IDEA Part B. In addition, parents must work together with school personnel to determine services that the child will receive to meet her unique needs.

First Things First: The All-important Individualized Education Program

To determine exactly which services your child needs, you will work with a team of specialists to complete a written document known as the *Individualized Education Program* (IEP). Every child who receives special education services must have an IEP. The IEP is the educational road map for children with disabilities. It spells out your child's goals and outlines the exact education, services, and supplementary aids that the school district will provide for your child.

Parents who feel their child might benefit from special education services should request an IEP evaluation from the school in writing. Your pediatrician can also help draft a letter of request. Parents should work with personnel from their child's EI program or provider to help with this transition. You can begin this process when your child turns 24 months of age.

An IEP is written after an evaluation. During the evaluation, current performance levels are established and documented. To be eligible for special education services, your child must be identified with a recognized disability (there are 14 different disability categories under IDEA) and the disability must adversely affect her educational performance.

Every IEP should have several key pieces of information. It should include your child's current levels of performance, measurable goals for the school year, and when reports about her progress will be provided. It should also discuss how well she's able to function in school, how your child will be included with peers with typical development, and how your child will be assessed on statewide and district-wide tests. In addition, should your child qualify for extended school year services, the IEP should lay out the kinds of interventions that your child should receive when school is not in session. The IEP establishes dates and locations of when services will begin, where they will be held, and how long they will last. The IEP should also discuss what will be done when your child's needs change. In addition, the IEP may outline whether your child gets "related services" such as special transportation, speech-language therapy, occupational therapy, and counseling.

The IEP is written collaboratively by a group—often called an *IEP team*—made up of the child's parents, a regular education teacher, a special education teacher, psychologists, therapists, a school administrator, and possibly other school personnel. A meeting to discuss the IEP must be held within 30 days after a school determines that a child needs special education services. Parents may invite anyone to this meeting, including personnel such as an advocate or the child's case

A Parent's Story: Barbara

Having 2 boys with autism prompted Barbara to do a lot of research into interventions. She concluded that for her family, applied behavior analysis (ABA) was the best therapy. But when she learned ABA wasn't a therapy option in her school district, she decided to advocate for its inclusion in her son's Individualized Education Program.

"As the parent of a child with autism, you have to learn to negotiate. You have to be persuasive and positive. You have to prepare for a legal fight but hope you don't have to. You have to keep good records.

"I always brought solutions to the table too. When they asked who should be my son's teaching aide [TA], I told them I had someone in mind. When the room he was using for speech-language therapy got taken away, I told them I didn't care if they used a closet. In fact, he did wind up in a small room without windows.

"Of course, you also have to realize that you won't always get your way. For instance, I wanted them to assess Sam's ability to work in a group. But the TA wasn't willing to take that data, and I had to be willing to put [up] with that."

The bottom line, according to Barbara, is that schools are required to meet your children's needs. "As the parent of a child with autism, I didn't care if I had to beg and grovel for what was important to me. It was for my sons."

manager from the EI program. The IEP is evaluated at least every year to determine whether goals are being met and may be adjusted if your child's needs change.

Unfortunately, research has showed that many IEPs for children with ASD are lacking and do not meet requirements of IDEA. Many IEPs omit important information and may not provide services to a child outside of the traditional school year. Many do not adequately describe how goals are to be measured or how certain goals will help the child in school. Many IEPs also fail to say how teachers intend to motivate the child or how they would engage the child in developmentally appropriate tasks or play. Some IEPs may not include important parent concerns.

When formulating your child's IEP with your school district, it's important to know exactly what your rights are and what to do if you are not happy with the resulting IEP. Before going to your first IEP meeting, do your research. Become familiar with your state's education laws, and know the types of interventions available to your child that are based on her needs. A good reference to start with is the *Individualized Education Program (IEP): Summary, Process and Practical Tips* guide published by Autism Speaks and available for download on its Web site, www.autismspeaks.org. You may also want to visit the US Department of Education one-stop shop for resources related to IDEA and rules and regulations concerning the IEP process at http://idea. ed.gov. See Appendix A for more information.

The TEACCH Method

In the 1960s, Eric Schopler and his colleagues at the University of North Carolina created an educational approach for teaching children with ASD known as *TEACCH* (Treatment and Education of Autistic and related Communication-handicapped CHildren). Schopler believed that autism was a lifelong disability but that things could be done to help a child adapt to the school and community. The program uses a variety of strategies to accommodate the needs of children with autism and also includes elements of different behavioral and developmental interventions, including applied behavior analysis; the Developmental, Individual Difference, Relationship-based approach; and social skills training. The program stresses the importance of identifying individual strengths and weaknesses and uses structured teaching methods that play to the child's strengths and interests. In particular for children with ASD, it focuses on 4 main concepts to enhance learning.

- *The organization of the child's physical environment:* The layout of a classroom—where the furniture is placed, the boundaries between work and play areas, and how items are labeled—is critical to how well a child with ASD learns. TEACCH stresses the importance of creating an environment that minimizes distractions. Work areas, for instance, should not be placed near windows. Leisure areas should not be located near exits. Pieces of tape may be placed on the floor to show where chairs should be situated while seated. The TEACCH method encourages teachers to create an environment with a lot of visual cues that will help children with ASD better understand directions and rules, better transition from one task to another, and better remain focused on the activity at hand.

- *A predictable, though flexible, routine:* Students with ASD have a strong need for consistency and routine. Many of them experience high levels of anxiety if those routines are disrupted, which can interfere with their learning. Providing a clearly illustrated (visuals are always best) schedule helps a child know what to expect in his day.

- *Structured activity systems:* Children with ASD thrive on structure and like it when tasks that are expected of them are clearly laid out. It's important to create a step-by-step process that's easy for them to understand. Early on, the system might be a series of pictures showing what tasks need to be done and in what order. Later, the system might involve the use of simple words or phrases. In some cases, the task may be arranged from left to right. As with any system, however, the student should be closely supervised by an adult, such as an aide, or the teacher.

- *An emphasis on visual learning:* Children with ASD do much better with visual cues, such as pictures, than they do with verbal or auditory ones. A visual schedule with pictures, for instance, may be helpful for outlining the day's activities. Color-coding subject areas can help a student stay organized. A chart with photographs or cartoons may show a child options for appropriate behavior when a classroom gets too noisy. Colored floor mats help him know where to sit for certain activities.

TEACCH is one of the oldest and most widely used programs in schools, and in North Carolina it has been the official form of publicly funded education for children with ASD since 1978. Although no other state abides by the principles of TEACCH as closely, elements of the program have seeped into classrooms throughout the world.

National Professional Development Center on Autism Spectrum Disorder

In 2007, the National Professional Development Center (NPDC) on Autism Spectrum Disorder was founded with funding by the US Department of Education Office of Special Education Programs. It is a multi-university program, and among its goals is to promote evidence-based practice—meaning effective treatments based on scientific research—for children and adolescents with ASD. The NPDC works with states to provide professional development to teachers and practitioners who serve individuals from birth through 22 years of age with ASD.

Using very strict criteria, the NPDC does an extensive literature review to determine which studies would be effective for a given service provider. The NPDC then develops a variety of resources and materials, including online modules and implementation checklists, giving service providers access to evidence-based practices. The NPDC updates the literature review periodically so that it reflects recent research and keeps practices current.

Included in evidence-based practices is structured teaching as well as interventions discussed in Chapter 4. To learn more, visit http://autismpdc.fpg.unc.edu.

Teaching Children With Autism Spectrum Disorder

Educating a child with ASD is not like teaching children with typical development. As you now know, children with ASD process information differently. Exactly where and how a child is educated in a school varies widely, depending on the child's needs, the child's age, and what is available in your school district. Some children may require a self-contained special education classroom, while others may be included in a mainstream class with peers who do not have ASD. Often, children who have ASD have a mix of specialized experiences and inclusive experiences at school. But even the highest functioning students often still need special supports to help them with organization, assignment comprehension, and other essential skills such as learning to manage social and peer relationships.

Every child's educational experiences will vary, just as the difficulties and talents of a child will differ. But like children with typical development, those who have ASD will have some general concerns that apply to each grade level.

Preschool

Between the ages of 3 years and 5 years, your child will most likely attend a preschool program for young children identified under IDEA Part B (Section 619) and often referred to as *early childhood special education (ECSE) programs*. These are typically half-day programs. Depending on your child's level of ability, he may be placed in a self-contained classroom, which is made up only of other children with special needs, with a small student to teacher ratio and where services such as speech-language therapy, occupational therapy, and social work may be integrated into the classroom experience. If appropriate and available, he may be in a blended classroom where he will be part of a class with children who have disabilities and those who do not. In a blended classroom, he may have a higher ratio of students to teachers, and he will be exposed to peers with typical development. He may also have the opportunity to receive specific therapies, such as speech-language or occupational, but these may be pullout services and not implemented directly within the classroom setting.

For some high-functioning children with ASD, parents and educators may choose to place them into a mainstream preschool, where they are exposed entirely to typically developing children. Specific therapies may be delivered privately after school in the home or community, or they may be done by an aide who works privately with your child in the school setting. Some school districts employ an autism consultant who works with preschool staff to provide modifications that support your child's success in a mainstream setting. As with all educational services, exactly how your child's preschool experience is structured will vary depending on his needs, strengths, and challenges, as well as resources available in your community. During this time, you may also choose to work with private practitioners (for example, behavioral specialists, speech-language pathologists, occupational therapists) to which your child's pediatrician refers you. Ideally, these practitioners will coordinate their services with those who work with your child in the school setting.

A Parent's Story: Nora

When Nora's daughter Rory was first diagnosed as having autism spectrum disorder at 24 months of age, Nora and her family felt as if they were on their own. But they found a developmental pediatrician who was a wonderful resource.

After spending a few months with a private therapist, Rory went to an applied behavior analysis (ABA) class. But it was not a good fit for her.

"Another mother suggested a private tutor that she had been using, who was a preschool teacher for children with autism. We always say she turned out to be Rory's Annie Sullivan. That woman got her in line. Carolyn didn't give up. That first day, Rory wanted her milk and Carolyn said, 'I'll give you your milk, but you have to say milk.' Rory screamed and cried and after about 20 minutes said, 'Milk.' It was incredible.

"Psychologists who evaluated Rory all agreed that she is very bright and capable of learning. She's known her alphabet since she was 24 months. She continued her private ABA lessons until she turned 3 and was sent to a private autism preschool that does 30 hours a week of ABA. She is now 5 and attending the same program but at the local elementary school. She also gets occupational therapy and speech-language therapy in school."

The bottom line to Nora's story: it will take time, energy, and patience, but to make progress, it's important to determine what therapy and therapists work best for you and your child.

Elementary School

Moving from preschool to an elementary school can be an exciting transition, but for children with ASD, it can also be a challenging one. More people may be involved in your child's education, and there may be more transitions in a day than he had in preschool. Socializing with peers and interacting with more adults also becomes a bigger part of the day. Extracurricular activities may become part of the schedule too.

According to law, children with disabilities must be placed into what is called the *least restrictive environment*, which requires school districts to educate children with ASD among children who are "nondisabled" and in "regular classes" as much as possible. The goal is for the child to be taught in the most natural setting possible while still making progress. Some people call this *mainstreaming*, while others refer to it as *integration* or *inclusion*.

Why the push for the least restrictive environment? Experts believe that being in an inclusive setting allows children with ASD to interact more frequently with people outside the special education environment. That means spending time with everyone from their typically developing peers, to support staff, to the custodial staff. Exposure to different groups allows for more social interactions, which can bolster a child's social skills, communication abilities, and confidence. Providing opportunities for inclusion of children with ASD has benefits for their typically developing peers as well, who become attached to their peers with differences and learn to support them in school and in their communities.

Of course, parents and others might not agree on the ideal classroom placement for a child with ASD. Different school districts will have different policies about what works best. It's also possible for a child's needs to change over time. But wherever a child is placed, it's essential that supports are in place to help him do his best. Possible classroom options include

- *Self-contained classroom:* The child is placed in a class only for children with disabilities.
- *Partial mainstreaming:* The child spends part of his day in a self-contained classroom and the other part in a regular classroom.

- *Full mainstreaming with support:* The child spends the entire day in a regular classroom with help from an aide.
- *Full mainstreaming without support:* The child spends the day in a regular classroom without an aide.

Integrating a child with ASD into a classroom with his mainstream peers often requires some form of disability awareness training for the teachers and possibly for other students he will see during the day. Ideally, the classroom teacher will know about autism and will take the necessary steps to make the room a comfortable environment for your child. She should also take some time to talk to your family about what works best for your child. It's important that teachers assist your child as he transitions between activities and do what it takes to help him navigate social and communication challenges. For instance, the teacher may help identify peers who could be paired up with your child during lunch and recess so he receives support from classmates during 2 of the more social parts of the day.

Many children with ASD also benefit from having the specialized therapies you read about in Chapter 4. For instance, your child may attend speech-language therapy to bolster his communication skills or occupational therapy to help with fine motor and self-care skills.

Some children may benefit from participation in a social skills group. A social skills group could help your child understand and practice his social interactions. Although the school setting is perfect for social skills training, it is also a difficult place to provide the amount and type of training that most children with ASD may require. Previous studies on social skills training have shown that most formal programs in schools may not be enough to make a difference in improving a child's social skills, while a more recent study published in 2016 suggested that participation increased peer engagement and decreased isolation during recess.

Even if your child is involved in a social skills group at school, it is important for you to work on these skills with your child at home as peer interactions start to become more complex. Games that encourage cooperation, for instance, can teach children how to get along better in group settings. Role-playing different social situations can help prepare your child for real-life situations in school. Presenting appropriate behaviors in the form of a story—also known as *social stories*—can be helpful as well. Explicit instructions for coping with tough situations, such as how to deal with a bully, may be helpful. You can also use drawings to teach your child how to read moods, books to teach manners, and home videos to show how to behave in different situations.

For some children, it is appropriate to have an aide or a paraprofessional within the classroom. The aide can ensure that your child spends as much time in an inclusive setting as possible. Children at this level may also be given special academic accommodations to help them succeed. For instance, they may be allowed to do just the even-numbered problems on a math assignment. In this case, the child is able to show what he knows while not getting too frustrated doing a task that may increase anxiety and frustration. Your child may be eligible for adaptive physical education to increase participation through accommodations for social, communication, or motor difficulties. Some kids may be given a designated cooldown area if they experience increased anxiety during certain times of the day.

To enhance your child's elementary-level education, it's important to involve him in other activities such as recreational programs, after-school clubs, and special interest groups. You may also want to enroll him in religious education, if that is important to you and your family. These groups not only tap into your child's interests but create additional opportunities for him to practice and hone his social and communication skills while participating in the life of his community. Your child's pediatrician and school team may be aware of extracurricular activities that are adapted for children with ASD and other disabilities within your community. See Chapter 9 for more information on community-based activities for children with ASD.

Middle School

The transition between elementary school and middle school can be even more challenging for some children with ASD. For starters, your child will now be switching classes every period instead of staying in one classroom for all subjects, which will place greater demand on her organization skills and ability to transition efficiently. She'll also be getting more time to complete longer-term assignments. Socially, your child may become more vulnerable to bullying as children become more aware of differences. Her peers may choose to avoid her so they aren't associated with the "weird" kid. Any differences in her personal hygiene and habits may become more obvious as adolescents become increasingly self-conscious about their appearance. To make it even more challenging, early hormonal changes in puberty might make her emotions less predictable and more volatile, which can make it harder for her to regulate her fluctuating emotions. Your young teen may become moody, irritable, and hostile. She may have changes in eating and sleeping habits and may even lose interest in things that used to fascinate her.

Some children may require additional supports for these vulnerabilities, which should be spelled out in their IEP. Different schools will use different methods for providing that kind of support. In some schools, for instance, children with ASD may be paired up with peer buddies who can help them navigate peer relationships. You can read about local friendship programs offered through Best Buddies at www.bestbuddies.org. Extra effort from school staff and parents may be necessary to help a child stay organized. A child with ASD may be placed into a supervised study hall staffed by a teacher, preferably with a special education background, who actively participates in helping the student organize assignments, directing the student's efforts to complete homework, and serving as a resource to assist the student in completing her work. The study hall teacher maintains communication with the student's regular teachers to make sure assignments are being recorded properly, completed, and handed in. Some districts may step up their efforts to communicate with parents.

Sexuality may become an issue at this age too. Important topics include sex education (including sex abuse education), self-care, hygiene, and intimate relationships. It's important to start these discussions early and regularly so when issues come up, it's possible to have a good, deep conversation that is at a level that your child understands. Helping children with ASD and other developmental disabilities understand rules about touch, affection, and boundaries can be difficult. If your child has difficulty understanding social norms such as keeping private parts covered in public, you will need to discuss that with her. If you have trouble discussing these topics, take advantage of your child's pediatrician and professionals at the school, who can help you figure out the best ways to raise these issues and have meaningful conversations about them.

Social challenges may become more of an issue at this age, as peers begin to play a more important role. Some children may be overly sensitive to what their peers say or do, while others may be entirely indifferent. Others become prey for bullies.

With greater self-awareness, your child may begin to notice that she is different than others, so you should be prepared to discuss your child's diagnosis with her in an appropriate way. (See the "Discussing an Autism Spectrum Disorder Diagnosis With Your Child" box on pages 109–111 later in this chapter.)

To help your child navigate the social world of middle school, make sure to continue working with her on her social skills, especially if the school no longer has these programs available. Some schools have peer programs in which certain typical students are selected and assigned to interact with specific students with ASD regularly. If bullying is widespread, the district may conduct disability awareness training and school-wide anti-bullying programs for all students.

Remember that these are the years when your child may have more unstructured time outside of her school day. Use this as an opportunity to help her explore activities that appeal to her interests and goals, even those that may someday lead to a vocation or career. Look for ways to modify interests that may no longer seem age appropriate and adapt them so they are. For instance, if a child loves to mold clay, consider enrolling her in a sculpting class. It's also important at this age to begin encouraging your child's independence and self-sufficiency. The more your child is able to do, the easier it will be for her later on to secure a job and live on her own.

High School

Entering high school is a big change for any teen and marks the transition to adulthood. These are the years when you begin planning for life after school. Will your teen go to college? Begin training for a job? Live on his own? While you are working through these important questions, it's essential that you continue to revisit your teen's IEP so his educational program remains current and reflects his ongoing progress as well as any new concerns.

When your teen starts high school, around the age of 14 years, it's important to begin the process of planning and setting long-term goals that will lead to development of a transition plan. Under IDEA law, an individual's IEP is required to have a transition plan by the time he is 16 years old. The transition plan identifies the services your teen will need to prepare for life after high school and describes his goals as he enters adulthood. The plan should reflect his personal desires and interests while also discussing practical concerns such as employment options, continuing education, health care, long-term care, sibling support, and need for community, state, and federal resources.

To create a transition plan that promotes success after school, it's important to involve your teen as well as teachers, siblings, friends, and any other people who are intimately familiar with his skills, talents, and shortcomings. Conversations about the transition plan should include questions that assess academic skills (reading, math, and writing) and personal skills (social strengths, interests, and reliability) such as

- What does your teen like to do?
- What are his dreams, goals, and interests for work?
- What are his strengths? What can he do?
- What are some areas that he still needs to explore and learn?
- What does he need to learn to reach his goals?
- What are some future education goals?
- How do you and your teen feel about him getting a job?
- Where are some viable places for employment?
- What kinds of transportation does he have available to him?
- Where will he live?

- What kind of health insurance will your teen have down the road?
- Does he require supports in developing friendships?
- Is he well-known in the community?
- Does he need help structuring his recreation time?
- What hobbies and interests does he have?

When formulating your teen's goals, it's important to think about his learning skills, communication skills, and ability to deal with sensory input. Is he a slow learner? Does he have a strategy for communicating that is effective, even if he doesn't speak clearly? Is he able to deal with new sights, sounds, and smells that he may confront in the community or workplace?

In considering any future employment opportunities, it's important to consider what kinds of job training or postsecondary education your teen will want. Some teens may have very specific goals in mind that may require more long-term planning. Your current school district may work with agencies and community partners to help your teen secure the support and training he will need. It's also important to know that several colleges and universities now offer programs geared specifically toward students who have ASD and other disabilities.

Difficulties in School for Children With Autism

School can be a wonderful place for learning, friendships, and honing the life skills that any child will need to succeed. But for some children, it can also be a challenging place, filled with stress, social anxieties, and performance concerns. These problems may be more commonly experienced by children who have ASD.

Challenging Behaviors

As anyone who has ever gone through school knows, good behavior is critical to a student's academic performance. But children with ASD may struggle with behaviors that are counterproductive to their progress and even disruptive to other students.

If your child is having behavioral problems, a team of professionals may do a *functional behavior analysis* (FBA). As you may recall, an FBA

Discussing an Autism Spectrum Disorder Diagnosis With Your Child

Parents may wonder about when and whether to tell their child about his or her autism spectrum disorder (ASD) diagnosis. Following are some commonly asked questions about discussing the diagnosis with a child with ASD:

Should I tell my child about his diagnosis?

Parents may fear that finding out about ASD will be hard on their child. Some children can initially find the news upsetting, especially if they are very sensitive to any suggestion that they are different from their peers. Many individuals with ASD, however, have shared that learning they were on the autism spectrum suddenly made it clear why so many things had been difficult or why they had been treated differently. With increased awareness of ASD, a diagnosis may also provide a reason for their behavior that they think other people might understand. For some, the diagnosis can take away the notion that past problems had all been the result of some personal failing; replacing this with the notion of a legitimate condition helps explain their challenges.

When should I tell my child that he has ASD?

While it is important to tell an individual with ASD about the diagnosis, there is no correct age or time to tell a child. A child's personality, abilities, and social awareness are all factors to con-sider in determining when he is ready for information about his diagnosis. For example, a parent may decide to talk about ASD when the child begins asking questions such as "Why am I different?"

Considering the potential effect of the information, how can a parent best explain to a child that he has ASD?

- *Before you begin, assess what your child already knows and how well he will be able to take in a discussion about ASD.*
- *Pitch the news at the right level.* Prepare to explain ASD in terms your child can grasp. Too vague of an explanation may not satisfy an inquisitive teenager, while too technical of an explanation may confuse or frighten a child of any age. If circumstances lead to a very early first discussion about your child's differences, you may

Discussing an Autism Spectrum Disorder Diagnosis With Your Child (*continued*)

Considering the potential effect of the information, how can a parent best explain to a child that he has ASD?* (continued)**

choose not to use the actual ASD label but discuss how some children learn differently or need help with certain things at school. Disclosing a more specific diagnosis can wait until your child's understanding grows.

■ *Be positive.* When sharing news of a diagnosis with your child, you will want to keep things very positive. It's also a good idea to choose a time when you and your child are feeling good and when you won't be interrupted or distracted.

■ *Tailor your explanation of ASD to your child's own situation.* Start with the positive; then address the negative. It's important to tell your child that you love all the "good stuff" about him, that is, his special abilities, qualities, and interests, and you wouldn't ever want him to change. Undoubtedly, your child has been struggling in some areas because of ASD. It's OK to acknowledge these difficulties while emphasizing that it is not his fault that some things are difficult for him.

■ *Describe ASD as a different kind of disability.* If the child understands the concept of "disability," you might identify ASD as just a different kind of disability. You can explain that people have a disability when something about them works differently from the way it does for most children, and they need help because of ASD. You might explain that like how people are different on the outside, they are all different on the inside too. People with ASD, for example, might need extra help in understanding others and making friends. It may be helpful to illustrate how all children learn differently by giving examples of children they know who get extra help in other areas.

■ *Stress that you'll be there.* You should emphasize that you and other family members, teachers, and therapists are going to be there supporting him as he works on things that are hard for him. You'll encourage him when it's tough and cheer when he has a success. You'll celebrate the good stuff while helping with the not-so-good stuff.

Discussing an Autism Spectrum Disorder Diagnosis With Your Child (*continued*)

Considering the potential effect of the information, how can a parent best explain to a child that he has ASD? **(continued)**

- *Let your child know there are a lot of other people with ASD.* Your child is definitely not alone, and it is important to let him know this. Your child may be interested in and benefit from meeting others with ASD. Introduce him to positive role models of people with ASD, both famous people (via books or movies) and people in your community.
- *Raise your child's awareness.* Even before you discuss your child's diagnosis with him, it may be helpful to read books in which characters have ASD and other disabilities and watch shows with your child in which characters have disabilities so that awareness of individual differences is presented as a part of everyday life.

Sharing information about ASD in a positive, matter-of-fact, and age-appropriate way helps set the stage for a child's ability to understand, accept, and adapt to the reality of ASD in his life. Keep in mind that the whole concept of "being on the autism spectrum" is a lot to take in. It's going to be a process that takes some time, with new questions asked and deeper understanding gained as a child matures.

For additional information on discussing ASD with your child, see Appendix A. Make sure your pediatrician knows about your questions and concerns, and share the information you find in your research. You might ask about a referral to a mental health professional for some additional therapy for your child and for some ongoing parent coaching as well. Remember, you and your pediatrician are partners in your child's health.

Adapted with permission of Kennedy Krieger Institute, Baltimore, MD. This information appeared originally at www.iancommunity.org/cs/articles/telling_a_child_about_his_asd.

identifies the antecedents and consequences surrounding a specific behavior and creates a plan for intervening that will alter the behavior, as well as ways to gauge whether the intervention is working. The IEP team can arrange for the FBA. In fact, IDEA law requires that an FBA be done when a child is having behavioral problems.

The process begins with identifying the problem behavior in clear, concrete terms. For instance, rather than say that "Johnny is rude," an FBA would say, "Johnny shoves, kicks, and hits other children during transition time." The description should be expressed in specific, observable, and measurable terms.

Next, you need to create a plan to collect data. Gathering data may be done in 1 of 2 ways, directly or indirectly. Collecting data directly involves observing circumstances surrounding the problem behavior. Does the problem occur just before lunch when the child may be hungry? Does it arise whenever she's in a crowded auditorium? Is she more apt to act out when new lessons are being taught? Are behaviors preceded by the same incidents each time? Find out how often the problem behavior occurs and in what kind of intervals. Doing an ABCs of the behavior (antecedent, behavior, and consequence) observation form can help too. Each time a child misbehaves, record the inappropriate behavior and what happened just before it, which are the *antecedents*. Then record what happens after it, which are the *consequences* of that behavior. Record only what you see and hear without interpreting the behavior.

Gathering data may also be done indirectly using student records, questionnaires, or checklists to see how others perceive the behavior. It may involve interviews with other staff members to find out who's present when the problem behavior occurs, when and where it tends to happen, and what's happening before and after the behavior. This information should be collected from several sources including teachers, counselors, and after-school supervisors.

After a few days, you should begin to see a pattern that links the child's behavior to her environment. You'll be able to predict events that lead to the problem behavior and identify consequences that perpetuate it.

Remember, most problem behaviors serve a purpose and are done to attain something or avoid something.

In addition, it is critical to understand that certain aspects of a child's ASD may be the underlying cause of a behavior. For example, a child with oversensitive hearing may act out during a noisy gym class. So an intervention needs to consider sensory and biological problems that manifest because of ASD.

The next step is to develop and implement a behavioral intervention plan (BIP). Children generally respond better to methods that are positive and that encourage and teach appropriate, alternative behaviors. You might try modifying the physical environment, adjusting the curriculum, or changing antecedents or consequences for the problem behavior. It's also helpful to teach a more acceptable behavior that serves the same purpose.

Once you implement the plan, make sure to monitor the child's progress over time. If interventions aren't working, you may need to go back and devise a new strategy.

If a behavioral problem becomes so severe that teachers recommend a child be expelled or moved to a different setting for 10 days or longer, your child may be given a manifestation determination hearing to determine whether the behavior was related to your child's disability. The manifestation review is conducted by the school district, the parent, and other members of the IEP team within 10 days of the suspension or change in placement. If the behavior was related to the disability, your child is returned to the classroom. The IEP team must then do an FBA and a BIP within 10 days of the manifestation determination, or modify the existing one to address the problem behavior.

Stress and the Rage Cycle

Children who have ASD are prone to anxiety and stress. In fact, anxiety is one of the most common coexisting medical conditions in children with ASD. Children with ASD may be thrust into confusing social situations that are difficult for them to understand or handle. Their sometimes rigid rules about injustice and their innate emotional vulnerability make it difficult for them to manage certain events that other children may readily dismiss. As a result, they may experience a lot of stress, which causes them to withdraw or become preoccupied with obsessions and thoughts. They may also become hyperactive, aggressive, and difficult. To compound the situation, many of these children have difficulty recognizing the stress they feel and see no problem with their behaviors.

Experts such as Brenda Smith Myles, PhD, have called the sequence of events around stress the "rage cycle." In the right setting with the right triggers, almost all of us can become entrapped in a rage cycle. But most children with typical development create strategies for dealing with situations that make them angry. And certainly by adulthood, most of us can better handle upsetting stressors.

Children with ASD, however, are more vulnerable to outbursts because they are naturally more prone to anxiety and have less self-awareness. It's important to understand that the meltdown occurs for a reason— there is often a reason for or cause of the angry behavior. That's why FBAs are so important to understanding the behavior of a child with ASD. Exploding into a tantrum is not something a child wants to do, but it's often the only way the child can express himself because his communication skills are inadequate.

Parents and teachers can help reduce the child's anxiety and stress by understanding the rage cycle and deploying strategies that help children manage their stress. (It's also why it's so important to improve your child's understanding of social situations, arm him with the skills for living and working in a world with other people, and help him master communication skills that will help him express himself.) The rage cycle has 3 distinct phases—rumbling, meltdown/rage, and recovery. Early in the cycle, there are distinct strategies for preventing or decreasing the problem behavior.

Rumbling

The rage cycle begins with the rumbling stage. At this point, you may notice some minor behavioral changes that have little to do with the impending meltdown. The child may clear his throat, lower his voice, tense his muscles, or tap his feet. Facial expressions may give away feelings of unhappiness. Other behaviors may be more obvious. The child may withdraw physically or emotionally from what's going on around him, or he may lash out physically or verbally at someone else. If it's happening in a classroom, the child may attempt to engage in a power struggle with the teacher.

Nipping the problem at the rumbling stage is critical to preventing a meltdown, and teachers and parents have several strategies at their disposal. These include

- *Removing the child:* If the problem occurs in school, the teacher can send the child on an errand. If it's happening at home, the parent can ask the child to retrieve an object. The brief absence can help the child regain his calm so that when he comes back, the problem has usually lessened.

- *Moving closer to the child:* When a teacher senses a child's distress, she can simply walk over and be near the child. Parents can do the same. Simply putting yourself in close proximity to the child can lessen his stress without disrupting other students.

- *Signaling the child:* A teacher who has a child prone to rage can work out a signal in advance that lets the child know she is aware of the situation. Making the signal, which can be as simple as tapping the desk or putting a pencil behind her ear, can be reassuring to the child and may be used just before removing the child from the situation.

- *Supporting his routine:* A child with ASD may rely on predictability. Having a visual schedule of events in the day can make him feel safe and ease his stress. It also helps to let him know ahead of time about any schedule changes.

- *Redirecting:* Shifting the child's attention to something other than what's upsetting him can often help reduce his stress. While it's OK to postpone a new activity in some situations, in others he may need to be redirected immediately. The child may also be redirected to a pre-rehearsed calming sequence or use relaxation techniques that have been practiced with a therapist beforehand.

- *Giving him a safe place to go:* Some experts call this a *home base,* a place where the child can go to escape stress. The safe place should have minimal distractions, and activities in the area should be soothing, not stimulating. In school, there could be a safe place in the classroom, such as a table in the corner, and when that is not enough, another safe haven outside the classroom might be the counselor's office. At home, it might be the child's bedroom. Wherever it is, the safe place should be viewed as a positive retreat, not an area used for time-outs or special play. It might also be used as a place for the child to regroup during the recovery phase of the rage cycle.

- *Acknowledging difficulties:* When the rumbling stage is triggered by a challenging task, it can sometimes help to simply acknowledge that the task is hard and then encourage the child to proceed anyway. A simple verbal acknowledgment may be enough to prevent the child from having a tantrum.

- *Walking, not talking:* Taking a short, silent stroll with a distraught child can sometimes help soothe a child on the brink of a meltdown. The accompanying adult should say nothing while allowing the child to vent any upsetting emotions without consequence.

As you can see, these strategies are not difficult to do and are, in fact, sometimes quite simple. But the effect they have on a child's impending tantrum can be huge. The key is knowing which one to use in which situation and not allowing yourself to become part of the struggle. It's also important to avoid certain behaviors that can escalate the child's rage and almost guarantee a meltdown. These include raising your voice, focusing on who's right, preaching, being sarcastic, using physical force, acting superior, pleading, bribing, and insisting on having the last word. An adult should also never attack the child's character, make unsubstantiated accusations, compare the child with others, or insult or humiliate the child.

Meltdown/Rage

If you aren't able to diffuse the situation in the rumbling stage, the child will go into the meltdown, or rage, stage. Behavior at this point is erratic and out of control. The child no longer has the ability to process information and may be quite physically aggressive—hitting, kicking, and biting—or verbally abusive. He may hurt himself or others or damage property. In some cases, the child may completely withdraw. Most times, the meltdown will have to run its course.

The focus at this point should be the safety of the child, his classmates, and adults. It's also important to try and help the child regain some semblance of control by whisking him off to his safe place or enlisting the help of other people on the school staff. Ideally, a plan should be in place before a tantrum occurs so staff and teachers are fully prepared.

Recovery

When the tantrum subsides, the child may feel badly about what's happened. He may also not fully remember what has just occurred. He remains fragile and may need time to rest before rejoining the class. The recovery period is not the time to teach the child new lessons or lecture on what has just occurred. Rather, the best thing to do is to help the child simply fall back into the routine of the class. A teacher can do this best by leading the child to a task he enjoys and does well.

By understanding the stages of the rage cycle, teachers and parents alike can help a child with ASD deal with stress and prevent bad situations from escalating into full-blown tantrums. It often takes time to figure out which strategies work best with each child and with which situation. Over time and with practice, the child may even learn to generalize strategies that work best and be able to apply them to other stressful situations.

Understanding and using educational services and strategies are important to help your child feel successful in a school setting. In some cases, though, strategies that involve medications may also be helpful. In the following chapter, we review the most common medications prescribed for children with ASD and factors to consider when evaluating this option.

᠍᠍᠍ ᠍᠍᠍ ᠍᠍᠍ ᠍᠍᠍ ᠍᠍᠍

Autism Champion: Brenda Smith Myles, PhD

BRENDA SMITH MYLES, PHD, has always spent time with children on the autism spectrum—one of her first playmates had autism, though Dr Myles was never told so. As a graduate student, she still remembers a little boy who threw a tantrum and stormed out of the room when she didn't draw a dinosaur correctly. "I ran after him, and from that moment on, I was intrigued, challenged, and in love with autism," she says.

That was back in 1982 when autism was less well-known. As a graduate student in special education, Dr Myles was the associate director of a clinic at the University of Kansas that trained master's degree students how to work with children who had learning disabilities and behavioral challenges. None of them had been diagnosed, but Dr Myles learned to recognize these students as having high-functioning autism. "Every place I turned, it seemed I should be working with kids with autism and their families," she says.

Which is exactly what Dr Myles did. She wrote the first federal grant in the country that created a master's degree program in Asperger syndrome (autism with typical or advanced verbal skills) at the University of Kansas. She also went on to write more than 150 books and articles on autism spectrum disorder (ASD), including *Asperger Syndrome and Difficult Moments: Practical Solutions for Tantrums, Rage, and Meltdowns*, a book she wrote in 5 days with her colleague Jack Southwick.

It was Dr Myles who coined the term "rage cycle," which describes the pattern of behaviors that result in the tantrums that are common in children with ASD. "Originally, we were going to call the book *Asperger Syndrome and Rage*, but parents wouldn't say it was rage," Dr Myles recalls. "So we changed it to *Difficult Moments*. Parents influence everything I do."

Dr Myles, who is a parent to a typically developing 25-year-old, has garnered numerous accolades for her efforts. In a survey by the University of Texas, she was named the second most productive applied researcher of ASD in the world. She is currently the president of AAPC Publishing, a small niche company that publishes books on autism. In addition, she is a consultant with the Ziggurat Group, an organization that provides assessment, consultation, and training to benefit individuals with ASD across the life span. She lectures globally about ASD and has given more than 1,500 presentations. "There are many countries doing a nice job with individuals on the spectrum," she says. "But I think the United States is certainly putting forth the tremendous effort to meet their needs."

Her goals are to encourage more collaboration so that individual institutions, states, and even countries aren't always reinventing the wheel and have the right information about autism. In this regard, she helped create standards for teachers of children with ASD, which were accepted by the National Council for Accreditation of Teacher Education. "It's all about bringing organizations and people together to collaborate and making sure individuals with autism reach their potential," she says. "I know that sounds idealistic, but I am from Kansas—a place where anything can happen. Just ask Dorothy."

CHAPTER 6

When Other Therapies Aren't Enough: The Role of Medication

As WE HAVE reviewed in previous chapters, the main treatments of children with autism spectrum disorder (ASD) are behavioral, developmental, and educational interventions. Currently, no medications directly target the social communication challenges and repetitive behaviors that are at the core of ASD. Still, medications may help address other medical conditions that are encountered more commonly in children with ASD compared with those without ASD, such as sleep problems, gastrointestinal (GI) conditions, and seizures. In children with ASD, we call these conditions *associated medical conditions* or *co-occurring conditions* because they are common medical conditions that often accompany ASD.

There are also associated psychiatric conditions, such as attention-deficit/hyperactivity disorder (ADHD), anxiety, and mood disorders, all of which are also more commonly seen in children with ASD. While behavioral therapy is considered the first line of treatment for these psychiatric conditions, medications may be considered in addition to behavioral therapy, especially if the symptoms disrupt your child's learning, socializing, health, safety, or quality of life. Medications may be the primary therapy for some of the associated medical conditions and can be an option for associated psychiatric conditions if behavioral treatments alone are not sufficient.

In this chapter, we look at the most common medications prescribed for children with ASD for both associated medical conditions and associated psychiatric conditions. We also look at factors to consider when making a decision about starting a medication for your child.

Whether or Not Medication Is Warranted

Insurance and Medicaid data indicate that 56% to 65% of children and adolescents with ASD are treated with medications to address associated psychiatric conditions and behavioral problems. These medications, often called *psychotropic medications*, are more commonly prescribed in older children who have ADHD, anxiety, and mood disorders. These medications are more likely to be used in older children and in those with fewer self-help, or adaptive, skills; less social awareness; and more-challenging behaviors. We discuss some of these medications later in this chapter.

So if medications aren't the primary treatment of ASD, why are so many children taking them? Many children with ASD have accompanying psychiatric conditions such as ADHD, anxiety, depression, or mood instability that, when left untreated, interfere with significant aspects of their lives. Treating these associated psychiatric conditions makes it possible for children with ASD to function at a higher level than they otherwise would. It may also enable them to more successfully navigate the demands of their daily routines and enjoy a higher quality of life. In the past, it was thought that some of these conditions, such as ADHD, were simply part of autism. Our mind-set has now shifted with the understanding that children with ASD are more likely than the general population to have associated psychiatric conditions and that treatment of these conditions can be targeted separately.

Even so, the decision to start medication for a child with ASD is not something done lightly. Here are some things you should do before moving in this direction.

● Before starting your child on any medication to address a challenging behavior, it's important to work with your pediatrician to see whether a medical condition may be the underlying cause of your child's behavioral problems. For example, a child with ASD and constipation may communicate her discomfort by yelling, screaming, or even hitting if she has difficulty verbally communicating with her caregivers. Many medical issues that cause pain or distress, such as infections, allergies, GI disorders, or dental issues, may increase behavioral problems in children with ASD. Likewise, children who are not sleeping well at night are more prone to daytime irritability. Even something as simple as an ear infection may cause a child to behave disruptively.

● Look at what else is going on in her life. It's important to consider that changes in the environment may be causing the problem behavior. Be on the lookout for new demands on your child, changes in her routine, or new transitions, all of which may upset her. The arrival of a new teacher at school, for example, may be causing your child to lose sleep, which, in turn, might make her more prone to repetitive behaviors.

● Thoroughly assess the problem behavior. Identify how long it has been going on and how long each episode lasts. Do certain factors or situations seem to trigger it? How has the problem behavior changed over time? Is it increasing, decreasing, or somewhat stable? Determine what kind of effect it is having on your child. Is it affecting her ability to learn? Is it hindering academic progress, affecting her relations with peers, or putting her or others at risk of harm? Understanding the ABCs of the behavior—meaning looking at what happens before and after a challenging behavior (antecedent, behavior, and consequence, as described in Chapter 4)—is also very helpful. Here's an example.

— *Antecedent:* Requesting the child to do a chore.
— *Behavior:* Throwing a tantrum and hitting.
— *Consequence:* The child escapes the task of doing the chore.

In this scenario, the behavior (tantrum/hitting), even though it may seem "bad," is functional for your child because it results in your child's desired outcome (getting out of doing chores). Until this is addressed through behavioral intervention, it is unlikely that a medication alone will change this behavior.

Therefore, always consider behavioral strategies first before thinking about medications. In many instances, a medication may be used to supplement a behavioral intervention. For example, if a child is very anxious she might have less tolerance for the inevitable frustration we all feel when trying or learning something new. If a medication decreases her anxiety, she may be more tolerant of frustration and less likely to engage in problem behavior when facing new challenges.

Treating Associated Medical Conditions

We next describe what you need to know about some of the more common associated medical conditions in children with ASD that may make you consider, or may in fact require, using medication.

Seizures/Epilepsy

When abnormal or excessive electrical impulses occur in the brain, your child may have a *seizure.* During a seizure, neurons in the brain may fire faster, more suddenly, and more out of sequence than normal. The abnormal brain activity may cause changes in sensation, perception, or physical movement. During a seizure, muscles may stiffen up or become completely relaxed. Some seizures involve the entire body, whereas others involve only one part of the body, such as the face, a limb, or one side. A child having a seizure may have rapid, violent movements and even lose consciousness. Less dramatic seizures may consist of momentary lapses of attention that can cause a blank stare for a few moments. Some seizures are so subtle that they go unnoticed.

Epilepsy and *seizure disorder* are terms used to describe 2 or more seizures that occur over time without an underlying cause such as an infection or a brain injury. Epilepsy may be diagnosed in individuals who have had just one seizure but also have a certain type of electrical abnormality detected by an electroencephalogram (EEG), a test that records electrical activity in the brain. Approximately 25% of all people with ASD may have at least one seizure during their lifetimes, and estimates of individuals with ASD who have epilepsy vary widely from 2% to 46%. It seems that differences between studies are likely caused by the characteristics of the children with ASD that were studied. For example, seizures and epilepsy are more common in children with ASD who are female, have intellectual disability, have genetic conditions, and have more-severe forms of ASD. The onset of seizures and epilepsy is most common in children before the age of 5 years or during adolescence.

If your doctor suspects your child is having seizures, she may do an EEG. Though an EEG is generally not recommended as part of the routine evaluation for a child with ASD, doctors may recommend it for symptoms that suggest seizures. Symptoms that may warrant an EEG include unexplained changes of consciousness, abnormal movements that are not typical in children with ASD, or an atypical pattern of regression. Some children may have abnormal EEG results without having seizures.

Treating children who have ASD and epilepsy follows the same principles as in other children with epilepsy and involves medications to prevent seizures called *antiepileptic medications*. There are numerous medicines in this category; some of the most common include levetiracetam (Keppra), oxcarbazepine (Trileptal), lamotrigine (Lamictal), valproic acid (Depakote), topiramate (Topamax), zonisamide (Zonegran), and phenobarbital. Antiepileptic medications can prevent seizures or decrease their frequency or intensity, but some may also have serious side effects. Treatment should be closely monitored to determine the most appropriate medication and dosage for your child. Your child may need periodic blood tests after he starts a medication to make sure enough is in his system and to monitor for side effects. He may also need an occasional EEG to see how well the medicine is working. Medication is usually weaned gradually after he has had no seizures for 2 years. In some cases, though, seizures may persist indefinitely, or it may take longer for a child to cease having seizures.

Whether or not your child needs to be on a daily medication to prevent seizures, your doctor may recommend a rescue medication to be kept at home and school and given in the event of a prolonged seizure. You may be given a seizure action plan to carry with you and give to your child's school so all people caring for your child know what to do in the event of a seizure and when and how to give the emergency medication.

For further information on seizures, visit the following Web sites: Epilepsy Foundation of America at www.epilepsy.com and Medical Home Portal at www.medicalhomeportal.org/diagnoses-and-conditions/seizures-epilepsy.

The following resource may be helpful for preparing your child for an EEG: Autism Speaks toolkit, *Having an Electroencephalogram: A Guide for Parents*, www.autismspeaks.org/tool-kit/atnair-p-having-electroencephalogram-eeg-guide-parents.

Tics

Some children with ASD have *tics*, or brief, involuntary movements or sounds. Tics are common in typically developing children but are usually temporary. When multiple kinds of tics occur in a child and last longer than a year, the child may meet criteria for a neurological condition called *Tourette syndrome*. A child with ASD may have tics or tic-like behavior but not meet the strict diagnosis of Tourette syndrome. The 2 conditions can have a lot in common including echolalia, obsessive-compulsive behaviors, and abnormal motor movements. Some experts believe that the same brain abnormalities in people with ASD also exist in people with Tourette syndrome. Medications used to treat tics include α_2-adrenergic agonists (such as clonidine and guanfacine), antiepileptic medications (such as topiramate), and antipsychotic medications.

Gastrointestinal Problems

Many children with ASD experience gastrointestinal (GI) issues such as chronic constipation, abdominal pain, or diarrhea. In fact, studies report that children with ASD are about 4 times more likely to have GI problems compared with those without ASD. Some children with pain or discomfort from GI issues may act out by hurting themselves, throwing tantrums, or behaving aggressively. Many will have trouble sleeping. Gastrointestinal problems may also delay toilet training of some children with ASD.

The most common GI problem in children with ASD is constipation. While some wonder whether the GI tract is somehow different from those of other children, there are several reasons why children with ASD develop constipation that have nothing to do with any differences in the function of their GI tract. First, children with ASD are more likely to be selective eaters, generally preferring foods that lack fiber and lead to constipation. Second, the sensory processing difficulties experienced by many children with ASD can cause increased sensitivity to the discomfort of stool passage and lead to the withholding of stool. Third, children with ASD frequently take medications for associated psychiatric conditions that have a side effect of slowing down the gut's ability to move stool. Last, many children with ASD and anxiety are resistant to going to the bathroom outside their homes, which further increases the stool-withholding behavior. If constipation becomes chronic, the colon becomes very swollen with stool, eventually leading to a condition known as *encopresis* in which soft stool from above moves around the hard-stool impaction, producing accidents and streaks of stool in the underwear. The stool of children with encopresis is often so soft that parents mistakenly think it is diarrhea, even though the cause of the soft stool is constipation.

Approaches to treating GI issues vary, depending on the problem. Children with constipation, for instance, may require changes to their diet in addition to stool softeners. Those who have gastroesophageal reflux disease may benefit from a medication such as ranitidine

A Parent's Story: Ronny

"From the time C.J. was 6 months to the age of 3, he had had diarrhea. Doctors kept telling us it wasn't uncommon in kids with autism. But we finally took him to a gastrointestinal doctor. An x-ray showed he had an obstruction in his bowels [from chronic constipation].

"The doctor suggested he take MiraLax [polyethylene glycol], an over-the-counter laxative. Now he takes one scoop every day in his morning drink. Every 2 weeks, he takes 4 scoops throughout his day. The MiraLax continually breaks down the feces, and C.J. can have normal bowel movements."

(Zantac) or omeprazole (Prilosec) to reduce acid and heartburn. Children with lactose intolerance benefit from a lactose-free diet. Your pediatrician will work with you to implement a treatment plan to best meet your child's needs.

Sleep Disturbances

Many children experience sleep challenges at one time or another. In fact, 3% of all visits to pediatricians are to address sleep problems. But the problem is greater in children with ASD, with about 50% to 80% having sleep difficulties.

There are many different causes of sleep problems in children with ASD. Primary sleep disorders, such as obstructive sleep apnea, restless legs syndrome, and delayed sleep-phase syndrome, are reported in children with ASD. In addition, the core behaviors associated with ASD may predispose children with ASD to behaviorally based sleep disorders. Elements related to bedtime routines and the sleep environment, such as viewing television or playing video games close to bedtime, drinking caffeinated beverages, or having a room that is too warm, loud, or lit, may lead to sleep difficulties. Last, medical and psychiatric disorders, such as epilepsy, gastroesophageal reflux, anxiety, and depression, may be the cause of a child's sleep problem. **Table 6-1** has more information about common primary sleep disorders seen in children with ASD.

Sleep problems can manifest as trouble getting to sleep, trouble waking up at night, or both. For children with ASD, transitioning to sleep can be difficult because of hyperactivity, anxiety, and poorly regulated sleep-wake cycles. Some children with ASD wake in the middle of the night and can't get back to sleep. They may not have mastered the self-soothing techniques that help them drift off again when they awaken in the middle of the night during normal cycles of sleep. Any attention they receive during night awakenings, such as snacks or companionship, can worsen difficulties because children with ASD may become dependent on these routines to fall back asleep. Still others may be battling physical discomfort such as restless legs or acid reflux.

Identifying the cause of a sleep problem requires a physical examination and a thorough review of your child's health history. It may also

Table 6-1. Common Sleep Problems in Children With Autism Spectrum Disorder	
Condition	**Description**
Obstructive sleep apnea	Occurs when a blockage (sometimes from enlarged tonsils or adenoids) does not allow air to adequately enter into the lungs. Symptoms include loud snoring, pauses in breathing or gasping breaths, difficulty waking in the morning, and daytime sleepiness or irritability. If untreated, may lead to heart problems.
Restless legs syndrome	Restless legs syndrome involves an urge to move the legs or an uncomfortable sensation in the legs that typically occurs at bedtime. It is worse at rest and is relieved by movement. Children may report leg pain, have difficulty finding a comfortable position to fall asleep, or be restless sleepers.
Delayed sleep-phase syndrome	A disorder of sleep-wake cycles (circadian rhythm) in which the individual has difficulty falling asleep and may often have difficulty waking up the next morning. This condition may be more common in children with autism spectrum disorder because of insufficient melatonin production.

help to think about your child's nightly bedtime routine, your child's nighttime awakenings, and how you respond to those awakenings. What does your child do before bed every night, and how long does it take for her to fall asleep? Does she snore, or is she a restless sleeper? Where does your child sleep and with whom? What foods does she eat close to bedtime, if any? Does your child watch television or have screen time before bed? Do you lie down with her? What have you done to try and solve the problem?

All this information is important for understanding your child's sleep challenges and providing the right treatment. Keeping a sleep diary for 2 weeks to determine the nature and severity of the problem is also helpful (www.sleepforkids.org/pdf/SleepDiary.pdf). Occasionally, more tests may be needed. For example, if your pediatrician suspects a primary sleep disorder, she may recommend a referral to a sleep medicine specialist or arrange for a sleep study (also called *polysomnography*). A sleep study involves your child staying overnight in a sleep laboratory, attached to monitoring equipment. The information from this study will be used by your pediatrician or sleep specialist to better understand the cause and severity of your child's sleep problem.

Before Medications: Importance of Sleep Hygiene and Behavioral Treatments

Sleep Hygiene

No matter what the cause of your child's sleep problem, treatment always begins with good sleep hygiene, or habits that support healthy sleep. Your child's sleep environment should be cool, with as little light and sound as possible. Healthy daytime habits include regular physical activity and limiting caffeinated beverages and naps. Healthy evening habits include limiting screen time (video games, television, and computer) and having predictable bedtime routines. Good sleep hygiene is the first step in treating any sleep problems and sometimes works by itself to help such problems. If not, other steps may be needed.

Behavioral Treatments

Many types of sleep problems will respond to behavioral treatments. One technique, known as *graduated extinction,* may be helpful for difficulty in falling asleep and night awakenings.

Graduated extinction is basically planning an exit from your child's room at bedtime or after a nighttime awakening. It does mean that you will ignore any disruptive behavior by not returning to the room for a predetermined amount of time. If done consistently, it can be effective, even with children with ASD and other developmental disabilities. The process begins at bedtime when you say good night and give your child some praise for going to bed on his own. After that, you will check on your child at predetermined intervals and ignore any protests from your child in between these checks. Checks should be brief glances into the bedroom. If your child is still up, reassure yourself that he is OK but encourage him to go to sleep; then leave the room quickly without engaging him.

As the nights go on, lengthen the time between checks. Some parents decide to go in for their first check after 5 minutes, then over successive nights lengthen the interval of time between checks by a minute or even more. Before starting, make sure that all caregivers agree to adhere to the plan. Set a goal to do graduated extinction for a period of time, say, 2 to 3 weeks. You should expect that your child's protest may reach a fevered pitch around day 2 or 3 (called the *extinction burst*), but if you stick with it, improvements should be obvious by the end of the first week.

Depending on your child's sleep patterns and habits, you may also want to try other behavioral strategies. If your child is simply not tired at bedtime, temporarily moving bedtime later until she's really tired, for instance, may help. Over time, as she becomes more successful at falling asleep, you can gradually move up her bedtime to an earlier hour. If you've been sleeping with your child to help her doze off, you might try moving farther away from your child until she is finally able to fall asleep on her own in her own room. This may help her fall back to sleep on her own if she awakens at night.

Although difficult for some families, a technique known as *scheduled awakenings* may help alleviate frequent night awakenings. If your child awakens during the night at about the same time, you may want to try gently rousing your child (just get his eyes to open for a few seconds) 15 minutes before the time he usually awakens. After a number of nights of this, wait to see if he sleeps through the problem time. If so, you may have helped reset his sleep cycle.

If behavioral strategies and improved sleep hygiene don't work, you may want to make an appointment with your child's pediatrician to discuss other treatments. The evidence for using medication to manage sleep problems in children with ASD is limited. Except as otherwise noted, more studies are needed to establish the effectiveness of these medications for children with ASD. Medications that can help manage sleep problems include

- *Melatonin:* The body naturally produces this hormone, which helps regulate sleep cycles. A number of studies have shown that children with ASD may make less melatonin than typically developing peers.

Taking supplemental melatonin an hour before bedtime can help establish a normal sleep-wake cycle and help your child get to sleep. Melatonin is typically not long acting, so it is mainly useful for children who have trouble falling asleep; it is less effective for those who have problems with waking at night, although using a long-acting form may help with staying asleep. Side effects are uncommon but may include nightmares. Several high-quality studies have demonstrated that melatonin can be effective in helping children with ASD and sleep problems fall asleep sooner and have a longer total sleep time. While melatonin is available over the counter, there is a similar prescription medication called *ramelteon* (Rozerem). It is a melatonin receptor agonist, meaning that it works by mimicking the actions of melatonin. There are fewer studies of using ramelteon in children with ASD than there are of using melatonin.

- *Clonidine* (Catapres or Kapvay): Clonidine is in a class of medications called *centrally acting α_2-adrenergic agonist agents*, which are used to treat high blood pressure. It may help reduce hyperactivity, impulsivity, aggression, and tics while improving attention in children with ASD. If your child is prescribed clonidine, your pediatrician will monitor his blood pressure. The main side effect of clonidine is drowsiness. For that reason, it may be given at night as a sleep aid.

- *Guanfacine* (Tenex or Intuniv): Guanfacine is like clonidine, as it is also designed to treat high blood pressure. It is used for the same purposes as clonidine (to reduce hyperactivity and impulsivity) but may be less sedating than clonidine. For this reason, it may not be used as commonly as clonidine for sleep.

- *Diphenhydramine* (Benadryl): Diphenhydramine is an antihistamine with sedating effects. Although commonly used for sleep problems, diphenhydramine has not been well studied as a sleep medicine. While it may be safe and effective for short-term insomnia, it may cause dry mouth, next-day drowsiness, and rebound insomnia (when sleep worsens after treatment ends). In some children, it causes hyperactivity and excitation instead of drowsiness.

- *Hydroxyzine* (Atarax or Vistaril): Hydroxyzine is an older antihistamine that also has a sedating effect. Unlike with diphenhydramine, a prescription is required for hydroxyzine. It can cause the same side effects as diphenhydramine. While diphenhydramine and hydroxyzine can help with sleep because both have sedation as side effects, neither has been well studied specifically as a sleep aid for children.

- *Mirtazapine* (Remeron): This is a medicine used as an antidepressant in adults. It affects the neurotransmitter (chemical signal in the brain) serotonin. Because it induces sleep, mirtazapine is often prescribed for children with sleep difficulties; it has not been studied specifically as a sleep aid in children with ASD. It may also help with anxiety and mood symptoms. Side effects include excessive sedation, dry mouth, weight gain, and constipation.

- *Trazodone* (Desyrel): Trazodone is also used to treat depression in adults and affects serotonin. Because of its sedative properties, it has been used in low doses to induce sleep in children. Excessive sedation, dry mouth, nausea, and blurred vision may be side effects.

Tips for Good Sleep Hygiene

Sometimes, good sleep hygiene, or habits that support healthy sleep, is all it takes to overcome sleep difficulties in your child. Here's what you need to do.

- Have your child go to bed and get up at the same time every day, even on weekends.
- Create a relaxing routine in the hour or so leading up to bedtime.
- Make sure your child's bedroom is conducive to sleep, which means the room is quiet, cool, and dark and does not have a television, a computer, or other electronics.
- Do not engage your child in play at bedtime or use bedtime as a punishment.
- Teach your child to fall asleep in her own bed, alone.
- Teach your child to fall asleep in conditions that will help her back to sleep if she awakens in the middle of the night.

Very rarely, a condition known as *priapism*—a painful, sustained erection—has been reported in boys and men. Although it is occasionally used to address sleep problems, there are no studies on using trazodone for sleep problems in children with ASD.

Remember: Even if you do give your child a medication to address his sleep problems, it's still important to use behavioral interventions to help your child get into a good sleep pattern.

Treating Associated Psychiatric Conditions

Children with ASD are often prescribed psychotropic medications, drugs that affect the chemistry of the brain, to improve behavioral functioning. Children who have ASD are vulnerable to behavioral problems that may meet criteria for psychiatric conditions. Sometimes it can be difficult to separate the symptoms of autism from those of some of these other conditions. For instance, children who have ASD may become anxious when routines are unexpectedly changed and yet not be labeled as having generalized anxiety disorder. The important point is that when a symptom such as anxiety, hyperactivity, or aggression significantly interferes with function, is not caused by a medical condition, and does not adequately respond to behavioral therapy, a psychotropic medication can be considered.

The specific psychiatric disorders that are often seen in children with ASD are

- *Generalized anxiety disorder:* Generalized anxiety disorder is excessive and uncontrollable worry about everyday matters. The worrying is disproportionate to the actual event and interferes with daily functioning.

- *Major depression:* As many as 1 in 8 adolescents in the United States experiences major depression, which can be tricky to diagnose in children, especially in those with ASD. This disorder involves ongoing sadness, discouragement, loss of self-worth, and loss of interest in usual activities. Some children won't seem sad at all but may instead act out by misbehaving and getting into trouble.

Children with ASD may manifest depression in the typical way, while others may become more irritable, experience sleep problems, have unexplained crying episodes, or simply have less interest in the activities they used to enjoy.

- *Bipolar disorder*: Previously known as *manic depression*, bipolar disorder causes extreme mood swings that alternate between euphoric highs and despairing lows. In children, bipolar disorder may be seen as agitation with explosive behavior. During manic episodes, children with ASD may become more hyperactive, louder in their vocalizations, and irritable or aggressive, and they may have a decreased need for sleep.

- *Disruptive mood dysregulation disorder* (DMDD): This is a relatively new diagnosis in the field of children's mental health. Children with DMDD have severe and frequent tantrums that interfere with their ability to function at home, in school, or with their friends. Some of these children were previously diagnosed as having bipolar disorder, even though they often did not have all the signs and symptoms. Research has also demonstrated that children with DMDD do not usually go on to have bipolar disorder in adulthood. They are more likely to develop problems with depression or anxiety.

- *Obsessive-compulsive disorder* (OCD): People who have OCD become consumed with repeating certain rituals and behaviors and may become obsessed with certain thoughts.

- *Attention-deficit/hyperactivity disorder* (ADHD): This is a childhood disorder characterized by hyperactivity, impulsivity, and difficulty in paying attention. It occurs in approximately 9% of all children and in 41% to 78% of children with ASD.

Common Medications for Psychiatric Disorders

Many of the conditions described in this chapter are commonly treated with medication from the categories included in **Table 6-2.**

Table 6-2. Possible Medication for Children With Autism Spectrum Disorder

Coexisting Condition	Medication Considerations
Obsessive-compulsive disorder	SSRIs: fluoxetine[a] (Prozac), fluvoxamine[a] (Luvox), citalopram (Celexa), escitalopram (Lexapro), paroxetine (Paxil), or sertraline (Zoloft)
	Atypical antipsychotic agents: risperidone[a] (Risperdal), aripiprazole[a] (Abilify), olanzapine (Zyprexa), quetiapine (Seroquel), ziprasidone (Geodon), or lurasidone (Latuda)
	Valproic acid[a] (Depakene or Depakote)
Attention-deficit/ hyperactivity disorder Hyperactivity Impulsivity Inattention Distractibility	Stimulants: methylphenidate[a] (Ritalin, Ritalin LA, Methylin, Focalin, Focalin XR, Concerta, Metadate CD, Daytrana, Quillivant XR, or Cotempla XR-ODT), dextroamphetamine (Dexedrine), lisdexamfetamine (Vyvanse), mixed amphetamine salts (Adderall, Adderall XR, Dyanavel XR, Adzenys ER, Adzenys XR-ODT, or Mydayis)
	α_2-adrenergic agonists: clonidine[a] (Catapres or Kapvay) or guanfacine (Tenex or Intuniv)
	SNRI: atomoxetine[a] (Strattera)
	Atypical antipsychotic agents: risperidone[a] (Risperdal), aripiprazole[a] (Abilify), olanzapine[a] (Zyprexa), quetiapine (Seroquel), or ziprasidone (Geodon)
Irritability and severe disruptive behavior (aggression, self-injury, vocal outbursts, tantrums, or meltdowns/ rages)	Atypical antipsychotic agents: risperidone[a] (Risperdal), aripiprazole[a] (Abilify), olanzapine (Zyprexa), quetiapine (Seroquel), ziprasidone (Geodon), or lurasidone (Latuda)
	α_2-adrenergic agonists: clonidine[a] (Catapres or Kapvay) or guanfacine (Tenex or Intuniv)
	Anticonvulsant mood stabilizers: valproic acid[a] (Depakene or Depakote), topiramate (Topamax), carbamazepine (Tegretol), gabapentin (Neurontin), lamotrigine (Lamictal), or oxcarbazepine (Trileptal)

Table 6-2. Possible Medication for Children With Autism Spectrum Disorder (*continued*)

Coexisting Condition	Medication Considerations
Irritability and severe disruptive behavior (aggression, self-injury, vocal outbursts, tantrums, or meltdowns/rages) (*continued*)	SSRIs: fluoxetine[a] (Prozac), fluvoxamine[a] (Luvox), citalopram (Celexa), escitalopram (Lexapro), paroxetine (Paxil), or sertraline (Zoloft)
	β-adrenergic blocking agents: propranolol (Inderal), nadolol (Corgard), metoprolol (Lopressor), or pindolol (Visken)
Sleep disturbances	Melatonin agonists: melatonin[a] or ramelteon (Rozerem)
	Antihistamines: diphenhydramine (Benadryl) or hydroxyzine (Atarax or Vistaril)
	α_2-adrenergic agonists: clonidine (Catapres or Kapvay) or guanfacine (Tenex or Intuniv)
	Atypical antidepressants: mirtazapine (Remeron) or trazodone (Desyrel)
Anxiety	SSRIs: fluoxetine[a] (Prozac), fluvoxamine[a] (Luvox), citalopram (Celexa), escitalopram (Lexapro), paroxetine (Paxil), or sertraline (Zoloft)
	Buspirone (Buspar)
	Mirtazapine (Remeron)
	Benzodiazepines: clonazepam (Klonopin) or lorazepam (Ativan)
Depression	SSRIs: fluoxetine[a] (Prozac), fluvoxamine[a] (Luvox), citalopram (Celexa), escitalopram (Lexapro), paroxetine (Paxil), or sertraline (Zoloft)
	Atypical antidepressants: bupropion (Wellbutrin) or mirtazapine (Remeron)
Bipolar disorder or mood disorder	Anticonvulsant mood stabilizers: carbamazepine (Tegretol), gabapentin (Neurontin), lamotrigine (Lamictal), oxcarbazepine (Trileptal), topiramate (Topamax), or valproic acid (Depakene or Depakote)

Table 6-2. Possible Medication for Children With Autism Spectrum Disorder (*continued*)	
Coexisting Condition	**Medication Considerations**
Bipolar disorder or mood disorder (*continued*)	Atypical antipsychotic agents: risperidone (Risperdal), aripiprazole (Abilify), olanzapine (Zyprexa), quetiapine (Seroquel), ziprasidone (Geodon), or lurasidone (Latuda)
	Lithium

Abbreviations: SNRI, selective norepinephrine reuptake inhibitor; SSRI, selective serotonin reuptake inhibitor.

[a] At least one published double-blind, placebo-controlled trial supports use in patients with an autism spectrum disorder.

Adapted with permission: Scott M. Myers, MD; Chris Plauché Johnson, MD, MEd; and the Council on Children With Disabilities. "Management of Children With Autism Spectrum Disorders," *Pediatrics*, volume 120, page 1169, copyright 2007 by the American Academy of Pediatrics.

A Few Precautions

Most of the medicines listed in Table 6-2 have not been directly studied in children with ASD. Those that have the highest level of evidence to support their use in patients with ASD have been indicated with a superscript *a*.

Selective Serotonin Reuptake Inhibitors

Chances are you've heard about the selective serotonin reuptake inhibitor (SSRI) category of medications, which includes drugs such as fluoxetine (Prozac), escitalopram (Lexapro), and sertraline (Zoloft). These may be prescribed for repetitive behaviors, OCD, anxiety, and depression. Studies show that these medications may help in addressing irritability, tantrums, aggression, and difficulty with transitions. Potential side effects of SSRIs include hyperactivation (hyperactivity, agitation, and sleep problems), nausea, drowsiness, fatigue, abdominal discomfort, headache, and dry mouth.

Studies of SSRIs have shown a small increase in suicidal thoughts compared with placebo (an inactive substance used instead of medicine), particularly among adolescents and young adults. Please note, however, that according to statistics from the Centers for Disease Control and Prevention, overall rates of teen suicide are much lower since SSRIs were introduced in the late 1980s. While the safety and benefits of SSRIs far outweigh the infrequent side effects, using the medication warrants close monitoring of your child's response.

Stimulants

Some children with hyperactivity, impulsivity, and inattention are prescribed stimulants, including methylphenidate (Ritalin) and dextroamphetamine (Dexedrine). Many preparations are available, varying mainly in the duration of effect but also in how they are administered (liquid, chewable pills, tablets, dissolving tablets, capsules, and even patches placed onto the skin). Stimulants are most effective in children who have ADHD without ASD and less so in children who have ASD and ADHD. Stimulants may also cause more adverse side effects in children with ASD. Potential side effects include loss of appetite, insomnia, jitteriness, abdominal discomfort, increased heart rate, and irritability. They can also worsen tics and increase anxiety and repetitive behaviors. Concerns about potential serious cardiac side effects are restricted to adults, children with congenital heart disease, and those with a family history of sudden death.

α_2-Adrenergic Agonists

α_2-Adrenergic agonists are prescribed for high blood pressure, but in children with ASD, they may be used to control aggression, explosive outbursts, and self-injurious behaviors. They are used to treat hyperactivity, impulsiveness, and inattention. These drugs are also first-line agents for reducing tics. As mentioned earlier in the chapter, they can be used to ease sleep problems as well. Common drugs in this category include clonidine (Catapres or Kapvay) and guanfacine (Tenex or Intuniv). Possible side effects of clonidine and guanfacine include drowsiness, dry mouth, decreased blood pressure, dizziness, constipation, and irritability.

Selective Norepinephrine Reuptake Inhibitors

Atomoxetine (Strattera) is a different, non-stimulant medicine prescribed to reduce ADHD symptoms such as distractibility, hyperactivity, and impulsivity while increasing attention. It may be beneficial for children who are sensitive to the side effects of stimulant medication. Common side effects of atomoxetine include fatigue, headache, and stomachache.

Atypical Antipsychotics

Atypical antipsychotics, also known as *atypical neuroleptics*, are a newer generation of medicines used to treat bipolar disorder, schizophrenia, and pronounced agitation and aggression, as well as tics. This newer class of antipsychotics has fewer adverse side effects than those that were used in the past. These drugs include risperidone (Risperdal) and aripiprazole (Abilify), the only 2 drugs specifically approved by the US Food and Drug Administration as of this writing for use in 6- to 17-year-old children and adolescents with ASD and irritability. Side effects include type 2 diabetes, weight gain, high cholesterol, sleepiness, headaches, dizziness, movement disorders (some of which may be permanent), and changes in the way the heart keeps rhythm. These side effects require monitoring with periodic blood tests and in certain instances, electrocardiography.

Pharmacogenomic Testing: An Emerging New Technology

Testing for genetic variants that increase the likelihood of medication side effects is an emerging area for precision medicine. Certain genetic markers may be identified that would indicate medications to avoid in selecting a particular treatment. As of this writing, it is still considered experimental and in need of further study.

The Need to Use Medications With Caution

Using psychotropic medications in children with ASD is a serious step in managing your child's health. As the parent, you should be told exactly how the medication should benefit your child's behavior, when you may expect to see a difference, the side effects he might experience, and what you will do if the treatment does not work. You should work with your child's pediatrician or mental health practitioner to figure out a way to determine the success or failure of a medication. Evaluating a medication may involve talking to teachers, behavioral therapists, or other treatment team members who work closely with your child. It's also important to follow up with your child's doctor regularly to figure out whether adjustments in the medication are needed and whether it is possible to safely go off the medication. If any information is unclear to you, you should persist in asking questions.

Typically, medication is started at low doses and gradually increased as tolerated until you've reached a conclusion about its effectiveness. This is called the *trial period*. During this time, there will be frequent follow-up visits and phone calls to ensure safety and make sure your child is responding appropriately. Once the medicine begins working as desired, ongoing monitoring may be less frequent. If symptoms resolve or significantly improve after starting a medication, it is reasonable to consider the possibility of lowering the dosage or even discontinuing the medication. This is generally considered after 6 to 12 months of improvement on a medication and should be done only after consulting your child's prescribing provider.

What You Should Know About Medications

Putting any child onto medication requires close vigilance but is especially important for children who have ASD. Even over-the-counter medicines and supplements should be closely monitored. Here are some guidelines you should keep in mind.

- Always give the medication exactly as it is prescribed. Follow the dosage and timing requirements closely, and ask your pediatrician or pharmacist what to do if you forget to give your child the medicine on time.

- Do not stop, restart, increase, or decrease any medicine without discussing it with your child's doctor first. If a medicine stops working, your child may need a different dose or schedule. But never make the change yourself without talking with the pediatrician first.

- Keep all medicines out of your child's reach and stored in childproof bottles. Supervise him whenever he takes his medication. Call your child's pediatrician, the hospital emergency department, or the Poison Help line (800/222-1222) if you suspect he has taken too much of a medicine.

- Always tell your pediatrician about other medications your child is taking before he starts taking a new one. You should also tell the doctor about any vitamins, herbal medicines, or diet supplements. Taking more than one medicine at a time may cause more side effects than from either medicine alone and may also lessen the effect of one or the other.

- Alert your child's doctor if you suspect your child is taking street drugs or alcohol. You should also tell your doctor if you suspect your child is pregnant.

- Use one pharmacy for all your child's medications. Certain medications can interact with one another and cause reactions ranging from mild to fatal. If your child has more than one doctor prescribing medications, each doctor may not know about other drugs your child is taking. Using one pharmacy will allow the pharmacist to review all the medicines your child is taking.

- Store medications properly. Ask the pharmacist where you should keep medications. Some pills are affected by the humidity in a bathroom, while other liquid drugs require refrigeration.

- Measure your medications carefully. If it's in a liquid form, ask for a syringe or dropper. Do not use tableware.

While medications may help with conditions that are common in children with ASD, some parents may prefer other types of interventions. The next chapter addresses these treatments, more commonly known as *integrative, complementary, and alternative medicine.*

CHAPTER 7

The Role of Integrative, Complementary, and Alternative Medicine

WHEN MY SON was diagnosed with autism, my wife and I were like any other parents who'd just been told their child had a lifelong condition: we were prepared to do anything we could to help him reach his full potential. In addition to intensive behavioral therapy, we did a lot of research into nutritional supplements. Although the research showed the supplements were safe, it also said there was limited evidence that they would be helpful in reducing the symptoms of autism. Still, we did try various supplements. After some time, we realized that his progress with behavioral therapy was no better with the supplements than without, so we discontinued them.

—Paul Carbone, MD, FAAP

   ❧ ❧ ❧ ❧ ❧

IT'S NOT UNCOMMON for parents of children with special health care needs to consider integrative, complementary, and alternative medicine (ICAM). In fact, studies show that 28% to 74% of all children with autism spectrum disorder (ASD) have been put onto ICAM treatments.

Parents turn to ICAM treatments for many reasons. Many parents are afraid of putting their children on conventional medications and worry about the adverse side effects of these treatments. Some have had little success with conventional medications and therapies. Others cannot afford behavioral therapies or do not have easy access to them. Many people believe that ICAM treatments are more natural, simpler to use, and less invasive. Some people have benefited from ICAM treatments themselves and want to give their child the same opportunity to benefit. For others, ICAM treatments are easier to access.

In this chapter, we look at some ICAM therapies that are often considered for children with ASD. As any parent who has ever done research on the Internet can tell you, there are hundreds of Web sites that discuss alternative remedies for autism, many with unproven claims. The goal of this chapter is to help you understand what some of these treatments are, how they're supposed to benefit children with ASD, and how to make an informed decision regarding whether you should consider one of these therapies for your child. We also help you evaluate the safety of these treatments and assess whether the benefits are worth the risk.

What Integrative, Complementary, and Alternative Medicine (ICAM) Is

Integrative, complementary, and alternative medicine encompasses a host of different therapies. To understand them, it helps to dissect the terminology. *Conventional medicine* (sometimes called *Western medicine*) refers to treatments that a doctor of medicine or doctor of osteopathy, or MD or DO, is likely to prescribe. This is sometimes referred to as "mainstream medicine" and is the most widely used form of medical treatment in the US health care system.

Complementary medicine is a treatment or therapy used in combination with conventional medicine. For example, massage, guided imagery, and acupuncture may be used in addition to analgesic medications to decrease pain.

Alternative medicine is a treatment given in place of a conventional one; for example, some adolescents use herbs rather than antidepressant medication to treat depression.

Integrative medicine is the blending of complementary and conventional therapies. It is the practice of medicine that reaffirms the importance of the relationship between practitioner and patient, focuses on the whole person, is informed by evidence, and makes use of all appropriate therapeutic approaches, health care professionals, and disciplines to achieve optimal health and healing.

Taken together, *integrative, complementary, and alternative medicine,* or ICAM, represents a large and diverse group of health care systems, practices, and products that are based on philosophies and techniques other than those used in conventional medicine. Health care professionals who practice *integrative medicine* use a combination of conventional and complementary treatments to treat their patients.

When it comes to treating disease, conventional medicine relies primarily on biomedicine, which is based on the laws of science and the use of the scientific method for evidence. Most treatments are biomedical and based on research, in particular a model known as the *randomized, controlled clinical trial* (RCT). An RCT is designed to prove or disprove the effectiveness of a given treatment. In an RCT, some subjects are given a treatment and others are not, but the researchers do not know who receives the treatment and who doesn't until after the trial is complete. At the end of the trial, the outcomes of those who received the treatment are compared with those who didn't. This type of trial allows researchers to minimize the influence of "bias" on the results of the treatment. The results of this type of research are typically published in a peer-reviewed academic journal. This means they've been closely scrutinized by a panel of medical experts, specifically peers of the researchers who practice in the field that is being studied. The peer-review process is designed to maintain professional, ethical, and

More About Integrative Medicine

Integrative medicine is primarily relationship-based care. Integrative medicine reaffirms the importance of the relationship between the practitioner and the patient, emphasizes wellness and the inherent drive toward healing, and focuses on the whole person, using all appropriate therapies to achieve the patient's goals for health and healing. It combines mainstream and complementary therapies for which there is some high-quality scientific evidence of safety and effectiveness to promote health for the whole person in the context of the patient's family and community.

scientific standards and provide credibility to the study. In addition, peer review determines whether an academic study is suitable for publication in a peer-reviewed journal or another publication.

Many alternative remedies have not undergone such rigorous scrutiny. Instead, support for these treatments is often anecdotal, meaning it's based on casual observations or a story about a person or a situation. This evidence is not nearly as reliable as that from an RCT. All cases or anecdotes are not represented, and anecdotal data are difficult to verify as being an accurate representation of the situation. Sometimes an individual response is inappropriately generalized for all people. The scientific method cannot be used in most cases to investigate anecdotal data. The scientific method uses careful written observation and collection of measurable data to answer questions through carefully designed experiments. Anecdotal data can become a testimonial to help promote a product or an idea.

Just because an alternative treatment has not been subjected to an RCT does not mean it will not work. It simply has not been scientifically proven to work beyond what is referred to as the "placebo effect" in which the patient's faith in the treatment—or the practitioner delivering it—may be enough to bring about a positive effect without the treatment itself influencing the outcome.

For any parent considering an ICAM treatment for a child with ASD, the most important thing you can do is to become educated and use common sense. Know the potential benefits of the treatments and understand the risks involved. Your pediatrician can help you in this process, and together you can decide whether to pursue the treatment. It's also important to know the resources needed to start and maintain the therapy. Many of these therapies can be quite costly. It is important for parents to investigate whether an ICAM therapy has been researched in an evidence-based scientific study. You can often find these studies on university or national accredited Web sites such as the National Institutes of Health (www.ncbi.nlm.nih.gov/pubmed). The National Center for Complementary and Integrative Health at the National Institutes of Health is a good source of information on ICAM treatment of ASD (https://nccih.nih.gov/health/autism).

Gluten-free/Casein-free Diet

Back in the 1960s, a physician named F. Curtis Dohan speculated that people who had celiac disease were more likely to have schizophrenia. Celiac disease is an autoimmune disorder that causes the body not to tolerate gluten, a protein found naturally in wheat, as well as rye, barley, and sometimes oats that are processed in the same place as these other grains. Later studies have not established that reducing the amount of wheat in the diet of people with schizophrenia significantly reduces their symptoms. Dohan's writings marked the beginning of the proposed link between diet and psychiatric and neurological illnesses.

The suggested link between gluten and casein and autism emerged in the 1970s. The theory—which remains unproven—was that children who have ASD are unable to break down the dietary proteins in gluten and casein, causing the formation of opioid-like peptides (short chains of amino acids with properties like medicine that affect brain function). According to this theory, children with autism are also believed to have "leaky gut." Because of this syndrome, these peptides are then able to escape from the digestive tract, cross the intestinal membranes, enter the bloodstream, and go up to the brain, causing the neurobehavioral symptoms that we know as ASD. It was believed that by eliminating foods that contain gluten and casein from a child's diet (known as the *gluten-free/casein-free [GFCF] diet*), you could diminish the symptoms of autism.

Some parents say that the GFCF diet has lessened their child's symptoms. Research to date, however, has not shown support for the GFCF diet and leaky gut theory. Several studies of the GFCF diet in children with ASD have shown that removing gluten and casein from a child's diet did not improve social skills or communication, nor did it help with sleep duration and activity levels. Even so, it's possible that some children with ASD who have significant gastrointestinal problems may reap some benefits from the GFCF diet, especially if they, coincidentally, also have celiac disease (gluten-sensitivity autoimmune disorder).

Still, many parents try removing gluten and casein from their child's diet. In fact, the GFCF diet is the most popular ICAM intervention among children who have ASD. It's generally considered safe, and some parents report that the diet has actually made a difference in their child's behavior. But it's hard to know whether these behavioral changes are directly related to the GFCF diet or are the result of another intervention that the child may be undergoing at the same time.

It's possible, too, that some children are lactose intolerant, meaning they can't tolerate the sugar in milk, which may cause gastrointestinal distress leading to irritability. Others may actually have celiac disease, which can also cause behavioral disturbances. By removing lactose and gluten from the diet of children who have these conditions, you may also notice behavioral improvements. Other families have reported improvement of their child's overall diet and in their child's range of food acceptance after eliminating dairy and gluten-based starches.

Deciding Whether to Try It

While the available science does not support the GFCF diet, it is understandable that some parents will want to try this intervention. After all, it's something that you can control and do on your own, and it is thought to be relatively safe. Before you do anything, though, talk with your child's pediatrician. You may also want to speak with a nutritionist because the GFCF diet may place your child at risk for some nutritional deficiencies.

For example, eliminating all milk products from your child's diet removes a critical source of calcium and vitamin D, which are key nutrients that are essential for strong bones. New evidence suggests that vitamin D may also play a role in neurological health and in the immune system and preventing infections, cancer, and diabetes. In addition, your child may require additional sources of protein because dairy products are often a major source of protein in a child's diet. Of note, these needed minerals are not always included in the now-popular gummy-type vitamins.

Taking gluten out of your child's diet can pose challenges too. Removing grains such as wheat, barley, rye, and oats from your child's diet eliminates important nutrients such as the B vitamins, iron, and fiber. Children who do the GFCF diet may benefit from vitamin and mineral supplements to make up for the nutrients missing from their daily diet.

Carrying out the diet can be difficult too. Gluten isn't always easy to detect, and reading labels can be challenging. While some sources such as bread, pasta, and cereal may be obvious, others such as deli meats, salad dressings, and broths may be less so. And if your child is already a picky eater, it may be a challenge to convince him to adopt this new way of eating. Food preparation may be more time-consuming for children on a GFCF diet, and the cost of the diet can be higher than that of a traditional diet for children.

While the GFCF diet is certainly among the most popular eating plans used in children with ASD, you may also hear about other diets that restrict certain foods or nutrients. Before putting your child onto any type of diet, talk with your child's pediatrician. You'll need to make sure your child is receiving all the nutrients important for his growth and development.

Alternative Sources of Key Nutrients

If you decide to put your child onto the gluten-free/casein-free diet, it's important to pay attention to certain nutrients such as vitamin D, calcium, iron, protein, and fiber, which may be lacking in this eating plan. The following chart offers other options for getting these important nutrients:

Nutrient Needs	Alternative Sources
Vitamin D	Fortified rice, soy, and almond milks; cod-liver oil; tofu and eggs; short-term exposure to sunlight; and supplements
Calcium	Fortified rice, soy, and almond milks; fortified orange juice; beans, broccoli, spinach, kale, tofu, and tempeh; and supplements
Iron	Red meats, pork, chicken (mainly in dark meat), shellfish, egg yolks, spinach, soybean nuts, prunes, and raisins; supplements
Protein	Eggs, nuts and seeds, lean meats, beans, and peanut butter
Fiber	Legumes, fruits, vegetables, nuts, and seeds; supplements

Dietary Supplements

The number of children and adults taking nutritional supplements has grown significantly in recent years. Multivitamins are the most common ICAM treatment—as many as 41% of children take a daily multivitamin. Among teenagers, as many as 75% take herbal remedies and other dietary supplements. It is not surprising that parents of children with ASD are interested in these same treatments to support the health of their children.

Vitamin B_6 and Magnesium

Vitamin B_6, or pyridoxine, helps the body make serotonin and norepinephrine, 2 important chemical messengers in the brain. Vitamin B_6 also helps produce enzymes for metabolizing protein and red blood cells. Children who do not get enough vitamin B_6 are at risk for certain skin conditions, for nerve problems, for irritability, and for depression.

Magnesium is an essential mineral that is involved in more than 300 biochemical reactions in the body. It's required for proper brain and muscle function, metabolism, and bone and immune health. Magnesium helps convert the amino acid 5-hydroxytryptophan into serotonin, a chemical messenger involved in regulating mood and keeping depression and anxiety at bay.

Back in the 1960s, some experts began to suggest that certain forms of mental illness were linked to biochemical problems in the body and that using vitamins as therapy could correct them. In children with ASD, some people thought that the body was unable to convert vitamin B_6 into a compound required to produce dopamine, a chemical messenger in the brain that regulates movement and behavior. Many children with ASD were also believed to have low levels of magnesium, though there was no direct connection.

Giving children a high-dose combination of vitamin B_6 and magnesium is a common ICAM treatment of children with ASD but is based largely on observations, not strong science. Some studies using low doses showed no benefits. Other studies using higher doses suggested that there might be some improvement in language or attention, but the research was not well designed.

Always talk with your child's pediatrician before you attempt this kind of a therapy. Treatment has potentially dangerous side effects, including peripheral neuropathy (nerve damage that can cause numbness, pain, and burning) from too much vitamin B_6 or diarrhea and arrhythmia (an abnormal heart rhythm) from high doses of magnesium.

Omega-3 Fatty Acids

Omega-3 fatty acids, especially docosahexaenoic acid and eicosapentaenoic acid, are essential for healthy brain development and proper communication between brain cells. They occur naturally in fatty fish and certain plant foods. In recent years, these healthy fats have been widely touted for their effects in preventing heart disease and depression. Some studies have suggested that these essential fatty acids might help improve attention, focus, and activity in children who have attention-deficit/hyperactivity disorder (ADHD). Some people believe they may also have a beneficial effect on children with ASD, although it is not well understood why this would be.

Small-scale research studies have suggested that high doses of omega-3 fatty acids might help in reducing repetitive behaviors such as pacing or rocking, fixated interests, irritability, and hyperactivity in children with ASD. Evidence, however, is sparse. There is a need for larger scale research studies to better understand the possible benefit of omega-3 fatty acids for children with ASD.

If you want to give your child omega-3 fatty acid supplements, make sure to talk with your child's pediatrician first. Keep in mind, too, that these fatty acids may cause gastrointestinal problems such as diarrhea, bloating, and abdominal pain. Make sure to identify target behaviors before starting treatment and keep track of how those behaviors change during treatment, so you'll know whether the supplements are making a difference. (See Appendix D for a sample medication flow sheet.)

Probiotics

The intestines harbor a rich array of bacteria that are responsible for the healthy functioning of our digestive, immune, and nervous systems. Among them are probiotics, that is, nontoxic bacteria or beneficial yeasts that dwell in our gut and are found in certain fermented foods such as kefir, yogurt, and tempeh. Probiotics are also available in supplement form as liquids, powders, or capsules. Among the most popular forms are lactobacillus, bifidobacterium, and saccharomyces.

Studies show that about 25% of all children with ASD take probiotics. This is not necessarily for the core symptoms of ASD but for the gastrointestinal and allergy issues that many children, including those with ASD, face such as diarrhea, constipation, irritable bowel syndrome, eczema, or certain allergies.

A recent review of children who used probiotics showed that the probiotics can help reduce the length of viral diarrheal illness and prevent or reduce the severity of antibiotic-associated diarrhea. In certain preterm babies, probiotics may protect against a severe gastrointestinal complication known as *necrotizing enterocolitis*, but more studies are needed. More research is also needed before probiotics can be recommended to treat disorders such as irritable bowel syndrome, Crohn disease, colic, and constipation and to prevent common infections and allergy in children.

Probiotics are generally considered safe, but in rare cases, they may be unsafe in children who are severely debilitated or immunocompromised or who live in households where such issues exist.

Multivitamins

As mentioned, multivitamins are the most common ICAM treatment. Vitamins are chemicals that the body needs, in small amounts, for many important functions. Many diseases result in not having enough of a certain vitamin; in these cases, using a vitamin supplement can be beneficial. In the case of ASD, some suggest that very high doses of certain vitamins are needed. Currently, however, no high-quality scientific studies show that high-dose (above the recommended amount) vitamin therapy is beneficial for children with ASD. If you suspect that your child may be deficient in certain vitamins or minerals, speak with your child's pediatrician. Various studies have shown that children with ASD may be at risk for nutritional deficiencies because of dietary restrictions or from being extremely selective eaters.

In general, vitamins that are given in recommended amounts are safe. The problem is that sometimes children wind up taking too much of certain vitamins, which causes toxicity. If you decide to give your child multivitamins and supplements, it's important to read labels and not give your child too much of any individual vitamin, especially the fat-soluble vitamins A, D, E, and K. Know the tolerable upper intake levels for individual vitamins in healthy children, and make sure your child's daily intake doesn't exceed these levels (**Table 7-1**).

Vitamin C

Vitamin C is a water-soluble vitamin responsible for healing, immune function, and iron absorption. It plays a key role in producing the neurotransmitters (chemical signals in the brain) norepinephrine and serotonin and in the breakdown of dopamine, another chemical messenger. These neurotransmitters play important roles in regulating mood, attention, and coordination and managing stress.

One small-scale study showed that vitamin C in children with ASD reduced stereotypic behaviors, but there are no well-designed studies of the effects of vitamin C supplements in children with ASD. Vitamin C is rarely used as a sole treatment for autism, but it may be part of a regimen of supplements, especially if there are concerns about vitamin C deficiency. It is a relatively safe supplement, though high doses may cause gastrointestinal problems such as diarrhea and kidney stones.

Melatonin

Many children with ASD have trouble getting a good night's sleep. For those who have trouble falling asleep, melatonin may be a good option. Melatonin is a hormone naturally secreted by the pineal gland in the brain that helps regulate our body's sleep-wake cycles. Some studies have shown that children with ASD have low melatonin levels.

Melatonin has been found through RCTs to be safe and effective at reducing the amount of time it takes for children who have difficulties falling asleep to doze off and increasing the length of time spent sleeping. (It is not generally used, though, to *keep* a child asleep.) Better sleep in these children (and their caregivers!) may lead to better

Table 7-1. Beware of Too Much

Some vitamins can be dangerous at high levels. Here's what experts recommend daily, as well as daily upper limits.

Vitamin	Age	Daily Recommended Intake	Daily Tolerable Upper Intake Level
Vitamin A	Babies 0–6 months	400 mcg/1,320 IU	600 mcg/1,980 IU
	Infants 7–12 months	500 mcg/1,650 IU	600 mcg/1,980 IU
	Children 1–3 years	300 mcg/990 IU	600 mcg/1,980 IU
	Children 4–8 years	400 mcg/1,320 IU	900 mcg/2,970 IU
	Children and teens 9–13 years	600 mcg/1,980 IU	1,700 mcg/5,610 IU
	Girls 14–18 years	700 mcg/2,310 IU	2,800 mcg/9,240 IU
	Boys 14–18 years	900 mcg/2,970 IU	2,800 mcg/9,240 IU
Vitamin D	Babies 0–6 months	10 mcg/400 IU	25 mcg/1,000 IU
	Infants 7–12 months	10 mcg/400 IU	37.5 mcg/1,500 IU
	Children 1–3 years	15 mcg/600 IU	62.5 mcg/2,500 IU
	Children 4–8 years	15 mcg/600 IU	75 mcg/3,000 IU
	Children and teens 9–18 years	15 mcg/600 IU	100 mcg/4,000 IU
Vitamin E	Babies 0–6 months	4 mg/9.3 μmol	Not determinable
	Infants 7–12 months	5 mg/11.6 μmol	Not determinable
	Children 1–3 years	6 mg/13.9 μmol	200 mg/464 μmol
	Children 4–8 years	7 mg/16.3 μmol	300 mg/696 μmol
	Children and teens 9–13 years	11 mg/25.6 μmol	600 mg/1,392 μmol
	Teens 14–18 years	15 mg/34.9 μmol	800 mg/1,856 μmol

Derived from American Academy of Pediatrics Committee on Nutrition. Kleinman RE, Greer FR, eds. *Pediatric Nutrition.* 7th ed. Elk Grove Village, IL: American Academy of Pediatrics; 2013.

daytime behavior and less family stress. Potential side effects of melatonin include nightmares and nighttime waking. If your child is having difficulty falling or staying asleep, your pediatrician can help you decide whether melatonin might be helpful.

A Parent's Story: Ronny

"Bedtime was always a struggle for us. Our son C.J., who is now 4, would scream for 2 hours straight. So my partner and I would split up and each take one child. By the time he was done screaming and crying, the parent with C.J. would wind up asleep in his room. Once, he climbed out and crawled into his brother's crib.

"Our doctor suggested melatonin. Every night he gets a cup of milk with melatonin dissolved in it. Then we do his nightly routine. He brushes his teeth, reads a book, and says, 'Daddy, it's time for bed.' Melatonin has been a lifesaver."

Cannabidiol

Since the first edition of this book, the use of medical marijuana and cannabis-derived medicinal products has become more popular for an expanding array of medical conditions, including autism. Despite a lack of RCTs, autism is listed as an approved diagnosis for the use of medical marijuana in 4 states as of this writing, with additional states permitting doctors the latitude to prescribe marijuana for chronic debilitating conditions. Currently, RCTs are underway in Israel and the United States that test various cannabis-derived products, including cannabidiol (CBD) and cannabidivarin. These components of marijuana are closely related to each other and do not make people high. A US Food and Drug Administration (FDA) advisory panel recently recommended the approval of Epidiolex, a CBD preparation for the treatment of severe childhood seizure syndromes, including Lennox-Gastaut syndrome and Dravet syndrome, on the basis of impressive results from 3 RCTs. Until proper testing is conducted under US FDA guidelines with specific approval by the US FDA for use in children with autism, however, the use of cannabis by-products for the treatment of ASD is considered experimental and is not supported by research to date.

Supplements for Oxidative Stress

Some researchers believe that oxidative stress and toxicity—when our bodies produce and cannot get rid of toxic forms of oxygen—are the culprits behind proposed neuronal (nerve cell) problems in children with ASD. Certain supplements are believed to help rid the body of this oxidative stress and enhance immune function. These include

- *Dimethylglycine:* Dimethylglycine is a by-product of the amino acid glycine. It is found naturally in some foods, such as beans and liver, and is available as a supplement. Some early reports suggested that dimethylglycine might improve speech and behavior in people who have ASD, but more studies are needed. This supplement is generally considered safe but may cause hyperactivity as a side effect.

- *Methylcobalamin:* Also known as *methyl B$_{12}$,* this supplement is involved in the proper functioning of certain antioxidants such as glutathione and a chemical process in the body called *methylation.* Some people believe that autism is the result of faulty methylation, which results in the expression of genes that cause ASD. Methylation is also important for ridding the body of oxidative stress. There have been no well-designed, controlled studies of the effect of methyl B$_{12}$ supplements on the behavior of children with ASD.

- *Folic acid, folinic acid, and folate:* These are all forms of a water-soluble B vitamin and are best known for preventing neural tube defects in fetuses. Folate is sometimes given in conjunction with methyl B$_{12}$ to increase levels of glutathione. They are also believed to increase levels of S-adenosylhomocysteine, or SAM-e, which is important for the production, activation, and breakdown of several important chemical messengers in the brain. There have been no well-designed studies of the effect of folate, folic acid, or folinic acid supplements, with or without methyl B$_{12}$, on the behavior of children with ASD.

Amino Acids

Amino acids play a critical role in the brain. In fact, many neurotransmitters are amino acids themselves or derived from amino acids. Not surprisingly, amino acids are essential for mental health and well-being.

Two amino acids that have been used in children with ASD are carnosine and carnitine. Carnosine has antioxidant properties and is believed to benefit brain health. Carnitine is found primarily in meat and is responsible for cellular energy production. There are not enough high-quality studies to say that carnosine or carnitine supplements are helpful for children with ASD. So while both amino acids are generally considered safe and well tolerated, little science shows that they have any efficacy in children with autism.

Interventions That Eliminate Infections

Through the years, there has been no shortage of theories about what causes autism. A weakened immune system that falls prey to viruses, bacteria, and fungi has been suggested as a possible cause of ASD. Although the immune system may be affected in some children with ASD, no strong scientific evidence supports the theory that problems with the immune system cause autism.

Intravenous Immunoglobulin

Research in recent years has showed that some children who have ASD have different immune systems compared with their typical peers. For instance, research has found irregular levels of cytokines, that is, substances that regulate important bodily immune functions. As a result, some people believe that altering the immune system may affect symptoms of ASD and have tried giving their children oral or intravenous immunoglobulin (IVIG) treatment. Intravenous immunoglobulin, which comes from human plasma, is used to treat neurological diseases rooted in autoimmune problems such as myasthenia gravis and Guillain-Barré syndrome. Unfortunately, studies have generally shown that IVIG does not help decrease or eliminate symptoms of ASD. The treatment is also costly and may cause serious side effects, including infection from contaminated blood products (such as viral hepatitis or HIV), meningitis, anaphylactic shock, kidney failure, decreased urination, sudden weight gain, swelling of the legs or ankles, or shortness of breath.

Antiviral Agents

Although no specific virus has been identified as the cause of autism, some people believe that treating children with antiviral agents can help. The theory behind these medications is that autism is the result of a chronic viral infection of the central nervous system. No clinical trials at all show that antiviral agents are helpful in reducing or eliminating symptoms of ASD. In fact, overusing these agents may be dangerous and risks suppressing bone marrow, the thick inner part of bone that produces white blood cells, red blood cells, and platelets. Other side effects include nausea, dizziness, headache, abdominal pain, and depression.

Antibiotics

Looking back, many parents recall their child having several ear infections before being diagnosed as having ASD. These infections were most often treated with antibiotics that some people believe may have altered gut microflora. These microflora are believed by some to promote the growth of bacteria that harm the nervous system, which in turn contributes to the development of autism.

Certain antibiotics have been used to try and clear the gut of the presumed toxic bacteria, but currently, no research shows that antibiotics can help reduce symptoms of ASD. Using antibiotics for a prolonged time is discouraged because it can lead to antibiotic resistance and can cause colitis, a sometimes serious inflammation of the colon.

Anti-yeast Treatments

Although there is no evidence to support this theory, some believe that overgrowth of a particular yeast, *Candida*, in the intestines may play some role in the development of autism. It is believed that the excess yeast, in turn, causes the symptoms we know as autism. To tame *Candida* overgrowth, some people give their children antifungal medications, which may cause harmful side effects. Chronic use of fluconazole, a prescription antifungal agent, may result in liver toxicity and an itchy skin condition known as *exfoliative dermatitis.* Nystatin, another antifungal agent, may cause diarrhea. Furthermore, no clinical trials have been done to evaluate antifungal effectiveness in reducing ASD symptoms.

Nonbiological Interventions

Changing behavior may be possible with nonbiological therapies. Some of these techniques have been used in the hope of altering the neural connections in the brain. Among those used for ASD are

Auditory Integration Therapy

Auditory integration therapy is an intervention that conditions children with ASD to tolerate certain sounds by listening to filtered music in a sound booth over a period of time. It is designed to retrain the ear to process sounds in a more normal fashion without any distortions. The cost of these sessions can be quite expensive, however, and the evidence to date does not support its use in treating ASD.

Sensory Integration Therapy

Sensory integration therapy is a form of occupational therapy that you may recall reading about in Chapter 4. The therapist may place the child in a specially designed room that stimulates all her senses. During a typical session, the therapist works with the child to encourage movement and elicit appropriate responses to various sensory stimuli. Therapy is based on the assumption that the child is overstimulated or under-stimulated by her environment and that therapy can improve her ability to process sensory input.

Despite dozens of studies over the past 4 decades, research about the effectiveness of sensory integration therapy is still insufficient to move this popular intervention into the realm of standard therapies for ASD.

Behavioral Optometry

The chance that a child with ASD will have a vision problem is thought to be no different than in a child with typical development. Currently, there is inadequate evidence to suggest that eye or vision problems cause or increase symptoms of ASD. Some professionals, however, believe that certain vision therapies might benefit a child's behavior—especially those associated with learning disabilities, language disorders, and other developmental problems—by improving his visual functioning. It is based on the belief that the problem behavior is actually the result of faulty eye movement.

Behavioral optometry is generally not recommended in children with ASD or those who have learning disabilities. In fact, in 2011, the American Academy of Pediatrics, along with the American Association for Pediatric Ophthalmology and Strabismus and the American Academy of Ophthalmology, issued a joint technical report saying that "Scientific evidence does not support the claims that visual training, muscle exercises, ocular pursuit-and-tracking exercises, behavioral/perceptual vision therapy, 'training' glasses, prisms, and colored lenses and filters are effective direct or indirect treatments for learning disabilities."

Craniosacral Therapy

Craniosacral therapy involves applying pressure to manipulate the fluid around the brain. The practice is usually performed by a chiropractor or motor therapist. The gentle pressure is intended to improve the function of the central nervous system and relieve stress. Research, however, has shown that simply touching the area around the spine does not alter the pressure of cerebrospinal fluid. Craniosacral therapy is not recommended for children who have Down syndrome because of possible neck bone problems that risk injury to the spinal cord. Although massage can be an effective way to relax a child who has ASD, there is no evidence that craniosacral therapy has any benefits beyond those of massage alone.

A Parent's Story: Carly

"Our son Asher, who is now 7, suffers from a great deal of anxiety. For him, deep pressure on his body has always worked best at relaxing him. These days, he likes to put his head into my neck and just nestle against me. Then he wants me to wrap my arms around him and just squeeze.

"Not surprisingly, Asher always responded best to forms of massage, in particular therapeutic brushing and joint compression. Therapeutic brushing involves brushing a small surgical brush on his arms and legs in soft, rhythmic strokes. I had followed that with joint compression, in which I gently had pressed together the joints at his shoulder, elbow, knees, and ankles for quick counts of 10. For some reason, when I did those 2 things every 2 hours, it would make my son more focused. It's as if it triggered something in his brain that helped him form his mouth better to make sounds. Unfortunately, he grew immune to its effects after 6 months.

"I also used to lie [down] on his back or roll a yoga ball from his back down to his feet. The weight of my body and the yoga ball soothed him and reduced his anxiety. But he doesn't like those techniques anymore. He still wears a weighted blanket at times, which helps reduce his stress, but I don't think it's heavy enough. He has found that he enjoys the deep pressure much more in an upright position.

"We did try him on the gluten-free/casein-free diet for a while when he was 4, but it was hard because he saw his sisters and parents eating the foods he really wanted, which made him upset. Also, during those 3 weeks, Asher was very lethargic and solemn. My happy little boy who once had lots of energy and loved to play all of a sudden wasn't happy anymore. His teachers would tell me that he didn't want to play or participate and just wanted to sit in a corner alone. It was an awful experience. We discontinued it after 3 weeks.

A Parent's Story: Carly (*continued*)

"Now, we use melatonin every night. He takes [it] before bedtime. He winds up very tired, sleeps well, and wakes up refreshed. That has worked very well."

Carly's story illustrates how families are the experts in caring for their children and in determining how some of the complementary and alternative medicine therapies discussed in this chapter are beneficial for their children. As you consider various therapies, be sure to discuss all options with your child's pediatrician.

Alternative Therapies to Avoid

Over the years, parents of children with ASD have turned to numerous therapies with the hope of helping their children. Some of these treatments have turned out to be harmful and potentially deadly.

Chelation

For years, many people believed—and some still do—that autism was caused by thimerosal, a preservative that contains mercury and that was previously used in vaccines (still in some influenza vaccines) to prevent contamination with bacteria and fungi. This alleged link has been scientifically disproved in numerous studies and reports. Still, the notion spawned interest in a treatment called *chelation*, a treatment with an agent that binds to heavy metals in the body and allows them to be excreted in the urine. Chelating agents also bind to other metals in the body, including iron and calcium, which are important and essential nutrients. Chelation is approved by the US FDA for treating lead poisoning but is not approved for autism.

Several chelating agents are available, and some are sold over the counter. Two of the most common are ethylenediaminetetraacetic acid and meso-2,3-dimercaptosuccinic acid. Treatment may be given orally or intravenously or applied topically to the skin.

Because chelation is a potentially dangerous treatment, it should not be used to treat ASD. Using chelating agents intravenously is especially dangerous and has resulted in the death of a child. It has not been studied in people with ASD, and any reports of its effectiveness have been subjective.

Hyperbaric Oxygen Therapy

Hyperbaric oxygen therapy (HBOT) involves placing the patient into a large, non-portable container and increasing air pressure to levels just slightly higher than normal atmospheric levels and boosting oxygen levels to 100%. It's generally used to treat a condition in scuba divers known as "the bends," which occurs when they surface too quickly and develop oxygen bubbles in their blood. It's also used to treat carbon monoxide poisoning and burns. As a treatment of autism, HBOT is intended to correct the theorized abnormal oxygen metabolism in the brains of children with ASD and eliminate excess oxygen.

Most studies have shown that HBOT is ineffective in treating autism, and the treatment is potentially dangerous. Side effects include ear pain, reversible nearsightedness, and seizures. Because of the potential for harm and lack of good scientific evidence of its benefit, HBOT is not recommended to treat autism.

Secretin

Using secretin to treat autism has largely disappeared, but it enjoyed a great deal of popularity in the late 1990s. Secretin is an intestinal hormone that controls digestion. In 1998, an uncontrolled study (there was no control group to compare against subjects who received

Tests for Autism That Your Child Doesn't Need

In recent years, some parents have been urged to get their children tested in ways that are entirely unnecessary in diagnosing autism spectrum disorder. These tests include hair analysis, measurement of micronutrient levels (such as vitamin levels), intestinal permeability studies, stool analysis, measurement of urinary peptide levels, and measurement of mercury level. These tests are not needed and results are quite expensive to obtain.

treatment) involving just 3 children showed that secretin relieved some of the communication and social skill deficits of autism while also helping with gastrointestinal symptoms. Excitement soon died down, however, when more than 15 controlled studies consistently showed clear evidence that secretin lacked benefit. Today, it is no longer regarded as a treatment of autism.

Mind-Body Therapies

Children with ASD who are high functioning and have good language skills may benefit from some ICAM therapies that help a child regulate emotions and maintain a state of calm. Although these treatments do not yet have the science behind them, they do offer an alternative to psychotropic medications, which may cause unpleasant side effects and are often expensive. Among them are

- *Yoga:* This ancient physical and spiritual discipline and philosophy originated in India more than 5,000 years ago. Today, it's a popular form of exercise that uses poses or postures to strengthen and condition the body while calming and nourishing the mind. The practice is believed to improve concentration, discipline, and confidence while also enhancing flexibility, strength, and coordination. Yoga is already gaining popularity as a treatment for children with attention-deficit/hyperactivity disorder (ADHD), a condition that often exists in children with ASD too. It is also showing promise as a treatment of many other ailments such as arthritis, back pain, and insomnia. Emerging evidence is encouraging and suggests that yoga is deserving of further study for the treatment of ASD.

- *Neurofeedback:* Like any form of biofeedback, neurofeedback therapy (NFT) "feeds back" information about a patient's physiological functioning. In NFT, the patient learns to regulate or control physiological impulses in the brain and then change outward behaviors. Studies about whether NFT is effective are not conclusive. In some children with ASD, neurofeedback has reportedly improved behavior and reduced symptoms. The National Institutes of Health has significantly increased funding of studies of NFT over the past decade, including for children with ASD; at this time, however, there is not clear evidence that NFT improves symptoms of ASD. On the other hand, initial studies examining NFT for symptoms of ADHD suggest that there may be an improvement in brain function in people with that disorder. It may be that children with ASD who seem to benefit from NFT might be having improvement in coexisting ADHD symptoms rather than a true improvement in the core symptoms of ASD. This therapy has no side effects but is costly. The scientific evidence does not recommend its use for children with ASD at this time.

- *Music therapy:* Some people with ASD display remarkable talent for music, so it's not surprising that therapists have tried to use music to help children with ASD gain new skills in communication and expression. While some small studies have shown encouraging results, more studies are needed to know if music therapy is beneficial for children with ASD.

- *Massage:* Application of touch and pressure to the body, by either a caregiver or a therapist, for the purpose of relieving bodily stress or discomfort, has been shown by a small number of studies to have modest benefits in children with ASD. Since massage is easily accessible, has few adverse side effects, and may be administered by caregivers, this is a promising intervention and further research is warranted.

- *Equine-assisted therapy:* A variety of activities with horses, including riding and non-riding interactions, have shown promise in their impact on behavior, social interaction, and communication of children with ASD. The evidence thus far is considered preliminary and further study is indicated.

Finding an ICAM Practitioner

Locating a therapist who practices ICAM treatment isn't as difficult as it once was because these treatments have become increasingly common. For instance, many pediatricians are becoming more knowledgeable about integrative, complementary, and alternative therapies and can provide advice on these treatments. In fact, the American Academy of Pediatrics has more than 400 pediatricians who are members of its Section on Integrative Medicine.

If you are interested in seeking an ICAM practitioner, start by talking with your child's pediatrician. Your pediatrician can tell you whether a treatment is safe and may also be able to refer you to a licensed practitioner or therapist in your area. Don't be afraid to ask a potential practitioner about credentials, education, and experience. Ask whether the practitioner has experience treating children, in particular those with ASD. Find out how many children the practitioner has treated and how often they are treated now. Make sure to gather information about office hours, costs, and insurance coverage.

Also, check into your state's licensing requirements for different types of ICAM. Some states require a license to practice acupuncture, for instance, but others do not. In states that do not, check to see whether your acupuncturist has been certified by a national professional organization. In fact, it can be quite useful to check whether any practitioner, such as an occupational therapist, has additional certification in a particular ICAM treatment (such as sensory integration therapy).

If you decide on an ICAM treatment, make sure to let your child's pediatrician know. Tell the doctor about any vitamins, supplements, or herbs you give your child. This information is critical because combining these products with a prescribed medication can sometimes produce dangerous side effects. Also, do not stop any prescribed medications without first speaking with your doctor.

Whether or Not ICAM Is Covered

Getting an ICAM treatment can be expensive, especially if the therapy isn't covered by your health insurance plan. Some insurance companies are now picking up the tab for these treatments, but coverage depends on the insurance plan you have. Other therapies may be managed and offered by school districts. In some states, families may be able to receive financial assistance from developmental disability agencies. On the other hand, some treatments may not ever be covered, which means you'll have to pay for the entire treatment out of your own pocket.

Therapy That Is Too Good to Be True

Many integrative, complementary, and alternative therapies lack scientific proof that support their use as autism spectrum disorder (ASD) treatments and the many health conditions associated with ASD. Knowing how to spot a false claim is important to avoid being overly persuaded by a treatment with no evidence behind it. Here are 6 kinds of claims to avoid.

- Those that are based on overly simple scientific theories. Your child's pediatrician can help you look into the science behind a therapy.
- Claims that a therapy can treat multiple different and unrelated symptoms, diseases, or conditions.
- Claims that use case reports or subjective data rather than carefully designed studies to show their effectiveness.
- Claims that children will respond dramatically or even experience a cure.
- Claims that say there's no need for controlled studies or peer-reviewed references.
- Claims that the treatment has no potential or reported adverse side effects.

Before seeking an ICAM treatment, check with your insurance company to see whether it is covered. Ask practitioners what they charge and to specify exactly what will be done.

Final Word on ICAM

It's not unusual for parents of children with ASD to explore integrative, complementary, and alternative remedies for their children. Some of these treatments may even offer some benefit. Others, however, may not. Research on these remedies is sparse, and much of the evidence is subjective. But just because something doesn't have scientific evidence backing it up doesn't mean it doesn't work; it simply means that scientists haven't subjected the treatment to rigorous scientific study. Many treatments once considered complementary are now mainstream. As stated earlier, the most important thing you can do is to become educated and use common sense. Know the potential benefits of the treatments and how to measure those effects.

The bottom line is this: if you decide to look into an ICAM treatment for your child, do your research. Start by asking your child's pediatrician what she knows about it and whether she can help you understand the potential benefits and risks. Read articles about the treatment on reputable Web sites such as those of the National Center for Complementary and Integrative Health at the National Institutes of Health, the Academic Consortium for Integrative Medicine and Health, and the Association for Science in Autism Treatment. (See Appendix A for more information.) Find out what the benefits, risks, and potential side effects are of any treatment. And tell your child's pediatrician and other health care practitioners if you decide to use an ICAM treatment with your child. Being open and honest about your child's care, as you'll learn in Chapter 8, is the best thing you can do to ensure her health and safety.

Partnering With Your Pediatrician

IDEALLY, YOUR CHILD'S pediatrician has played a vital role in caring for your child with autism spectrum disorder (ASD). Your pediatrician may have been the one who listened to you when you had concerns about your child's behavior and development. She may have been the one to screen your child for ASD, refer you to a specialist or an early intervention (EI) program, and provide you with information and community resources on autism.

There are things you should be able to expect from your pediatrician, but the relationship with your pediatrician is a partnership, one that requires input from you, the parent, not just your child's doctor. We discuss how you can work with your child's pediatrician so your child receives the best care possible. Good care also involves input from the treatment team (including the pediatrician and staff from your child's primary care practice), behavioral therapists whom your child sees, and other medical, developmental, and educational specialists involved in your child's care. A medical home will help you bring together all the components of your child's care. In this chapter, we discuss the medical home concept and why it's so essential to the care and well-being of children with ASD.

Every child, every patient, is entitled to quality medical care, but it's especially important for children with special health care needs, such as those with ASD. Children with ASD tend to have more-frequent contact with the health care system. Often, treating children with ASD demands more of the pediatrician. It may require more time during an office visit to address the needs of the child with ASD and her family. Many of these children also have other associated medical and psychiatric conditions.

While some physicians have limited experience with children with ASD, most pediatricians report that they have an active role in screening for ASD and caring for children with ASD in their practice. Knowing what you can expect from your pediatrician and fulfilling your own responsibilities in this partnership will help ensure that your child gets the care she deserves.

What You Should Expect From Your Pediatrician

Pediatricians are important advocates for any child but especially for children with special health care needs such as ASD. Here are some key things your pediatrician may do for you if you suspect or know your child has ASD.

- Listen to all your concerns about your child's development, be it speech and language delays, delays in social skills, or the presence of unusual behaviors. Research has shown that most parents are usually correct when they suspect something is wrong with their child's growth and development.
- Give you a screening questionnaire that will probe more deeply into your child's development.
- Give you a screening questionnaire specific for ASD that is recommended at the 18- and 24-month visits.
- Refer to a professional, or team of professionals, who uses the latest diagnostic tools to help make a formal diagnosis.
- Refer for an audiology evaluation.
- Refer for EI services in your community even before there is a formal diagnosis (see Chapter 4).
- Persist in addressing your concerns even if a screening test result is negative.
- Pay close attention to and screen younger siblings of your child with ASD, given the increased rate of recurrence within families (see Chapter 2).

- Stay abreast of the most recent research and developments in the field of autism and be aware of local agencies, services, and support groups available to you and your children.

- Continue to follow up on the care of your child after the diagnosis, and be an active partner in your child's care by listening to your concerns, respecting your expertise as a parent, and collaborating on treatment decisions.

You need to be certain that you feel that you can talk with your pediatrician and that she is able to do these key things. But it takes more than just your pediatrician; children with ASD need medical homes.

Your Child's Medical Home

When we think of a home, we think of a building. But a medical home is not a physical structure. Instead, it's an approach to providing health care services that are *accessible, family-centered, continuous, comprehensive, coordinated, compassionate*, and *culturally competent*. The model was developed by the American Academy of Pediatrics and has since been adopted and promoted by other medical organizations. In this section, we look at what these terms mean and what you can do to help ensure that your child's medical team is living up to these standards. For more information, visit the National Center for Medical Home Implementation Web site at https://medicalhomeinfo.aap.org/tools-resources/Pages/For-Families.aspx.

Accessible

An *accessible* pediatric practice is one where the care you receive is provided right there in your community. The doctor or on-call provider should be available to you (at least by phone) after hours, on weekends, and during holidays, 24 hours a day, 365 days a year. At appointments, you and your child should be able to sit and talk with the pediatrician about any and all aspects of your child's care. The pediatrician and staff should be open and honest in their conversations with you while also listening to your concerns and questions. Because of this relationship, you and your family should become well acquainted with the pediatrician and other members of the office staff such as nurses, nurse

My son's pediatrician knows a lot about autism, but it's difficult to talk with her. How do we deal with this?

When it comes to a condition such as autism, a doctor who has the clinical skills, knowledge, and expertise in treating autism spectrum disorder is a definite plus. A doctor is also better able to treat your child's health concerns if she has an interest in that area of medicine. Her experience will ultimately help her direct you to resources and other experts in the community.

But if it is hard to speak with her or if you receive information that is hard to understand, ask that things be described in clearer terms. Or perhaps you can call later to go over your questions. Write a note or tell your pediatrician in person when you are not pleased. Many practices now have patient portals that allow you to communicate with your child's pediatrician electronically. Be as specific as possible so it can improve your child's care as well as that of other children. It may help to schedule an extended parent conference with your pediatrician to discuss issues in greater detail than is typically possible at a sick-child visit or a well-child visit (also called a *health supervision visit*).

Remember that every relationship has peaks and valleys. Your child's pediatrician is human, too, so give her a chance to make things better. Often, differences of style or other difficulties can be worked out over time. On the other hand, if difficulties cannot be worked out and your child's needs are not being met, it may be reasonable to interview other pediatricians to find one who is a good fit for your family. After all, you'll be more likely to ask questions and share concerns if you feel comfortable with your pediatrician. If a doctor is not as approachable, you may be reluctant to discuss important issues that affect your child's care.

practitioners, and physician assistants, and you should feel comfortable asking them for information and resources for your child's needs. The office should help connect you to family support organizations in the community.

Being able to afford to care for a child with ASD is also part of accessibility. If your pediatrician can no longer care for your child, the office should be able to accommodate you or refer you to another practice that provides the same kind of care.

Accessibility refers to physical access too. Being an accessible practice means that the facility is easy to enter and exit and meets the standards set by the federal Americans with Disabilities Act. If necessary and possible, the practice should be located near public transportation.

Family-Centered

In a *family-centered* medical home, the pediatrician is a familiar and trusted figure to the child and her family. But the family is regarded as the primary caregiver and source of support for the child. The relationship between the pediatrician and the family is built on trust and mutual sharing of information. Both parties share in the decision-making process. The pediatrician should ask you about your concerns, what you've observed, and what might be the cause of these concerns. The information you provide should always be given careful consideration.

Meanwhile, your pediatrician should give you and your family all your treatment options in a clear, unbiased fashion. While sharing her expertise, the doctor should always respect you and your child as the experts in your child's care. If you pursue an option that is not in line with her recommendations, she should feel free to ask why and to share scientific evidence about the risks and benefits of that option. But she should also respect that decision, even if she doesn't agree with it.

Continuous and Comprehensive

When it comes to caring for a child with ASD, consistency is important, especially for a child who does not like change. Ideally, the pediatric practice should have the same health care professionals taking care of your child from infancy to adolescence and into young adulthood. And if your child sees a specialist, your pediatrician should review the report from that provider so she can stay on top of all aspects of your child's care.

Although *continuous* care means your child should have access to a doctor 24-7, it does not necessarily mean that the doctor you talk with at midnight will be your primary care doctor. It's up to you to be familiar with the after-hours policies of your practice and to know who the other professionals are who may be involved in providing care.

When your child hits the teen years, continuous care may mean letting your child have a say in his own medical care. It can mean allowing him to take responsibility for his health care concerns, meet in private with his pediatrician, and take charge of his medications, appointments, and health records. (There is more about this in Chapter 11.)

Comprehensive care means the pediatrician is well trained and able to manage all aspects of your child's care while also serving as an advocate for your child. Comprehensive care doesn't mean just handling illnesses. The doctor should also be involved in preventive medicine, which includes immunizations, growth and development, recommended screenings (such as hearing, vision, lead, and cholesterol), and the proper supervision of care. The office staff and pediatrician should be open to advising parents on everything from health and safety, to parenting and psychosocial issues, to concerns about health insurance, Medicaid, and Title V state programs for children with special health care needs. If a family requires extra time to discuss these issues, the office should have a system in place to accommodate those needs.

Coordinated, Compassionate, and Culturally Competent

Pediatric care that is *coordinated* is central to the concept of a medical home. In a well-coordinated medical home, the pediatrician works closely with your family to develop an appropriate plan of care that meshes well with other health care practitioners, organizations, and agencies involved in your child's care. If others on your child's health care team make recommendations, the pediatrician should evaluate and interpret those recommendations for you.

A critical part of a coordinated care plan is the care notebook. The care notebook helps you keep track of all aspects of your child's care. Those same records should also be available in your doctor's office. We discuss more about the care notebook later in this chapter.

A Parent's Story: Jennifer

"As a single mom with 3 sons who have autism, I'm lucky to have a pediatrician who really listens. He is very patient and lets me carefully explain all of the minutiae of what is going on, no matter how insignificant the details may seem. Sometimes even the smallest details make sense to him and tip him off to something greater going on. He never makes me feel stupid for worrying or wondering or being tired or sad or confused. And he excuses me sometimes for the enormous burden that I face.

"I remember telling him one time just how hard homework was emotionally for my 7-year-old, who has an anxiety disorder. I told him I wished the school would just let him not do it because he was excelling academically. My pediatrician agreed with me but told me, 'I mostly agree that *you* don't need to do homework. Your days are hard enough, and your nights are hard enough.' So basically, my pediatrician gave me a hall pass from homework and we were all happier at home. Everyone's anxiety went down after that.

"He makes my job easier because he trusts me. He knows that I have been working with all 3 of my sons so intensely, full-time, for 8 years now, and that I have been hands-on, 100% involved. So he trusts me to make the ultimate decision regarding their care and treatment.

"At the same time, we are truly a team. All of the decisions, from medication to changes in therapy, are made by both of us. I can decide to eliminate a speech-language therapy, for example, and explain to him why, and he trusts that I made the right call. He might give me reasons to reconsider, but he understands that my motivations are pure, that I am an educated mom, and that my desire to help my sons be successful comes from the same place of science and love that his decision to practice with this particular population did. We are both highly educated, empathetic, and practical people who want the best for my sons and are dedicated to doing whatever it takes to get them there. It feels like a blended personal *and* professional partnership. I trust him."

Compassion comes in the way that the pediatrician and his staff treat you and your child. Concern can be verbal or nonverbal, but it should always be respectful and kind. Their concern should show up in the way they talk with you and listen to your concerns and in the amount of time and effort they put toward addressing your needs. The pediatrician should make an effort to really get to know your child and acknowledge the challenges that ASD imposes on your family.

Cultural competence refers to being sensitive to your values, beliefs, preferences, languages, and customs. The pediatrician and his staff should not judge you by your age, class, ethnicity, gender, race, sexual orientation, spiritual practice, or financial status. Of course, it is up to you, the parent, to convey the values, customs, and preferences that are important to your family. For instance, if you are Jewish and eat a kosher diet, you cannot assume that your doctor knows this about you until you share this with him.

If English is not your primary language, your pediatric practice should seek out ways to communicate with you that are more effective, such as involving a trained medical interpreter in your visit and providing written information in your primary language. Telephone access to medical interpreters is available if none are readily accessible in person. To make sure information is accurately conveyed, you may ask the doctor to provide a written document of what you discussed. You'll be able to cross-check the accuracy of what the interpreter tells you.

Being a Good Parent Partner

Like any partnership, you need to devote time and energy toward the relationship you have with your child's pediatrician. After all, you are your child's primary caregiver, you know her better than anyone else, and the information you have about her is vital, whether it's pinpointing a diagnosis of autism or determining whether a treatment is working. If you feel that you aren't being listened to, you may want to interview another physician who might be a better fit for your child and family.

To be a good parent partner, it's important to be an active player. If you choose, go to each doctor appointment armed with a list of questions and concerns. Be prepared to update your doctor about changes in your child's health and circumstances, such as changes in medications and treatments. Consider your pediatrician a key source of information, but always do your research and gather information from other sources too. Your pediatrician can also help you gain more knowledge by referring you to reputable Web sites, other parents, and books and articles (see Appendix A).

Don't be shy about telling your pediatrician of plans to ask other health care professionals for advice and second opinions. In fact, most pediatricians welcome a second opinion and may even give you a referral to another expert. And whenever possible, give your doctor feedback on how she is doing. Send a thank-you note for a suggestion she made that worked out well. Let her know when something doesn't go well too.

One of the most important things you can do is to keep good records of your child's medical and educational information. When several health care professionals are involved in a patient's care, it's easy for pieces of information to get overlooked or lost if a specialist doesn't send follow-up reports to your pediatrician. That's why your records are so important and warrant a discussion of their own.

Like any relationship, the way you conduct yourself can make a difference. If you want your doctor to listen to you, it's important that you listen to her. If you want to hear good news, make sure to share your good news too. Arrive on time so you help your doctor stay on schedule. Your child is but one patient in your pediatrician's busy day. If you need extra time for your visit, always let the scheduling staff know in advance.

Be clear with your pediatrician about how you want to work together and share in the decision-making process. Don't expect perfection from your pediatrician—doctors are human too. If you're generally happy with your doctor and her practice, it may be worth enduring some difficult periods when you may not agree on treatment or philosophy.

Keeping Good Records: The Care Notebook

Tracking all your child's health and medical needs is a daunting task and can be especially overwhelming if you have a child with ASD. Among all the therapies, health care specialists, and treatments, it can seem like a massive task just to stay on top of appointments, much less keep records of them. However, for the sake of your child's care, it's a task that should be done meticulously and regularly by you and your pediatrician.

That's where the care notebook comes in. A care notebook is an organizational tool that allows you to keep track of important information about your child's care. Having a comprehensive care notebook cements your role as the primary expert in your child's care. It is also a tool to help you communicate important information to your pediatrician. The care notebook should keep track of appointments and all aspects of your child's medical care as well as your child's special care needs, any community health services, records of his therapy, and issues at school, including the Individualized Education Program. More specifically, your care notebook should contain

- Medical summary (diagnoses, hospitalizations, medications, allergies, family medical history, names of doctors with phone numbers, list of current therapies and frequency, and names of therapists and phone numbers)
- Progress notes from routine doctor visits
- Immunization records
- Reports from specialists
- Medications, names, dosages, and frequency
- Laboratory tests and results
- Dietary changes
- Medical bills
- Insurance papers
- Types of activities of daily living that your child can do
- Notes about your child's social interactions, communication concerns, and ability to cope with stress

- Special transportation needs
- Early intervention services received
- Notes on conversations with school officials, including teachers
- Individualized Education Program and behavioral intervention plan
- Summaries or data provided by your child's behavioral therapist
- Transition plans
- Updated list of behavioral reinforcers or list of activities that can soothe or entertain your child

Bring your care notebook on all doctor visits, therapy sessions, and other appointments involving your child's care. You might also want to make a smaller version with the most vital health and medical information to take on vacation in the event of an unexpected illness.

Keeping the care notebook updated is an important task. Fill in details after each appointment and therapy session. Ask office staff for immunization records, doctor reports, laboratory test results, and any other information about your child that you require. For more information on how to build a care notebook, visit the National Center for Medical Home Implementation Web site at https://medicalhomeinfo.aap.org/tools-resources/Pages/For-Families.aspx.

The Doctor Visit

Going to a doctor, a dentist, or any medical professional can be stressful for all children—adults, too, for that matter—but for children with ASD, these events can be downright distressing. The idea of someone touching your face or skin and even poking and prodding your body can cause enormous anxiety for a child who may already be extremely sensitive to stimuli.

For starters, a doctor visit is a change in routine. It might mean pulling your child out of school early, interrupting a therapy session, or changing her meal schedule. The waiting room can be stressful too, especially if there are several other children and the wait is long.

The good news is, many practices are now becoming more sensitive to the needs of children with ASD at appointments. So if you need to ask office staff for special accommodations, you should feel comfortable doing so. If your child needs time with the doctor to make her comfortable, ask whether you can book a longer appointment. If sitting in the waiting room is too stressful, ask whether you can wait in the car and be called on your cell phone when the doctor is ready. Many practices now are making these and other accommodations for families of children with special health care needs.

Of course, it's important that you relate your concerns to the doctor or dentist before you arrive at your visit. Tell office staff what bothers your child, but also share what comforts and interests him. This information can help staff make accommodations that will help you and your child have a better visit. Tell them about previous visits, that is, what went well and what didn't.

It's also important to prepare your child for the visit. Talk to your child about what he can expect at a doctor or dentist visit. Look for books and videos that can show your child in a positive way what takes place. Try presenting appropriate behaviors in the form of a story (also known as *social stories*) with pictures about how to behave or react in a situation to teach your child. To make some of the procedures less frightening, practice some of them at home first. Take your child's temperature or blood pressure. Look inside his mouth with a tongue depressor. Peer inside his ears and nose. Listen to his heart with a stethoscope. Purchasing a toy doctor's kit beforehand can help him become familiar with the doctor's instruments. You might want to rehearse your visit in advance as well.

If your child has a hard time waiting, you might decide to book an appointment early in the day or immediately after lunch break, as these times tend to have shorter waits. You can also inform your pediatrician whether you prefer to separate procedure visits from routine examinations. Some children with ASD benefit from having a written schedule of procedures in the office on which items can be checked off as completed. This can be arranged with a nurse ahead of the visit and incorporated into a social story. If your child might need a vaccine or an uncomfortable procedure, talk with your pediatrician about how to best give that information to your child in a way that he can understand.

A Successful Doctor Visit: Dr Rosenblatt

"The good visit starts with an upbeat and welcoming staff who is sensitive to the child's special needs. This is followed by the doctor who takes time to bond with parent and child. The doctor should be flexible about the child's ability to handle the examination, which may take place on the parent's lap, on the examination table, or standing up.

"The examination starts as simply as possible. I save what the child may perceive as the most frightening aspects of the examination until the end. I like to start by checking the hands and feet and then moving to the trunk and head. Whenever possible, I try to make a game out of the necessary parts of the examination. I allow the child to handle whatever instruments I use and practice the examination before it starts. Humor helps with some children but may irritate others.

"In certain circumstances, no amount of charm or sensitivity will be able to calm a child's raging fear. In those situations, I try to express my empathy and complete the examination as efficiently as possible.

"I try to make up for invading the child's personal space by declaring an end to the hard part of the visit and allow the child to be comforted by her parent. I will provide tissues to wipe away tears and drippy noses and may try helping the parent console the child. Once the child is dressed and calmer, I may offer a special toy or activity for the child.

"After finishing my discussion with the parent, I check to see how the child says good-bye. From the children who respond to me, I will try to get a high five. If their response is forgiving, I will even try to get a hug. If they ignore or avoid my gesture, I will praise their bravery and say how proud I am of how they handled the examination. If the child is unable to understand what I am saying, I reassure the parent that we will try to minimize her child's discomfort in the future during necessary examinations and procedures."

Sometimes, even with all your best efforts, a doctor's appointment can be challenging, especially if your child didn't get enough sleep the night before or if he is fearful about an impending immunization. In this case, you simply have to do the best you can to keep the appointment moving so you can reduce your child's time at the doctor's office. Enlist help from your spouse or a friend to accompany you. Come prepared with written questions. Bring a favorite toy or object that your child finds soothing. Do what you can to calm your child during the actual visit. You may choose to finish the appointment with a special reward, which will help your child associate doctor visits with something positive and enjoyable.

The Health Care Team

Because autism is a complex condition, it's possible that your child will have specialist doctors, in addition to your pediatrician, involved in his medical care. A great deal will depend on your child's particular health needs and concerns. Many of these doctors are pediatric specialists who work specifically with children in their areas of expertise. Here are some other types of health care professionals you may need.

- *Neurodevelopmental and developmental/behavioral pediatricians:* These specialists see children with developmental and behavioral concerns that may be signs of a developmental disability such as ASD.
- *Neurologists:* Neurologists treat conditions affecting the brain and other parts of the nervous system. Children who have seizures, headaches, and other symptoms related to the nervous system may be referred to neurologists for further testing and treatment.
- *Geneticists:* These physicians specialize in genetic disorders and con- ditions. They may ask questions about your medical history, take a family medical history, and perform a detailed physical examination. They may also request one or more tests to provide information or confirm a diagnosis. Geneticists might refer you to other specialists such as genetic counselors who provide information and support to patients and families affected by or at risk for genetic conditions.

- *Gastroenterologists:* These medical doctors treat health problems associated with digestion such as chronic or recurrent constipation and diarrhea, abnormal stool patterns, and abdominal pain.

- *Psychologists and psychiatrists:* These health care professionals work with patients to address challenging behaviors that result from mental health conditions such as anxiety, obsessive-compulsive disorder, and depression. While a psychologist has a graduate-level degree in psychology, a psychiatrist is trained in medical school. Psychiatrists focus more on medications, while psychologists generally are involved in specialized testing and behavioral therapies.

- *Registered dietitians or nutritionists:* Many children with ASD are finicky eaters who may be at risk for nutritional deficiencies. A registered dietitian or nutritionist can help ensure your child gets the nutrients he needs.

- *Social worker or nursing care coordinator:* These health team members work with families to identify and acquire needed resources and supports in the community.

When working with these other health care specialists, ask that any information about your child be sent to your pediatrician. Remember to ask them for their reports, and keep a detailed record of your visits. Be prepared to go to these appointments with all the information and questions you normally take to your pediatrician, such as names and dosages of drugs that your child takes.

Final Word

While you play the most critical role, your pediatrician is a key player in caring for your child. Together, you should share one goal: to make sure your child receives the best medical care, therapies, and support available in your community. The key to meeting that goal is a solid relationship with your pediatrician, one that is built on mutual trust, respect, and understanding. In the next chapter, we go beyond your pediatrician and the rest of your medical team and look at the resources you may find in your community that will support you and your child.

🐿 🐿 🐿 🐿 🐿

Autism Champion: Jason Cherry

"On July 12th, 2016, I found myself surrounded by family grieving, confused, and scared—I had just been given the diagnosis of Hodgkin lymphoma stage 2 cancer. At only 19 years old, I was scared but also humbled by the presence of mortality. I thought to myself, 'I got this' and 'I can beat this.' How could a 19-year-old so confidently be able to swallow tragic news of learning his chest was filled with cancer? I realized that after the years of trials with my brother, Matthew Cherry, this was bound to be one of the easier journeys I would have to face.

"I am now 21 years old, a former professional race car driver, current business owner, founder of Siblings of Autism 501(c)(3), cancer survivor (like I said, I got this!), and younger brother to Matthew. My brother, Matt, was adopted from Russia at 3 years old, 2 years before I was born. He was quickly diagnosed with a multitude of complexities—fetal alcohol syndrome, attention-deficit/hyperactivity disorder, and the most predominant diagnosis of autism. This would change my world forever.

"Matthew, my younger sister (Samantha), and I were raised in a small 1,500–sq ft house with 9 beagles, 1 poodle, and 3 cats—as well as both of my parents. It was a typical day to witness my brother body-slam himself, punch his face till it bled, or run away from home. Samantha and I were in constant fear. Fear that Matthew would hurt himself too bad one time, fear that he would not come back, and fear to even bring our friends from school over to our house. It was difficult to accept his behavior in my younger years.

"As Matthew grew older and found his way into a state-funded, residential program (thanks to my mom!), I witnessed a change. A beautiful change—because for the first time in my whole childhood, I no longer feared Matthew or was embarrassed by his actions in public and was actually proud to call him my brother. The residential program was a blessing to our whole family. Matthew was around peers, receiving the proper support he needed, and was finally on the right dosages of medication—he was no longer the Matthew I had so much anger toward as a child.

"Now that I am older, I can look back and see the blessings in disguise. Matthew molded me—taught me about compassion, perseverance, and forgiveness. He made me fearless as I drove 150 miles per hour at racetracks all over North America. He prepared me to face 5 rounds of chemotherapy followed by weeks of radiation. He is the reason I founded Siblings of Autism and strive to help other siblings all around the world. He changed my life forever and I am eternally grateful for this lifetime of a lesson called *autism*."

Siblings of Autism is dedicated to supporting the siblings of individuals on the autism spectrum through scholarships, respite funds, and outreach programs. For more information, go to https://siblingsofautism.org.

CHAPTER 9

Services in Your Community

IF YOU LIVED in Chicago and had a child with autism spectrum disorder (ASD), you'd no doubt welcome a Web site such as the Rush University Medical Center Autism Resource Directory (www.rush.edu/services-treatments/psychiatry/autism-resource). The site hosts a comprehensive list of services for children with ASD, a list that includes everything from pediatric dental practices and therapy services, to parent support groups, to a Lego club geared just toward children with ASD. The site is a wealth of information for parents looking for ways to support their children, learn about ASD, and connect with other people, including other parents.

But not every city has a medical center such as this, and not every medical center has such a detailed Web site. In fact, if you live in a rural community like Ellen does, you're not apt to find much. Ellen lives in a rural town in Utah, where there are few organizations dealing with issues surrounding autism. Fortunately, a local support group for parents of children with ASD held a parents' night at her daughter's school, where she connected with the founder of the group. When that group was dissolved, she found a support group through a statewide organization that had local chapters. She also found resources through a program run by her state health department for children with special health care needs. It was simply a matter of looking, probing, and reaching out for Ellen to tap into the resources she needed to help her raise her son, who has autism.

Support for families with children who have ASD comes in many forms. It may be educational, emotional, or financial. It may be practical or spiritual. In this chapter, we highlight the kinds of services a community might offer to children with ASD and their parents and families. We also introduce you to some of the organizations involved in autism research and advocacy. Of course, it's impossible to cover every single type of service in every single community. But we hope this chapter will give you an idea of what's potentially available to you and ways for you to find these services. And if you're inspired, you may just want to launch something of your own to help other families in your own community.

The Many Forms of Support

Whether you're looking to meet other parents who have a child with ASD or you need information about the best therapies in your community, it helps to know about local organizations that assist children and families who are living with autism. The increase in the number of children with ASD has given rise to a number of organizations as well as many state and local groups. For many people, these organizations become vital sources of information and support. Here are just a few.

Autism Science Foundation

The Autism Science Foundation (www.autismsciencefoundation. org) aims to support autism research by providing funding and other assistance to scientists and organizations conducting, facilitating, publicizing, and disseminating autism research. The foundation adheres to rigorous scientific standards and values because it believes that outstanding research is the greatest gift it can offer families.

The Autism Science Foundation also provides information about autism to the public and works to increase awareness of ASD and the needs of individuals and families affected by ASD. Through educational programs, the foundation also brings together parents and scientists. These opportunities help individuals with autism, their parents and siblings, and students and scientists share their knowledge and expertise. Scientists benefit from hearing about the day-to-day experiences of families, and families hear directly about the latest in autism research.

Autism Society of America

The Autism Society of America (www.autism-society.org) is based in Bethesda, MD, and has chapters throughout the country. The group hosts a national conference, raises money for research, and strives to bring awareness to the issues surrounding autism. It also publishes a quarterly magazine and provides information about ongoing research.

Among its ventures is a partnership with AMC Theatres to provide sensory-friendly films every month for people with ASD and other disabilities. During a sensory-friendly film, the movie auditoriums will be better lit and the sound will be turned down. Families will be allowed to bring their own gluten-free/casein-free snacks, and the presentation will have no previews or advertisements. Audience members will be free to get up and dance, walk, shout, or sing.

Autism Speaks

Autism Speaks (www.autismspeaks.org) raises money to fund research into the causes, prevention, and treatments of autism. The organization also strives to increase public awareness of autism and its effects on individuals, families, and society. Autism Speaks publishes documents and toolkits about various aspects of autism. The toolkits address a wide range of topics, are written by ASD experts, and can help you find services as soon as your child is diagnosed (*100 Day Kit*) all the way through adulthood (*Transition Tool Kit*). Autism Speaks also offers an online community in which groups can chat about their concerns, ask questions, and share knowledge. An online resource library provides information about everything from safety products and assistive technology to books, magazines, and newsletters about autism.

Center for Parent Information and Resources

Perhaps you're looking for information about early intervention (EI) services, or maybe you need resources to help your teenager transition into adulthood. The Center for Parent Information and Resources (CPIR) is a good place to start. The CPIR offers information on disabilities and programs and services for infants, children, and youths with disabilities. It also has information on the Individuals with Disabilities Education Act and the No Child Left Behind Act that affects your child's education.

The CPIR Web site, www.parentcenterhub.org, can connect you to statewide organizations that can direct you to services in your community. The site also offers articles for parents like you on how to find services for your child, articles for teachers on how to discuss concerns about a child who may have a disability, and articles for employers on hiring people who have disabilities. You can find information about research and its importance in teaching children with disabilities.

Colleges and Universities

If you live in a town with colleges and universities that have robust education programs—especially those with a strong emphasis on special education—you may find support and programs on those campuses that benefit people with ASD. Some colleges offer programs for children and families in the community as a way to teach students who are majoring in special education.

You can also find support and information through the Association of University Centers on Disabilities (AUCD). The AUCD is a membership organization that supports and promotes a national network of university-based interdisciplinary programs. Network members are made up of

- University Centers for Excellence in Developmental Disabilities (UCEDD) Education, Research, and Service, funded by the Administration on Intellectual and Developmental Disabilities, work with people who have disabilities, their families, state and local government agencies, and community providers on projects that provide training, technical assistance, service, research, and information sharing.

- Leadership Education in Neurodevelopmental and Related Disabilities (LEND) programs, funded by the Maternal and Child Health Bureau, are training programs usually found in a UCEDD whose participants work with local university hospitals or graduate health care centers. Through LEND, children and their families can work with faculty and graduate students in their training to improve the health of children and adolescents with disabilities.

● Intellectual and Developmental Disabilities Research Centers, most of which are funded by the National Institute of Child Health and Human Development, strive to prevent and treat disabilities through biomedical and behavioral research. They also provide research training for scientists in different stages of their careers.

At least one of these programs exists in every state, and they are all part of universities or medical centers. They serve as a bridge between the university and the community and bring together the resources of both.The UCEDD, for instance, have been involved in many issues important to families with children who have ASD, such as EI, health care, community-based services, education, and transition from school to work. The AUCD also has a Web site with a lot of information and news related to autism and other disabilities. You can find it at www.aucd.org.

The Power of Support Groups

Want to know the name of a good psychologist in your community? The most autism-friendly restaurant in your neighborhood? The best way to work with your school district? Talk to other parents. Most parents agree: one of the most helpful sources of information about ASD—or any health condition for that matter—is other parents. You might meet these parents at school, at your doctor's office, or even out at a neighborhood playground. But one of the best places is in the context of a support group. A support group brings together people who are facing similar challenges, whether it's parenting a child who has ASD, trying to lose weight, or overcoming an addiction.

A good support group is valuable on so many levels. For starters, it's a wealth of information. Here you'll meet other parents who have walked the same journey that you are now on. Like you, many have looked for medical experts to help their children, and many had the same questions that you do about therapies, medications, and schools. Tapping into a good support group is like finding a library filled with resources and information while also connecting with good friends.

Being surrounded by other people who are raising a child with ASD helps you know what to expect while you move forward. It can be empowering and help you regain some sense of control over what may be a difficult situation.

But a support group does more than provide information. Run properly, it's also a tremendous source of emotional support. Learning that your child has ASD can be tough, and you may experience a lot of challenging emotions as you go about the task of raising your child. Having a good support group gives you a place to unload those feelings of frustration, anger, and grief. It's also a great place to share your victories, happiness, and laughter with people who truly understand. In return, you will hear from other members who can offer you advice and share their own experiences. For many people, a support group can alleviate sadness and stress.

Of course, not all support groups are good ones. Some may not be aligned with your approach to your child's diagnosis and treatment. You should also be careful not to attend support groups in which you are not comfortable. Those that are dominated by talks of a cure or overrun by overly negative members may not be in your best interest. There are also groups that use high-pressure tactics to sell products or services or require high membership fees. And groups that prescribe medical advice or those that are judgmental may not be a good fit either.

If you want to join a support group, ask your pediatrician for names of local organizations. You can also talk with other health care professionals, as well as friends, teachers, and therapists, for ideas. (See also Appendix A.)

Online Support

In the age of the Internet, you can find almost anything on the Web, including support for families who have children with ASD. Online support groups can be a great convenience if you don't have time to attend meetings or if you prefer the anonymity of the Internet. If you do choose to join an online group, know the terms of the Web site and how your personal information may be used. Steer clear of sites that aggressively market products or services. Be careful about giving out too much personal information, and understand that people may not be who they say they are. Here are a few you may want to check out.

Autism Hangout

Autism Hangout is an online discussion forum that features news stories, blogs, videos, and information for parents of children with ASD, as well as children and adults who have ASD and other caregivers. Discussion forums cover everything from medications and therapies to stories about life with autism. The site also invites members to share information about products and services as well as reviews of books related to autism. Community members get to know and learn from one another. The Web site is www.autismhangout.com.

Autism Support Network

According to its Web site, the Autism Support Network was founded with a simple mission: to connect, guide, and unite individuals and families faced with autism. In addition to providing a free online support community, the site provides a wealth of information about everything from diagnosis, therapies, and relationships to local resources in your state and community. It lists upcoming conferences, new research findings, and grant opportunities. The site also allows visitors to post questions to doctors. You can check out the network at www.autismsupportnetwork.com.

A Different Kind of Support: Service Dogs

For children with autism spectrum disorder (ASD) who are sensitive to sights and sounds around them, a service dog can be a soothing presence, that is, a welcome companion and dependable guide. Well-trained dogs can even prevent a child from wandering or running away and help a child master social skills. Many organizations train these dogs to work specifically with children with ASD, including 4 Paws for Ability (https://4pawsforability.org).

Special Playdate

When your child has ASD, giving her opportunities to learn social skills can be difficult. On Special Playdate, a free online service that links parents of children who have special needs, you can arrange playdates with other children who may have similar special needs. You can join the site and search for other parents by visiting www. specialplaydate.com.

Out 'n' About

Got a child who likes the water? If you live in Galveston, TX, you can enroll him in a sailing program called *Heart of Sailing*, designed just for people who have ASD. Does your child love horses? In Elbert, CO, you can sign her up for therapeutic horseback riding at the Pikes Peak Therapeutic Riding Center. Got a young thespian in middle school? If you live in Plainview, NY, you can enroll him in Discover Theater.

The growing number of children with ASD has spawned an industry of community services and businesses that cater exclusively to people with ASD, which is good news for parents raising a child with autism. Whether it's art, Lego building, or martial arts, you can find organizations all over the country that will cater to your child's interests.

The surge in autism awareness has also inspired existing services to make special accommodations for children who have ASD. Libraries, movie theaters, YMCAs, hotels, and theme parks are all offering special days or events for children with ASD. At some theme parks, families whose children have disabilities such as ASD may be eligible for an accommodation that allows them to bypass the long lines that become so distressful for children with ASD. Some restaurants now offer autism-friendly dining at which employees are trained to be more patient and tolerant if children have challenging moments. At zoos that have become autism friendly, you can find special maps and planning guides. Even hair salons are taking steps to make their services more accommodating to children with ASD.

To assist with family travel, some hotel chains now have autism-friendly rooms with special door locks, shorter strings on the blinds, and a set of books in the room to create a homier feel. Corners of dressers and tables are covered to guard against unexpected falls, and doors may be equipped with alarms that warn you when someone tries to leave.

Churches and synagogues around the country are coming up with ways to cater to children with ASD too. Many of them have formed inclusion committees to discuss ways to incorporate the needs of people with ASD into worship services. Some have created special services that are shorter in duration and allow children more freedom of movement and expression. Others have published religious books geared toward children with ASD.

A Parent's Story: Carly

"Our family is part of the Mormon faith. Our bishop is also the principal at the [school for children with special needs that] my son Asher attends. Because he sees a lot of children who have autism, our bishop often has great ideas on how to make life better for these children.

"Recently, he ordered a swing for my son, which we attached to a basketball hoop in the gym at the church. He can swing on it to let out his stress and anxiety whenever he is overwhelmed during services. The bishop also asked 6 different people at church who are strong enough to handle my son to take turns supervising him every sixth Sunday. That way, none of them have him during church all the time. They take a turn every sixth week, and it gives my husband and me the opportunity to do the things at church that we need to do.

"It has been a fabulous program. The support, love, and service that people have given us in the church can never be fully repaid. It's a way to get lots of help without having to worry about the burden of finances. I'm very grateful for this program that my bishop came up [with] for us."

Getting the Services You Need

Obtaining these services has gotten easier over the years but may still require some phone calls and research. Here is how to access the most important ones your child will require.

Accessing Early Intervention

All states have an early intervention (EI) program for infants and toddlers with disabilities. The federally funded program was designed to help children younger than 3 years learn important developmental skills. The program also teaches families the skills they need to best work with their child. Exactly how the program is run varies from state to state.

Anyone can refer a child for EI services including the parent, the child's doctor, or a child care provider. Your child does not need a diagnosis to receive EI services. All you need for a referral is a concern that your child is experiencing a delay, though in some states, a diagnosis can provide your child with more-specialized services.

Once your child is referred, a team of specialists will evaluate your child to determine whether he qualifies. The team will write an Individualized Family Service Plan (IFSP) that specifies the services your child needs. It also outlines goals, start and end dates of services, and steps to help your child and family transition to school services if your child still has developmental needs after he turns 3. A service coordinator will be assigned to your family to help coordinate services. Whenever possible, services will be administered in a place where your child is comfortable, such as his home or in child care.

Payment for EI services varies from state to state too. In some states, services are free of charge. In others, expenses are billed to the family's insurance plan. Some states charge according to the family's household income. Other states will provide services regardless of income. But all states must provide at least some services free of charge. These include screening for young children who have developmental or behavioral concerns, testing to determine the types of services that are needed, coordination of services, and development, review, and evaluation of the IFSP.

You can get information about your state's EI program from your pediatrician, the state health department, or the local school district. You can also find information on the Early Childhood Technical Assistance Center Web site at www.ectacenter.org.

Accessing School-Based Services

Once a child is 3 years old, she is able to receive services in the school with the help of the teaching staff. If a child has ASD and it affects her performance in school, she is likely to qualify for school-based services. Gaining access to these services usually begins when a parent or a member of the school's professional teaching staff refers a child for an evaluation to determine whether there is a disability. Parental consent is needed before an evaluation can be done. If an evaluation reveals that the child has a disability, she may be eligible for special education services.

The degree of services, however, can vary widely. Some children have difficulties learning with regular curricula, even if they don't have a disability. For them, the first step may simply involve the classroom teacher informally trying different teaching approaches. The teacher may also do a response to intervention (RTI). An RTI involves consulting with other teachers, providing the child with more-individual attention, or using other strategies to teach the child. All this can be done without additional testing of the child.

If a child needs more help than the classroom team can provide, a committee on special education may recommend using a Section 504 plan, which is named after the law that describes it. Section 504 guarantees that children with disabilities have equal access to an education, which means your child may receive accommodations and modifications that will support her ability to learn.

Some children, however, require an Individualized Education Program (IEP) tailored to their special needs. Individualized Education Programs are provided by the federal Individuals with Disabilities Education Act, which gives local schools funding for eligible students aged 3 to 21 years. An IEP outlines the educational program designed for your child and is written by the parents, the classroom teacher, a

A Special Note on Wandering

Wandering (also called *elopement*) is the tendency for a child to try to leave the safety of a responsible person's care or a safe area, which can result in potential harm or injury. Whether your child is at school, at the local park, or even at home, keep in mind that nearly half of all children with ASD between the ages of 4 years and 10 years wander. In some cases, wandering continues well into the teen years. Children elope for a variety of reasons. They may want to escape a frustrating situation or sensory disturbances. Some wander off in pursuit of a special interest, such as trains, or to visit a place they enjoy, such as the local park. Others elope for the simple pleasure of running or exploring.

Wandering is a serious safety concern for children with ASD, who often lack the social and communication skills to return to safety. That's why parents and other caregivers must be made aware of the potential for wandering. If necessary, install security measures inside your home such as dead bolts or alarm systems. If your child is wandering to get something or go somewhere, try to teach him other ways to obtain what he wants. Also, let your local police and neighbors know that your child wanders. Vigilant neighbors and first responders can act as your eyes and ears to help reduce the risk of harm.

You can keep your child safe by having him wear a medical ID bracelet or tag that includes his name, his telephone number, and any other important information. It's especially important to provide your child with some form of ID when you're on vacation, in case he wanders. Many local police departments have programs to help ensure the safety of children with ASD, such as tracking devices. Call to see what programs are available to you.

Of course, it's important to arm your child with basic safety skills. Teach your child to recite his name, address, and phone number. Get him into the habit of wearing his ID bracelet or tag whenever he goes out. Enroll him in swim lessons so he knows the basics of water safety. While you certainly want your child to explore and function in the world beyond his home, you also want him to be as safe as possible. For more information on wandering prevention and safety, visit the Autism Wandering Awareness Alerts Response and Education Collaboration at www.awaare.org.

special education teacher, someone from the school system, and others. You can read more about IEPs in Chapter 5 or at www.wrightslaw.com.

All these services are provided by your local school district at no additional cost. To find out more about school-based services, talk to your child's teacher or the special education staff at your child's school.

Finding Adaptive Sports and Recreation Opportunities

All children need physical activity to stay healthy, and children who have ASD are no exception. Regular activity is important for teaching gross motor skills and exposing children to social opportunities. The key is finding the right programs for your child.

Often you can find these programs through your local parks and recreation department. Many communities now provide adaptive sports and recreation programs that are specifically designed for children with ASD and other disabilities. These programs will take into account the unique ways your child learns and structure activities in ways that work best for your child. In fact, adaptive sports centers can be found around the country, offering everything from bowling and golf to skiing and outdoor adventure programs. Adaptive recreation allows children with ASD to become active, navigate social situations, develop motor skills, and most of all have fun.

Some communities have specially designed parks and playgrounds for children with ASD. If you're interested in finding parks designed specifically for children with ASD, call your local parks and recreation department, the state parks department, or the US National Park Service. Although all children and teens 16 years and younger are admitted to national parks for free, the US Geological Survey provides a free lifetime access pass for US citizens with a permanent disability that limits one or more major life activities. (Visit https://store.usgs.gov/access-pass for more information.)

Even major theme parks now provide accommodations for children with ASD and other special needs. Call in advance for information before you visit a park. The bottom line: children with ASD are entitled to the same recreational activities that other children enjoy.

Final Word

These days, most communities offer a wealth of services for children with ASD and their families. Seeking out these services can be richly rewarding for your child and for you and your family as well. The activities not only are more accommodating to your child's special needs and more enjoyable for your child but give you the opportunity to meet other parents who are also raising a child with ASD. We encourage you to look in your community for these kinds of services and to take advantage of the offerings.

ᴥ ᴥ ᴥ ᴥ ᴥ

Autism Champion: Denise D. Resnik

DENISE D. RESNIK suspected that something was wrong with her son Matthew. Soon after his first birthday, he stopped speaking, started carrying around a plastic shovel, and no longer responded to his name. Tests showed his hearing was fine. "My mom gave me the book, *Let Me Hear Your Voice: A Family's Triumph Over Autism,* by Catherine Maurice, about a family's struggles and triumphs with autism," Denise recalls. "After the first few pages, I knew what we were dealing with."

At 20 years of age, Matthew was a human GPS, a math whiz, and a young adult who eagerly helped out with chores such as emptying the dishwasher, folding laundry, and taking out the trash. Now at 27, he still watches toddler movies to soothe himself, sneaks into his parents' bedroom several nights a week, and eats only a handful of different foods.

Like the lives of many other parents whose children have ASD, Denise's life has been largely defined by her son's diagnosis. In 1997, she cofounded the Southwest Autism Research & Resource Center (SARRC) in Phoenix, AZ. What started as a mother's support group and coffee shop gathering evolved into a nationally recognized nonprofit working with thousands of children, adults, and families affected by ASD each year, along with physicians, educators, professionals, and paraprofessionals. With more than 160 employees, the organization provides lifetime support to individuals with ASD and their families, and it also advances research. In 2012, she founded First Place AZ to advance new, innovative housing and community options for adults with autism and other neurodiversities.

"Through the years, we've been growing up with our kids and doing our best to respond to the ever-increasing demand," says Denise, who owns a marketing and communications firm. "For us, it doesn't mean just directing individuals and families to SARRC for services or First Place for housing; it's about being a catalyst and expanding support and options within the community through quality education, training, and evidence-based working models. It's also about advancing discoveries into the causes and most promising interventions for children and adults."

Denise is convinced that with the proper support, adults with ASD are capable of becoming engaged citizens. "Like most parents, my husband and I continue to wrestle with pressing concerns like how Matt will continue to progress and become a productive, contributing member of our community. How can we be assured he'll be safe, secure, and accepted when we're no longer here to watch over him?"

Through the decades, Denise envisioned Matthew living in a home with friends, pursuing his education and skill development, working someplace where he is valued, and continuing his volunteer work. That dream is now being realized through the completion of First Place–Phoenix, set in the heart of the supportive community dubbed by PBS NewsHour as "the most autism friendly city in the world."

"Matt is one of the hardest working young adults I know," says Denise. "With his work ethic, results-driven focus, and kindness, he'll be an excellent employee and a very good neighbor."

CHAPTER 10

Accessing Care

Annabelle lives in Wisconsin where her son with autism has received financial assistance for therapy sessions. Because of his disability, her son had qualified for waivers that helped pay for camps, social skills training, and in-home therapy. Household income wasn't a factor. All it took was some perseverance and research for Annabelle to secure the money.

❧ ❧ ❧ ❧ ❧

Let's face it: raising a child with autism spectrum disorder (ASD) is expensive. Research published in 2014 has shown that the estimated cost of caring for someone with autism is between $1.4 million and $2.4 million over a lifetime. Children who have ASD typically require more visits to the doctor's office, an array of therapy services, multiple medical treatments, and special education services. Behavioral therapies alone can rack up $32,000 or more annually in costs during early childhood. Indirect costs include all the lost time and wages by parents who must take time off from work to care for their child.

For some people, affording the care can be a major struggle and even a hurdle to securing the help their child needs. In this chapter, we look at the various sources of financial assistance available to you, be it government programs, grants from private organizations, or insurance coverage for ASD services. We also look at the laws that govern your access to these services so you know what you are entitled to receive. With a little initiative and persistence, you may be able to access the kind of resources that Annabelle was able to obtain for her son.

Government Programs

Financial assistance is available from federal and state government programs, but each has its own set of rules, regulations, and procedures.

Supplemental Security Income

Supplemental Security Income (SSI) is an important source of financial support for low-income families who have children with special health care needs and disabilities. According to the US Social Security Administration (SSA), 1.2 million children and teens younger than 18 years were receiving SSI in 2018. In most states, being eligible for SSI qualifies your child for the state Medicaid program, which provides access to health care. Supplemental Security Income is administered by the SSA, funded by the federal government, and in some places also receives state support.

To qualify, a child must have a medically determined physical or mental impairment or a combination of impairments that results in marked and severe functional limitations. The disability has to have lasted or be expected to last at least 1 year.

To determine whether your child's disability makes her eligible for SSI, you will need to have your child evaluated. This process is handled by Disability Determination Services (DDS). Every state has its own name for the agency that handles the DDS, but they are all overseen by the SSA. To make a decision, a disability examiner and medical or psychological professional will gather information from parents, physicians, hospitals, psychologists, teachers, schools, social workers, friends, relatives, and anyone else acquainted with the child who may provide information about her impairments and functioning. Medical records from your child's pediatrician are especially important for reaching a decision. The disability examiner and medical or psychological professional must then determine whether the disability is in fact "severe" enough to qualify for SSI services.

Eligibility and the actual amount of financial support you receive depend on family income, whether it's a 1- or 2-parent household, how many siblings there are, and financial assets. A child may be denied SSI if the child herself is engaged in "substantial gainful activity," meaning she's working and earning more than a certain amount of money. The total figure that is allowed is determined annually. Supplemental Security Income can be an important source of support and health benefits for young adults in transition. For more information about SSI, contact the SSA at 800/772-1213 or check out its Web site at www.ssa.gov.

Social Security Disability Insurance

Supplemental Security Income is not to be confused with Social Security Disability Insurance (SSDI), which is given to any unmarried child or teen younger than 18 years (or any young adult between 18 years of age and 19 years of age and still in high school) whose parents are disabled or retired and receiving Social Security retirement or disability benefits. Unlike SSI, the SSDI program is funded through Social Security, using monies collected through the Federal Insurance Contributions Act (FICA). There are no income and asset limits to receive SSDI, but payments are based on the parents' employment history and amount they have paid into Social Security.

Fast Fact

Title V of the Social Security Act created maternal and child health programs throughout the United States. Children who qualify are eligible for health care services as part of the provision for children with special health care needs. These programs are usually managed by state health agencies and come by many names, including Children's Special Health Services and Children's Medical Services. Most of these programs are offered through clinics, private offices, hospital outpatient and inpatient treatment centers, or community agencies.

If your child does not get Social Security Income, you may still be able to get help from one of these programs. Contact your state or local health department, your social services office, or a local hospital and find out how you can contact your local program for children with special health care needs.

In certain circumstances, such as the following, the adult sons and daughters of parents who paid FICA may continue to receive SSDI as adults:

- An adult disabled before age 22 may be eligible for a child's benefits if a parent is deceased but worked long enough under Social Security or is currently receiving retirement or disability benefits.

- An adult son or daughter who received dependent benefits on his or her parents' Social Security earnings before he or she turned 18.

An adult receiving SSDI benefits becomes eligible for Medicare after a 2-year waiting period. To qualify, an adult must have an appropriate medical diagnosis and be able to demonstrate that his disability interferes with his ability to secure gainful employment.

If your young adult is 18 years or older, his disability will be evaluated in the same way it would be for any adult. The decision is made by your state's DDS.

Applying for SSI or SSDI

To apply for the SSI or SSDI program, you need to visit your local Social Security office or call the toll-free number 800/772-1213. If you are applying for SSI payments for your child, you should bring her Social Security number and birth certificate with you. If you are applying for SSDI benefits for your child, bring along your own Social Security number as well as your child's Social Security number and birth certificate.

The SSA will contact your doctors to obtain your child's medical records, but you can help by providing as much information as possible about your child's medical condition. It's not necessary for you to request information from your child's pediatrician and other doctors, but it does help if you can provide as much information as possible about your child's medical condition, records of her doctor and hospital visits, and patient account numbers that will help the SSA obtain her medical records. If you do have copies of any medical reports or information, you can also present those to the SSA.

You may be requested to bring other documents and information too. For instance, if you're applying for SSI for a child or teen younger than 18, you will need tax records and employment papers to show your income and assets as well as those of your child. The SSA may also ask you to describe how your child's ASD affects her ability to function daily, and the SSA may ask you for the names of teachers, family members, and child care providers. You may want to bring along any school records to your interview with the SSA.

Many communities now have special arrangements with medical providers, social service agencies, and schools to help the SSA obtain the evidence it needs to process your claim. But anything you do that helps the SSA get the records it needs will help it process your application more quickly.

Home and Community-Based Service Waivers

Some individuals may qualify for services and supports through the Home and Community-Based Services (HCBS) Waiver program, also known as *Section 1915(c) of the Social Security Act,* which was signed into law in 1981. Home and community-based services are provided by state Medicaid programs and funded through a combination of federal funding and state funding. The waivers allow states to waive certain Medicaid restrictions, such as income, so individuals can obtain medically necessary services in their home and community that might otherwise be provided in an institution, as the Section 1915(c) program requires an individual to meet institutional level-of-care requirements. Services that are covered help support people with disabilities, including ASD, and are designed to help them live more-independent lives. The waivers allow states to cover an array of HCBS, such as respite care, modifications to the home environment, and family training, that may not otherwise be covered under a state's Medicaid plan.

A small number of states even offer autism-specific 1915(c) waivers. The ages of the children who can receive waivers vary by state, as do the types of services that are covered. In Maryland, for instance, the Medicaid waiver provides intensive individual support services, respite care, and other services. But the program, as with most HCBS waivers,

Special Needs Trust

If your child receives a substantial amount of money as a gift or through another person's will, you may wish to create a document called a *special needs trust* (SNT) (also called a *supplemental care trust*). It is a legal tool that ensures that inheritance money is available to your child when he needs it. The SNT provides for the needs of your child without disqualifying him from benefits received from government programs such as Supplemental Security Income (SSI) and Medicaid. If the money is left in a traditional will, the person must use that money first for living expenses and health care until the money is depleted. To be sure that needed government assistance continues, assets must be placed into the trust and set up correctly.

Money placed into the SNT can be used only for items and services not covered by Medicaid, SSI, or other state or federal funds, but funds cannot be given directly to a person with a disability. Instead, they must be given directly to a third party to pay for goods and services to be used by the person with a disability. The trust may be used for expenses such as transportation, materials for a hobby or recreational activities, computers, and vacations. The funds cannot be used for food, shelter, or clothing.

The money in the trust can be invested and earn unlimited money. Assets and earnings belong to the trust, not the child. Parents can establish and fund the trust and act as trustees while they are alive, or the trust can be written so it is established by the parents' will and starts to function after the parents' death. There are numerous advantages to establishing a trust early, even before your teen turns 18. If you wish to create an SNT, make sure to contact an experienced lawyer. Ask your pediatrician for a referral or contact your local bar association. You may also find help from related nonprofit organizations.

An ABLE Account

In 2014, Congress passed the Stephen Beck Jr., Achieving a Better Life Experience (ABLE) Act, which allows families of children with disabilities to save in an account that will not be taxed. The beneficiary of the account (your child) is the account owner,

Special Needs Trust (*continued*)

An ABLE Account (continued)

and contributions can be made by any person (such as family or friends). As with SNTs, funds in an ABLE account do not affect eligibility for SSI, Medicaid, or other public benefits. To be eligible, an individual must have a disability with an age of onset before 26 years. You may need a letter from your child's pediatrician to document your child's functional limitations. The money in an ABLE account is used for "qualified disability expenses" such as education, housing, transportation, employment training and support, assistive technology, personal support services, health care expenses, and other expenses that help improve health, independence, and/or quality of life. The current annual limit on how much can be contributed to an ABLE account is $15,000.

There are differences between ABLE accounts and SNTs. Determining which option is the best for your child and family will depend on individual circumstances. For some families, both of these options may be beneficial. More information on ABLE accounts is available from the ABLE National Resource Center (www.ablenrc.org).

is available only to a fixed number of individuals. In states without an autism waiver, individuals may be able to qualify for services under another program. In some instances, HCBS have created access to highly specialized services for children and adults with ASD.

In general, HCBS waivers fund specific programs and services and do not directly give funding to individuals. But some states have established self-directed programs that allow individuals to use the funds to purchase the services they need themselves and hire and fire the staff they want. Generally, the waiting period for services can be long, sometimes taking several years.

The best thing you can do is to call your local or state Medicaid office as soon as your child is diagnosed as having ASD to begin the process. You should ask your pediatrician for the name of the agency that handles HCBS. Once your child is approved for funding, you will work with a case manager to create an annual service plan that pinpoints the exact supports your child requires. Depending on your state, the waiver may apply to medical equipment, home remodeling for safety concerns, and therapy services. The case manager oversees your plan and makes sure that you are receiving quality services while ensuring that you are complying with the rules as well. From time to time, your case manager may call you and make sure your needs are being met.

The process for submitting a waiver application is different in each state just as the types of services available to you will vary depending on where you live. For more information, contact your state or county offices of the departments of health and human services, mental health, and intellectual disability or the state developmental disabilities organization.

Tax Equity and Financial Responsibility Act of 1982

Some states offer Medicaid coverage to certain children with disabilities through a program called the *Tax Equity and Financial Responsibility Act* (TEFRA) of 1982. This might also be referred to as a *Katie Beckett waiver* in your state, named for a girl whose mother helped spearhead passage of TEFRA. TEFRA provides Medicaid coverage to children who have more severe forms of disabilities but whose parental income would otherwise disqualify them. Funding is intended to benefit children whose disabilities may require care in an institution but whose family has chosen to care for them at home. Some states, such as Pennsylvania and New Hampshire, offer programs like TEFRA. Again, you should contact your state Medicaid agency to determine whether TEFRA is offered.

Government Health Insurance

Most people who have full-time jobs have health insurance. Perhaps your insurance covers your child's many needs for his ASD. But if you don't have private health insurance, you may be able to get help from state and federal government programs. Here are a few programs to look into.

Medicaid

Medicaid is a joint program of the federal and state governments that provides medically necessary services to low-income families and children who meet specific eligibility requirements. The numbers of children who have special needs and receive Medicaid have risen significantly in recent years. For many eligible children, Medicaid is often their sole source of health insurance. In some cases, individual participants may be asked to share in the cost for certain services.

Although Medicaid is a federal program, each state sets its own guidelines and determines who is eligible and which services are covered. In 2014, however, the federal government directed states to cover all medically necessary treatment for autism through their Medicaid programs. This new obligation is part of the Early Periodic Screening, Diagnosis and Treatment program, which mandates basic preventive and therapeutic health services that are deemed appropriate and necessary for children. For children with ASD, this may mean that behavioral interventions, such as applied behavior analysis, may be covered by Medicaid.

To understand what your state offers, visit your state's Medicaid Web site, the Centers for Medicare & Medicaid Services (CMS) Web site at www.cms.gov, or the CMS Medicaid-specific Web site at www.medicaid.gov. You can also get information from other parents and disability organizations; see Appendix A for suggestions.

Children's Health Insurance Program

The Children's Health Insurance Program (CHIP), provides free or low-cost health insurance to children from working families with incomes that are too high to qualify them for Medicaid but too low for them to afford private health insurance. The program covers prescription drugs, vision care, hearing assistance, and mental health services and is available in all 50 states and the District of Columbia. It also covers routine checkups, immunizations, hospital care, dental care, and laboratory and x-ray (also called *radiograph*) services. Children get free preventive care, but low premiums and other services may require you to pick up some of the costs.

Each state creates its own CHIP and determines eligibility, benefits, premiums, and application and renewal procedures. In general, in 2018, a family of 4 with an annual household income of up to $49,200 a year is eligible for coverage.

To find out more about CHIP in your state, contact your state Medicaid agency. You can also get information on the Internet at www.insurekidsnow.gov or by calling 877/KIDS NOW (543-7669).

Private Health Insurance

In previous years, almost all private insurance policies did not cover the behavioral and developmental treatments that are the cornerstones of effective ASD therapy. Through the hard work of parents of children with ASD and autism advocates, coverage of ASD interventions has significantly changed over the past 15 years. As of this writing, 48 states have enacted autism insurance reform laws that require private health insurance companies to cover autism treatments such as applied behavior therapy, occupational therapy, and speech-language therapy. These laws don't cover every type of insurance policy, so you should call your insurance provider to find what specific ASD services are covered under your policy.

If you don't live in one of these states, don't automatically assume that your child's services and therapies are not covered. You may be able to obtain coverage if your insurance company is based in one of the states that has an autism insurance mandate or by showing that the treatments are medically necessary. And if you are receiving services for

---

Private Insurance Update

The Patient Protection and Affordable Care Act contains several provisions within private insurance reform that benefit families of children with disabilities. These include

- Eliminating lifetime and annual caps on benefits
- Guaranteeing coverage through elimination of preexisting condition denials
- Expanding dependent coverage up to age 26 years

another condition besides autism, you may be able to secure coverage by stating that problem as the reason for the services.

> ### A Parent's Story: Nora
>
> "Last summer, my daughter Rory received a grant from the Jewish Social Service Agency to pay for weekly horseback riding lessons. Now I'm waiting to hear about my application to receive money from the Low Intensity Support Services [LISS] program through the Arc, which serves people with developmental disabilities in Maryland. The LISS money would help us pay for a day camp this summer and would cover participation for 2 weeks. I had to fill out applications for both grants, but the effort was well worth it.
>
> "I learned about these funding sources from the parents in Rory's class. They've also helped me find sensory-friendly movie theaters, good places for haircuts, and support groups. The best sources of autism information of any kind, I've found, are other parents."

Assistance From Private Organizations

Numerous organizations around the country offer scholarships, family grants, and other types of funding for people with ASD to help pay for expenses related to autism. Finding these organizations takes some digging, but if you don't mind doing the work, you may be able to find funding. Autism Speaks maintains a current list of family grant opportunities at www.autismspeaks.org/family-grant-opportunities.

When you apply for a scholarship or grant, read everything carefully. Make sure you satisfy all the requirements and send in the information it needs. Check to be sure that you fit the criteria before you even put pen to paper. Pay close attention to deadlines. Keep a copy of whatever you send in. If you don't get funding the first time, you can use that information to apply again in the next cycle.

🐌 🐌 🐌 🐌 🐌

Autism Champion: Lorri Shealy Unumb, Esq

WHEN LORRI SHEALY Unumb's son Ryan was diagnosed as having autism spectrum disorder (ASD), his therapies added up to $75,000 a year out of pocket. But Lorri knew she had no choice. "My husband and I are both lawyers and, compared with most lawyers, we don't make a lot of money, but we made enough to sacrifice one salary to get therapies for Ryan," she recalls. They also moved to a less expensive house and began cutting costs.

Lorri, who also has 2 typically developing sons, was acutely aware that other families weren't so lucky. "I'd go to these support groups with other moms, and they didn't have an extra salary to sacrifice," she says. "It drove a stake through my heart thinking how difficult it must be. It just wasn't fair. They couldn't afford therapy for their child, but they were still paying insurance premiums every month."

The injustice inspired her to pursue changes in insurance coverage for ASD services in South Carolina where she lives. Lorri recruited other parents, began visiting legislators, and wrote a bill in 2005.

The battle wasn't easy. "When you're an autism parent, many days, it's all you can do to get through bath time and bedtime before you collapse," she says. "The last thing you have energy for is to battle insurance companies."

In 2007, the law was passed. Ryan's Law—named for her son and in memory of her father, Ryan Shealy, a former state legislator—requires insurance coverage for ASD services and served as a catalyst for nationwide ASD insurance reform.

"In many ways, autism has been a blessing in my life," Lorri says. "I can't say I'm glad my child has autism. At the outset, all I wanted to do was figure this out and grieve. Now I have a different perspective. I can appreciate the way autism has changed my life and given my life meaning. I'm almost 48, and I see people around my age struggling to find meaning and purpose in this life. That's something I don't have to struggle with. It brings a certain fulfillment, and for that, I'm grateful."

CHAPTER 11

Adolescence and Beyond

WHEN HER SON PAUL was first diagnosed as having autism in 1994, Charlotte didn't know whether Paul would ever ride a bike or talk on the phone. As for herself, she decided to put her journalism career on hold to care for her son and spent hours driving him to various forms of therapy. During his early teens, she homeschooled him for 2 years.

Growing up was scary for Paul, now 20. Unlike most teenagers, Paul didn't want a cell phone. He didn't want to carry a wallet, and he didn't want a job. Girls? They terrified him.

In his late teens, all that began to change. He had his first girlfriend, landed a job of bagging groceries at the local supermarket, and graduated from high school. But his parents were still uncomfortable with the idea of Paul moving into a precollege independent living situation. "We feared he'd spend too much time alone," Charlotte says. "We weren't sure he'd advocate for himself."

Charlotte and several other parents banded together and began discussing all the challenges that confront teens with autism once they turn 18 and become adults. They decided to do research into their options and to share the information. Together, 3 of the families decided to create a transition program. They rented a house, hired a director, and assigned each boy to a bedroom. The goal of the program has been to train the boys to live independently and to master skills such as banking, cooking, cleaning, shopping, and navigating public transportation. They also do social skills training, visit a gym twice a week, and do yoga 5 days a week. Recently, Paul and one of his housemates began taking driver's education in the hopes of getting their drivers' permits.

Charlotte has since decided to formalize the program for other young adults with autism. And Paul is making plans to attend a boarding school for young adults with disabilities and take classes. He hopes to become an artist someday. "It blows my mind to see the distance he has traveled," Charlotte says of her son. "It literally inspires me every day."

~~ ~~ ~~ ~~ ~~

MOVING FROM CHILDHOOD into adolescence is a major step in any child's life. These are the years when your child starts thinking about his future, what he'll do for a job, where he'll live, and how he'll live as an adult. These are also the years of significant physical changes as hormones shift and your child slowly evolves into an adolescent and then an adult. And then there are the changes in social expectations as friendships become more central and the possibility of dating looms.

As any parent of a teenager will tell you, adolescence is a critical turning point. Your teen is approaching young adulthood, and along with it comes a host of physical, mental, and emotional changes. A teen who has autism spectrum disorder (ASD) will experience changes as well, with some, such as Paul, making great strides in their social skills and experiencing a lessening of their symptoms.

In this chapter, we give you an idea of what many adolescents with ASD may experience during these years and what you can do to help promote a smooth transition from childhood through the teen years and into adulthood. We look at the all-important transition plan as your teen begins to look forward to his adult life in the community. We also discuss some of the practical steps you can take to help your child live more independently. In addition, we explore some of the physical, emotional, and social changes that are occurring that may affect your child's well-being.

As we address these issues, keep in mind that transition from childhood to adulthood will be unique for each individual. For example, children with ASD and intellectual disability may have different goals and expectations than those without intellectual disability. This is all the more reason to work in partnership with your pediatrician to make sure these changes are thoughtful and respectful of each adolescent's level of development.

The Transition Plan

Remember the Individualized Education Program (IEP) that laid out all the details of your child's education while he was in elementary school? As you may recall, the IEP was created as part of the Individuals with Disabilities Education Act (IDEA), which gives your child access to special education services. One of the basic goals of IDEA is to prepare students for employment and independent living. To that end, the law requires that all students who receive special education services have a transition plan in place by the time they turn 16 years old. Ideally, the process should begin at age 14. Once your young adult turns 21 (22 in certain states with extended eligibility), he is no longer eligible for special education services offered under IDEA, but he may be eligible to receive services until that time.

In short, the transition plan is the road map that could help prepare your teen to participate as much as possible in community life once school is completed. Individuals with ASD have a range of options once their education is completed. Some may benefit from a highly structured vocational or day program, while others may pursue employment in a sheltered, supported, or competitive setting. Still others may wish to pursue some form of higher education or trade school before joining the workforce. The most important thing is that for many people, adults with ASD included, having a job helps define and give meaning to their lives. The transition plan outlines your teen's specific goals as he prepares for adulthood. It should also address his health care needs, job and career options, community participation interests, and plans for continuing education.

The thought of your adolescent getting a job might seem too far in the future for you to contemplate right now. It might also be difficult to imagine your teen holding down a job. But in reality, adolescence is a good time to start talking to your teen about what he wants to do in the future. You might want to start by discussing different jobs and skills that are of interest to him. You may want to talk about people he knows who are going to college, getting a job, or living on their own. Some adolescents may find the prospect of striking out on their own rather frightening. To make the discussions less anxiety ridden, you may want to set aside a time and day every week to discuss your teen's future. Knowing that it's on his schedule will help him plan what he wants to discuss and ease his anxieties about the discussion.

In drafting the transition plan, you need to take into account your teen's learning capacity and then consider several questions, such as

- What does your teen like to do?
- What are your teen's dreams and goals in life?
- What is your teen able to do? What are his strengths?
- What does your teen need to explore?
- What does your teen need to learn to reach his goals?
- Does your teen have future education goals?
- How do you and your teen feel about him getting a job?
- What are some possible job options for your teen?
- What are the skills and supports needed for a job?
- What kinds of transportation does your teen have available to him?
- Where will your teen live?
- How will your teen get health insurance?
- Are supports necessary to encourage friendships?
- Do people in the community know your teen?
- Does your teen need supports to structure time for recreation?
- Does your teen have a system for communicating that is effective?
- Does your teen require additional strategies to improve his communication?
- What other supports might your teen need?

When creating the transition plan, it's important to consider your teen's existing support systems, financial planning needs, long-term care needs, and access to community, state, and federal resources. You should also take into account the kind of support he has from family members, including siblings. The plan you ultimately create should be outcome oriented and based on your teen's strengths and areas of need. It should set realistic goals and specific strategies for meeting those goals, especially if your teen has challenges that need to be addressed. It should also be laid out on a timeline so the plan has details about when important events are coming and which resources are needed to address goals.

Keep in mind that the transition plan is a work in progress, one that should be revisited several times a year. Over time, your teen will continue to grow and learn, and the transition plan should be adjusted accordingly. But start the process early so you can tap into the educational resources available to you. And make sure to include others, such as your teen's educators and therapists, in the process.

Whatever you do, make sure your teen is involved in the process of creating the transition plan as much as possible. The process can be a way to develop your teen's self-advocacy skills, which will become increasingly important as he ages. Of course, different teens will be able to participate at different levels. Some, because of challenges with cognitive skills and communication, may need more assistance than others. The important thing is that your teen should be encouraged to participate in planning about the future to the fullest extent possible. Ideally, your teen should know about his disability and be able to discuss it with others. (See the "Discussing an Autism Spectrum

Fast Fact: Members of the Transition Team

Many people may be involved in your teen's transition planning, including

- Your teen
- You and other caregivers
- Special education teachers
- Other teachers
- School administrators
- Therapists and other service providers
- Representatives of outside agencies that may support your teen after the transition
- Other individuals who can support your teen

Disorder Diagnosis With Your Child" box on pages 109–111 in Chapter 5.) He should be able to tell others about any special accommodations he needs.

Boosting Your Child's Self-advocacy

Every parent wants his child to be able to speak up on her own behalf, whether it's ordering a meal in a restaurant or standing up for herself when she thinks she's been treated unfairly. Self-advocacy is the ability to take responsibility for your choices and decisions and to express your needs and ask for help. These are all vital skills that a child acquires gradually over time. The ability to advocate for yourself is essential to any child's growth and development.

For most of your child's life, you may have been her primary advocate, which means you've made many decisions for her. You chose the therapies she required, told her when to get out of bed, and sent her to activities that you thought suited her personality and interests. But as your child gets older, the goal is to have her learn to advocate for herself to the extent that she can, which means assessing a situation, realizing that something requires action, and speaking up about what she needs or wants. It means knowing her rights and responsibilities and using the proper resources to reach a decision. For children who have ASD, self-advocacy also means being aware of their disability and being able to communicate it to others verbally or through the use of pictures, written words, or gestures. Although all children with ASD may not be able to fully advocate for themselves, the goal should be to work to achieve the highest level possible.

Like everything else you have taught your child, teaching her about self-advocacy will require patience, time, and the understanding that it's a process, not a quick lesson. Encouraging self-advocacy starts with giving your child choices in life, from the cereal she eats for breakfast to what shirt she wears. As she gets older, you will be able to give her even more choices. When should she clean her room? What time should she go to bed on a Friday night? What activities should she participate in?

Breaking down the process of decision-making into simpler steps can help too. According to the Wisconsin Department of Public Instruction handbook *Opening Doors to Self-determination Skills: Planning for Life After High School*, these steps are

1. What is the decision you need to make?
2. What decisions could you make? (In other words, what are the possibilities from which to choose?)
3. Evaluate each choice. What are plusses and minuses of each choice?
4. Pick the best choice. Describe which choice you think is best for you.
5. Evaluate. Did you make the best choice for you?

Carefully considering decisions in a step-by-step fashion will help your child become more aware of the many choices she faces and better understand her options. Eventually, making decisions will come more easily and be less of a regimented process.

For teens who want to become more active on a community level, participation in self-advocacy groups such as the Autistic Self Advocacy Network (ASAN) may be an option. This group provides community organizing, self-advocacy support, public policy advocacy, and education for "autistic youth and adults." ASAN also works to improve the general public's understanding of autism and related conditions.

When and how do I tell my child he has autism spectrum disorder?

Talking with your child about his diagnosis is a process, not a onetime conversation. The whole concept of "having autism spectrum disorder" is a lot to take in. It's going to take some time, with new questions asked and deeper understanding gained as your child matures. There is no exact age or time that is correct to tell a child. Your child's personality, abilities, and social awareness are all factors to consider in determining when he is ready for information about his diagnosis. For example, a parent may decide to talk about autism spectrum disorder when the child begins asking questions such as "Why am I different?"

(For more information, see the "Discussing an Autism Spectrum Disorder Diagnosis With Your Child" box on pages 109–111 in Chapter 5.)

The organization is "run by and for autistic adults" and appropriately maintains that "autistic people are equal to everyone else, and important and necessary members of society." Groups such as ASAN are part of the neurodiversity movement, which is described as a civil rights movement for people with diverse neurological conditions, including autism, which are the result of "normal variations in the human genome" and not necessarily disorders to be cured; rather, they are to be recognized and respected as any other human variation. For more information, see Chapter 4.

Encouraging Your Child's Daily Living Skills

All your child's life, you've been gently nudging him toward greater independence to the best of his ability. And hopefully, you've been doing that with an eye toward his future and the knowledge and abilities he will need to navigate his way through the world. If you haven't done that, now is the time to really build these skills. As your child reaches adolescence, it becomes more important to think about the skills he'll need to live and work independently, now and in the future. For instance, it may be important to teach him how to ride public transportation and to show him how to use money for purchases.

To encourage your child to absorb these skills for daily living, keep in mind that people learn best when skills are taught in the setting where they are used. It's best to apply these lessons using actual objects and to do it at the time these tasks are most often performed. For instance, if you want to teach your child how to use money, take him to a store and teach him how to pay for something. Don't use only play money at home. If you want to teach your child to wash his face before bed, give that lesson at bedtime, not in the middle of the day. It's also important to recognize that children with ASD often learn best when they are motivated to obtain something or gain access to an activity that they highly desire.

Medical Concerns During Adolescence

The medical conditions commonly seen in children with ASD that are discussed in Chapter 3, such as sleep difficulties and gastrointestinal problems, may continue during the teenage years, but there can be some new challenges. Puberty can be tough, even among children with typical development. In children with ASD, the body changes that occur with puberty can create new challenges. Adolescence is a peak time for teens with ASD to develop seizures, the other time being the preschool years. (For more information on medical issues in a child with ASD, such as sleep difficulties and gastrointestinal problems, see Chapter 3.)

Likewise, a child with ASD who has tics may find his tics worsening upon entering adolescence. If your child has been an extremely finicky eater, he may experience difficulty in keeping up with the growth demands of adolescence. It is important to continue to work with your pediatrician on these and other medical conditions, such as sleep, because treating them will help your child prepare to meet the challenges of adolescence.

Data from recent national studies also indicate that teens with ASD may be more likely to have an unhealthy weight (overweight or obesity). Adolescence may be a vulnerable time for individuals with ASD to gain excess weight because of lower levels of physical activity, preference for higher-calorie processed foods, and the need for medications to manage psychiatric conditions that may increase appetite. Make sure to schedule yearly health supervision visits with your teen's pediatrician so weight and body mass index can be closely monitored. This is important because teens with an unhealthy weight (especially those with ASD) are at higher risk for disorders such as type 2 diabetes, high blood pressure, and high cholesterol level. These conditions place adults at risk for cardiovascular events during adulthood such as heart attack (also called *myocardial infarction*) and stroke.

Adolescence is also the time to start preparing for the transition of your teen's medical care to an adult health care professional. National professional organizations, including the American Academy of Pediatrics (AAP), recommend that families of children with disabilities begin planning and setting long-term goals for the future health care needs of their children at age 12 years. (See the "Private Insurance Update" box on page 212 in Chapter 10 for information on the Patient Protection and Affordable Care Act that addresses health care needs of individuals with disabilities.) A health care transition plan should be developed with health care professionals by the time a teen is 14 years old. Starting early allows for time to teach self-management skills and prepare teens and families for the choices they will need to make.

Privacy and the Adolescent Examination

As your child gets older, you may need to consider privacy during physical examinations. Properly addressing this issue during the examination of an adolescent with autism spectrum disorder (ASD) depends greatly on the teen's developmental level. If his cognitive skills are those of a young child, it may not be appropriate for the parent to leave during the examination. In such a situation, a parent may be a source of reassurance and comfort, the same as the parent would be to a younger child with typical development who is not yet protective of his body's privacy in front of his parent.

For adolescents—and certain preadolescents—with ASD who are already physically modest with family or who are in the process of learning to be more modest, it is customary for the parent to step out of the room for the physical examination.

It is critically important to communicate in advance what the physical examination involves. Effective communication will help ensure that there is no misunderstanding about the reasons for and conduct of the examination.

If the patient is an adolescent or a young adult and the examination requires visualizing or touching sensitive private areas, the American Academy of Pediatrics recommends a chaperone. The chaperone is usually a nurse or medical assistant rather than a friend or family member. However, using a chaperone should be a shared decision between the patient and the physician. The patient's preference should be given the highest priority when deciding whether to use one.

If a medical chaperone is necessary and the patient refuses, the patient and parent should be given alternatives. These could include not performing the complete examination, performing the full examination at another time, performing it without a chaperone, or seeking care elsewhere.

It is important to plan this transition with your teen's pediatrician well in advance to avoid lapses in meeting your teen's health care needs. Many families have found it difficult to find adult providers with experience in treating adults with ASD. Your pediatrician can help you in the process of identifying adult primary care practitioners and specialists who will be part of the adult medical team. Once that happens, a plan can be made to transfer important health information between providers and a date can be set for when the transition takes place. More information on health care transitions is available on the AAP National Center for Medical Home Implementation Web site (www.medicalhomeinfo.org) and the Got Transition/Center for Health Care Transition Improvement Web site (www.gottransition.org).

Safe Travels by Young Adults With Autism

Parents of adults with autism spectrum disorder need to make sure that their adult sons and daughters are safe travelers, whether the adult drives, rides a bike, walks, takes public transportation, or has another way of getting around the community. Even as a passenger, they must be able to self-monitor and refrain from distracting the driver and must be comfortable wearing a seat belt.

Behavioral Concerns During Adolescence

Certain psychiatric disorders such as anxiety, depression, and mood disorders may become more pronounced as your child ages. Some children may be prone to anxiety or depression, especially if they become more aware of being different from their peers. Children with greater behavioral volatility may become more unsafe as their bodies mature and develop. For example, the tantrum of a 3-year-old boy with ASD may be no different than that of a 13-year-old boy, except that when the older boy hits, it may be more injurious to himself or those around him.

If your child is struggling with difficult behaviors that are affecting her daily functioning and ability to learn, it's important to talk with your child's pediatrician. In the setting of sudden behavioral change, especially in children with limited communication skills, it will be important for the pediatrician to check that no medical problems are making your child uncomfortable and contributing to her irritability such as an ear infection, a dental problem, or constipation. The pediatrician will also consider sleep problems or seizures, which may contribute to challenging behaviors, as well as any psychiatric conditions that may be present. It may be helpful to involve your child's entire team when behavioral problems arise. You may talk with your child's pediatrician about coordinating with educators, therapists, psychiatrists, and other specialists to develop a plan to help your family and your child.

Budding Sexuality

While children who have ASD will have the same body changes during puberty that other children have, they may have a harder time understanding those changes. It's important to talk about sexuality with your child, using language that she can understand. This should start well before the teenage years when differences between the sexes are explained, social skills are developed, and the importance of good personal hygiene is stressed. Talking about sexuality with any child might be uncomfortable for any parent, and it may feel especially awkward if your child has ASD. Some parents may even think they can overlook discussions about sexuality if their child has ASD, but every adolescent deserves to be well-informed about topics such as abstinence, contraception, and pregnancy. Talking about sexuality has important safety aspects as well.

Children and youths with disabilities, including ASD, have an increased risk of being sexually abused. Some children with ASD might be more vulnerable to sexual abuse because of dependence on others for care, less-developed social skills and judgment, and difficulty in defending themselves or reporting abuse. These fears lead some parents to shelter their children from social opportunities or knowledge about sex. Yet lack of education means more risk for children with ASD and other disabilities. Studies have shown that when sexual questions are addressed openly within families, the risk of abuse is lowered. Children with ASD can learn to protect the privacy of their own bodies if they are given the knowledge to do so.

So it is clear that frank discussions about sexuality may be even *more* important for children with ASD because they may be less likely to learn it from their friends, movies, and other sources. Much of the information that other children pick up is subtle and indirect as opposed to clear-cut and direct, making it harder for children with ASD to grasp. In reality, it's best that children—all children, in fact—get the information from their parents. Two important aspects to discuss are sexual safety and the social issues surrounding sex.

Sexuality education isn't just about sexual intercourse. It's about your child's body and all its impending changes, the difference between public and private, appropriate touching and boundaries, and how to prevent sexual exploitation. In reality, you began teaching your child about sexuality when you taught her to lock a public bathroom door and to change in the appropriate locker room. Over time, it evolves into discussions about menstruation in girls and nocturnal emissions ("wet dreams") in boys. Eventually, your conversations will turn to talk about sexual intercourse and other sexual activity. Along the way, it's also important to teach your child about touch, specifically about why some forms of touch are appropriate and others are not and what your child can do if she is inappropriately touched.

The best time to broach these subjects is well before your child reaches puberty and should be based on what your child can understand. The same instructional tools and skills you used to teach your child about other topics can be used now to teach your child about sex and

Teens With Autism Out in the World

Adolescence is the time when most teens become increasingly interested in the world beyond their family and home. Peers and friendships may take on greater importance, and your teen may want to explore new activities and become a greater part of the community. Eventually, your teen may be interested in dating, driving, and getting a job. At the same time, some of these interests may be intimidating and frightening. Fortunately, you can help your teen embrace some of these interests at her own pace along with some additional coaching from you.

sexuality. That means you may want to use visual aids, books, and stories. It might also mean breaking down lessons into a sequence of events. Most important of all, make sure you are direct and clear in your instructions. Children with ASD like information that is clear-cut and straightforward, not nuanced and vague. And make sure to always give your child the opportunity to ask questions and to let her know you are open to questions later on. Autism Speaks has published a free adolescence and puberty toolkit for parents (www.autismspeaks.org/toolkit) that addresses a wide range of topics including body changes, self-care, hygiene, and menstrual cycles that can provide some guidance on how to address these topics with your teen. The University of Michigan has a list of additional resources that can help you get started at www.med.umich.edu/yourchild/topics/disabsex.htm. Finally, here is a link to the *Healthy Bodies* toolkit for parents published by the Vanderbilt Kennedy Center: https://vkc.mc.vanderbilt.edu/healthybodies.

Strengthening Social Skills

During the teen years, the growing significance of friendships in your teen's life could lead to much turmoil. For teens who have ASD, the lack of strong social skills may be an obstacle to making and keeping friends. Like with all teenagers, these challenges may become more apparent to your teen at this age, and feelings of being different and lonely may become more acute and more painful. Your teen may also be teased or become the target of bullies.

Helping your child develop better social skills is a lifelong process. It begins with making sure your child understands what friendship is and how friends behave toward each other. For instance, your child should understand that a friend is someone who spends time with you and treats you kindly, not someone who hangs around only when other people are not available, when she needs to borrow money, or when she needs help with homework. It also involves learning how to read body language, subtle social cues, facial expressions, warmth, sarcasm, and hostility in another person's speech.

Fortunately, social skills seem to be something that you can teach your child. Researchers at the University of California, Los Angeles (UCLA), developed the Program for the Education and Enrichment of Relationship Skills for motivated children and teens in the 7th through 12th grades who are interested in learning ways to help them make and keep friends. It is a 14-week program that uses evidence-based interventions to help teens learn important social skills and practice these skills in sessions during real play activities such as sports and board games. Parents are taught how to help their teens make and keep friends by providing feedback to their teens through social coaching during weekly socialization homework assignments.

Topics in the program include how to use appropriate conversational skills, finding common interests by swapping information, using humor appropriately, and entering and exiting conversations. The program also looks at how to handle disagreements, gossip, rejection, teasing, and bullying. In addition, it looks at ways to be a good host, make phone calls, and choose the right friends. A 2009 study looking at the program found that it helped boost the social skills of children with high-functioning autism, which suggests that social skills can, in fact, be taught.

Of course, not everyone can be in the program at UCLA, but your child's pediatrician may be able to refer you to programs or classes in your area that can help. (For more information on how to access resources in your community, see Chapter 9.) You can also help your child socially by providing opportunities for her to interact with peers her age in groups and activities in which she can share her interests. Encourage potential friendships by allowing your child to host get-togethers. And if your child is interested in technology, consider helping her use appropriate social networking sites to make connections and teach her safe Internet practices. Honor these as friendships, but teach her the right way to use this technology by sitting down with her at the computer. To find Web sites that provide discussion forums in which people with autism can share their experiences, ask questions, and engage in chats, see Appendix A.

Fast Facts: Theory of Mind

Theory of mind is the ability to attribute mental states—beliefs, intentions, and desires—to other people, a skill that most typical children develop and sharpen with age. Children who have autism spectrum disorder may not have well-developed theory of mind skills, making it hard for them to be empathic toward other people's experiences and feelings. It is one reason why they may struggle socially. Parents can help their child develop theory of mind skills by asking what characters in books, movies, and television shows are thinking or feeling, engaging in role-play, and talking about their own thoughts and feelings.

Strengthening Community Connections

Whether we live amidst the tall skyscrapers of a city or the rural countryside of a farming town, we all live in a community, and most people need to be a part of it. Adolescence is a good time to help your teen develop ways of connecting to his community. It's especially important to help your teen tap into his interests and use those interests to find outlets outside the classroom.

To help your teen zero in on the right activities, think about his interests. Does he love animals? Reading? Playing sports? Does he collect certain objects or play certain games? What motivates him? What are his challenges and struggles? What goals do you want to see him reach when he participates in this activity?

Some of these activities may be found in school. Most schools offer all kinds of extracurricular activities, be they sports, music programs, or chess clubs. But many of these activities can also be found in your community. The local YMCA, for instance, may offer inclusive fitness activities. Craft stores may offer classes on sewing, scrapbooking, and other arts and crafts. Churches and synagogues may have youth groups.

There are also community activities specifically for youths with ASD. Best Buddies, an international nonprofit (www.bestbuddies.org), helps link people with ASD to people in the community, such as corporate and civic leaders, college students, and high school students, for one-on-one friendships that can ultimately lead to employment, social opportunities, and leadership roles. Special Olympics offers the opportunity for your child to participate and compete in athletic events (www.specialolympics.org). Let your child's interests be your guide when it comes to choosing community activities.

Entering Adulthood

When your teen becomes a young adult, both of you will face many decisions that will shape how she lives the rest of her life. The key is to talk about these options with your young adult and help her understand what she can do and what she wants to do. Like other young adults, she may be asking some important questions: "Should I go to college?" "What should I study?" "Where will I work?" Helping your young adult answer these questions is an important job for parents. Knowing your options will help.

Education After High School

Not all people with ASD want to stop attending school after they graduate high school. Some want to pursue higher education, be it at a college, a community college, or a vocational school. Many 4-year universities and community colleges are now offering more support services for students with ASD.

There are 3 main kinds of postsecondary education models for young adults with disabilities. In the *mixed/hybrid model*, students are in classes, for credit or audit, with students who do not have disabilities but also take life-skill classes with other students who have disabilities. Students also get work experience on or off campus. In the *substantially separate model*, students participate solely in classes with other students who have disabilities. They may participate in social activities on campus and may acquire some work experience on or off campus. In the *inclusive individual support model*, students get individualized services such as an educational coach, a tutor, or technology in college courses, certificate programs, or degree programs, for audit or credit. Services and employment experiences are driven by the student's career goals.

It is important to work with the office of special services at the school before enrollment and assess whether they are truly set up to meet the needs of a student on the autism spectrum, which would include

Lingering Questions About Teens With Autism

My son has become interested in dating. How can we help him successfully do this?

Some teens with autism spectrum disorder (ASD) will not have an interest in dating, but others, such as your son, do become interested in pursuing a relationship. Unlike other activities your emerging adult will want to pursue, it will be hard for you, as the parent, to control his romantic interests and whether the feelings are reciprocated. What you can do is help your teen learn basic social skills such as what to say when you want to ask someone out, how to behave, and what's appropriate. Like most people, your adolescent may learn the sorrows of heartbreak and the joys of falling in love.

Is it safe for a teenager with ASD to drive?

It depends on your teen. Some teens—both typically developing and with ASD—are not ready to be safe drivers and should wait until they are older before getting a driver's license. Gauge your teen's ability to focus, coordinate his motor skills, regulate his emotions, and understand what other drivers and vehicles are doing. If you're not sure, talk with your teen's pediatrician, therapists, teachers, and others involved in his care for their input. Specialized providers in the field of occupational therapy within your community may offer formal driving evaluations and training.

Where will my teenager live?

Adults with ASD have several housing options. Some may wind up living completely independently, while others may live in supported living, supervised living, or group homes, each with varying degrees of supervision, assistance, and support. In choosing where your teen will live, consider his safety skills, phone skills, and ability to maintain and clean a home. Other important skills include grocery shopping, cooking, budgeting, and doing laundry.

not only educational supports but social, emotional, and residential supports as well. The coaching necessary in a residential setting may be more important than the educational support for some students in order to help with time management, cleanliness, nutrition, exercise, and socialization. A program that provides only some of those supports may reduce the student's overall chance for success. Depending on where you live, you may be able to access programs that prepare students for college life and help facilitate successful transitions to the chosen school.

Preparing the transition plan can help your teen zero in on her interests and goals. It's also important to have regular discussions about her future plans. Don't hesitate to consult experts such as your teen's pediatrician, a school guidance counselor, college admissions professionals, and even parents of those with ASD who have already transitioned to young adulthood.

Job Options

Like most people, young adults with ASD may someday seek employment. Some may first attend community college or college, but others may go directly into the workforce. The desire to be trained in a skill or profession and become gainfully employed is a major transition, one that shapes a lot of your teen's future.

Transition planning in the IEP was designed to get you and your teen to start thinking about possible job directions. One of the best things your teen can do is to explore job options while still in middle and high school. Learning about career opportunities that exist, participating in school-to-work activities such as internships, and identifying specific areas of interest will help your teen prepare for a job and get the training she might need if she is in need of further skill development. Your county or school district may provide vocational rehabilitation (VR) or planning services. (See the Vocational Rehabilitation section on the next page.) Your teen may even be able to get some work experiences right in school by helping with light office duties, staffing the school store, or assisting in the cafeteria. Your school may even have formalized programs that support these types of job experiences, which you should explore. Outside school, your teen may be able to secure a paid or unpaid internship.

Individuals on the autism spectrum can be desirable employees because of strengths that are common in those with ASD such as attention to detail, perseverance on repetitive and monotonous tasks, ability to adhere to highly structured tasks that involve a lot of rules, and enthusiasm for tasks in their area of special interest. Several major corporations have set up special departments to accommodate workers with ASD since they can be valuable members of the workforce.

People with ASD and other disabilities may have different work environments that vary in several ways. The job setting your teen chooses will depend on the extent of her abilities and interests. Some adults with ASD, for instance, may work in competitive employment, with market wages, typical job responsibilities, and no long-term support. Some may benefit from working in supported employment, which offers competitive employment but with support services on the job. Another option is secured or segregated employment, in which individuals with disabilities work separately from workers without disabilities and do tasks such as sorting, assembling, and collating. Sheltered employment is similar in that workers are segregated, but this type of work provides training and services that help workers develop life skills.

Vocational Rehabilitation

In addition to protecting people with disabilities from discrimination, the federal Rehabilitation Act offers vocational rehabilitation (VR), a program that funds training and education so a person with disabilities may secure a job. Vocational rehabilitation programs are managed by individual states and funded largely by the federal government.

To be eligible, you must have a physical or mental impairment that may limit your ability to secure a job and show that you require VR services to become employed. You must also prove that you intend to work.

To participate in a VR program, your teen must first submit an application. Once the application is approved, your teen will complete an Individualized Plan for Employment (IPE). The IPE outlines goals and the services offered to meet those goals. Vocational rehabilitation offers a range of services including career counseling, skills assessments, job training, and assistive technology. Services end, or are *closed out*, after you have been at your job for at least 90 days. The services may also be discontinued if it seems the goal of securing a job cannot be met or if the individual chooses to drop out of the program.

In recent years, growing numbers of people with ASD have been accessing VR services, according to a report by the Institute for Community Inclusion. In fact, the number of young adults with ASD who closed out of VR more than tripled between 2003 and 2008. The study showed that young adults with ASD (without intellectual disabilities) were more likely than those with intellectual or other disabilities to receive assessment, job placement, and on-the-job support. Those who received these services were also more likely to get a job.

Adult Day Program Services

Youth who are unable to transition into a full-time job for whatever reason may benefit from participating in an adult day program. These programs vary in what they offer, but generally serve as a place outside the home for individuals to remain active in the community and have contact with peers under appropriate supervision. They allow time for caregivers to work outside the home or tend to other personal or family needs. The services may include recreational activities, exercise, life skills training, vocational training, volunteer opportunities, and health services.

Down the Road

Perhaps the most critical—and often most frightening—question that parents face is "Who will take care of my child someday when I am no longer around?" Some adults with ASD will be able to hold down a job, live independently, and even have a family. Others will be able to do so with supports and assistance. Still others, however, will benefit from living in residential facilities that offer more support, such as group homes. Again, it is advisable to include your young adult in the process of making these important decisions as much as possible depending on his or her capacity for participation.

Planning for your child's future often involves meeting with attorneys, financial planners, and others who can help you work out the specific details. If you think your child will require long-term care and living arrangements, you should start making plans before he turns 18 and is legally an adult. If, at age 18 years, your young adult is not able to make responsible decisions, a formal evaluation should be done to determine whether he needs a legal guardian. Guardianship is not an easy issue, especially if your adult son or daughter has difficulty with problem-solving skills in some areas but can make some decisions on his or her own in others. Guardianship means that other people will help your young adult make decisions about his health and other aspects of his life. So it should be pursued only when you are sure that your young adult is unable to make well–thought-out decisions for himself about health care choices as well as choices related to daily life and finances. Alternative options include supported decision-making and power of attorney. You may want to talk with your young adult's pediatrician, service coordinator, school team, and immediate family members about this decision. An attorney may also be helpful. For more information, search for guardianship at the Got Transition/Center for Health Care Transition Improvement Web site (www.gottransition.org).

It's also important to make sure your adult son or daughter receives adequate health care coverage and is financially secure. Establishing a special needs trust or an Achieving a Better Life Experience, or ABLE, account can help do this (see the "Special Needs Trust" box on page 208 in Chapter 10).

Accessing appropriate resources in your community is necessary to help pave the way for a smooth transition from childhood through the teen years and into adulthood. By working with your transition team to create a plan well ahead of any major changes, you will help ensure that your teen has the skills and supports he will need to feel successful and fulfilled during his adult life.

🐾 🐾 🐾 🐾 🐾

Autism Champion: Tim Page

TIM PAGE HAD always been passionate about music, even at the tender age of 24 months when a song could ease an unruly tantrum. As a child, he played piano and composed music. He went on to become a Pulitzer Prize–winning music critic for *The Washington Post*. But his childhood was fraught with challenges. "I flunked almost everything," Tim recalls. "I was still peeing my pants when I was 12. I was unable to concentrate in class. I couldn't understand why teachers would want me to do this or do that. I was incredibly awkward and couldn't play any sports."

Tim grew up in the 1950s and early 1960s, when autism was less recognized and poorly understood. He hated being made to learn things that didn't interest him and always preferred it when people explained why they did what they did. His father insisted he make eye contact. But it was difficult for him to give or receive hugs and touches from anybody outside his family, a need that had it been addressed, he says, would have made a big difference in almost every aspect of his life.

Reading *Emily Post's Etiquette* helped him understand social nuances and why people behaved the way they did. When he was finally diagnosed as having autism spectrum disorder (ASD) at 45, everything made sense. His experience became his memoir, *Parallel Play*.

Today, the 64-year-old divorced father of 3 sons—one of whom has ASD—is the Professor of Music and Journalism at the University of Southern California. He talks openly about his experience with ASD and says children with ASD are better off when they're left to pursue their own interests, which for Page was music, old records, and silent films.

As an adult, he says he has mastered the art of "playing Tim Page" and can speak to large audiences with ease. But he still struggles with social situations in which he doesn't know anyone, he rarely attends social outings with his colleagues, and he generally prefers his own company to that of others. He continues to dread any form of overstimulation, be it loud noises, busy conversations, colors, or lights, and struggles with eye contact when discussing anything he feels deeply about or listening to music with others.

"What I've done is find ways I can be at my best and not at my worst," Tim says. "I know what I can do easily, and if I have to do something that is more difficult, I find a way of talking myself into it. These days, I usually come through."

CHAPTER 12

Putting It All Together: Everyday Strategies for Helping Your Child

IMAGINE IF YOU COULD anticipate your child's every move, every day. You'd know exactly what would upset him in any situation. You'd know his every mood and anticipate all his needs. You'd know exactly what to expect at any social gathering, public event, and outing. And you'd have a strategy on hand for dealing with every problem that arises.

Of course, as you know, real life doesn't work that way, especially when children are involved. Like anyone, your child with autism spectrum disorder (ASD) is full of surprises, good and bad, and you never know just what will happen on any given day. It's important that you accept that fact right from the start, which will make unexpected and unwanted behaviors less daunting.

Then you need to come up with a collection of strategies for coping with different situations. Keep in mind that even if you do find something that works, you have to realize that what works for your child in one situation may not continue to be effective at another point in time. It's important that you are prepared with plan B—and while you're at it, thinking about plans C, D, and E. Remember that problem-solving requires being creative, flexible, and patient.

Dealing successfully with whatever the challenge might be involves being prepared for the unexpected. It's also about knowing that there are multiple ways to tackle any problem. There is usually no single universally correct solution for most challenges faced by parents of children with ASD.

In this chapter, we provide some practical strategies for parents on how to help their child with ASD navigate the world. We can't possibly identify every situation or provide solutions for each one. But we hope these personal stories will help you come up with your own strategies and ideas. The key is to think creatively and find a solution that works for you and your child at any given moment.

Getting Through the Day

All of us have routines and schedules that we must follow, even children. When children have problems with their routines, it can be difficult for you, as the parent, to get through your day. Simple tasks such as getting dressed, eating a snack, or getting into the car can become a monumental challenge, and you wind up feeling stressed and exhausted.

Most parents who have children with ASD have come up with ways to deal with these difficult moments. In this section, we hear from these parents and learn how they have managed.

≥● ≥● ≥● ≥● ≥●

A Penchant for Routine

"LIKE MOST CHILDREN WITH AUTISM, my 4-year old son Quennedy likes predictability. When he came home from school, he used to run and run. He was filled with anxiety.

"So when I saw him at school using a visual schedule, I decided to try this at home. We drew up a schedule with pictures of washing hands, going potty, eating a snack, and reading a book. Then, we'd end every evening with a short movie or video.

"Having this visual schedule has calmed him right down. If he wants to know what's next, all he has to do is look at the schedule. If there are unexpected activities like a dentist visit, I make a new visual icon and show him the picture. So when we took him to his first dental visit, I drew a stick figure and a chair and showed him what was coming.

It didn't work great the first time. But he was much better on his second visit."

—Tracey, Cincinnati, OH

Being on Time

"WHEN TERRY IS LATE, he gets very anxious. It used to cause serious meltdowns. Over the years—he's 14 now—I've learned to make sure we leave super early for anything Terry does and that we build plenty of travel time into our plans when we go to movies, appointments, dinner dates, and other outings.

"We recently went to see a play and had to leave directly from church. My husband and I both knew we'd get there in plenty of time. But Terry was anxious the whole way there. Every red light, every slow car, and my husband's wrong turn all ratcheted up his anxiety. By the time we got there, he was so tense. To make matters worse, we had to deal with very tight crowds, and our seats were in the middle of the row. Everyone was chattering, and the whole event turned into a real struggle for him.

"My second adaptation, I have decided, needs to be getting aisle seats for these kinds of events so he can get up and move without disturbing people and he doesn't feel claustrophobic."

—Delia, Voorheesville, NY

Brushing Teeth

"MY DAUGHTER ANNIE, who is now 9, always hated to brush her teeth. She didn't like the way it felt, didn't have the patience to sit still for me while I did it, and was terrified of going to the dentist. To help with brushing and dental visits, we started counting very slowly—so I have enough time to brush—from 1 to 5 on the bottom teeth and 6 through 10 on the top. When I get to 5, she repeats it, and then I move on to 6.

"Counting gives her predictability, it gives her an end in sight, and she has to participate, or I keep brushing until she makes an attempt to communicate. Counting, in general, soothes her. Singing songs like

ABCs, 'Itsy Bitsy Spider,' and 'Five Little Ducks' has also been helpful for her."

—Amy, Exton, PA

Tying His Shoes

"WHEN MY SON WAS YOUNG—he's now 34—he insisted on tying his own shoes. The laces always wound up loose and large. He didn't like the laces to touch the floor, so he constantly stopped to retie them, often in midstream and where people would run into him.

"This didn't work because he couldn't tie them tight enough. We decided to permanently tie them with a double knot. We made the laces loose enough so he could slide his foot in and out of the shoe easily but tight enough so the shoe wouldn't come off his foot."

—Phyllis, Kansas City, KS

Being Away From Home

"TRAVELING, PARTICULARLY OVERNIGHTS, can be very trying on kids with autism. If there was a sink in the same room, Annie always wanted to play with water. To solve this, we put her in a 5-man tent in the room and called it 'Annie's own tent.' We also put a blow-up air mattress in it. She loves it. She knows it's her own space, and she feels very safe being enclosed in it.

"I also bring a plastic container with her favorite toys in it, so she has her own playbox, and her special blanket or whatever stuffed animal she likes at the time. Then we fasten the zipper and tie a bow around the 2 zippers so she can't get out. We invested in a video monitor that we angled at the tent, so we could hear and watch everything Annie did. This has proven to be a very effective way to make a safe environment for Annie and allow me to sleep."

—Amy, Exton, PA

Driving Different Routes

"My son Sam loves routine, like most children on the spectrum. Whenever we break from routine, he gets very anxious. He used to get anxious if I took a different route to get somewhere. To break him of that, I'd deliberately take a different route and then give him a reward. He came to associate changes in routes with getting a reward."

—Barbara, Ann Arbor, MI

Teaching Him to Get Dressed

"Our son C.J. is 4 and learning how to dress himself. To teach him, we created a visual schedule that outlines the order of what he puts on— underwear, socks, shirt, and pants.

"He starts by looking at the schedule and then walks over and retrieves the first item. Then he looks at the second item and gets that. And so on. Sometimes it takes a long time for him to get dressed, but he is learning how to do it. It just has to be at his own pace."

—Ronny, Cincinnati, OH

Helping Her Identify Herself

"Because Annie is nonverbal, she can't tell someone where she lives if she is lost. So we have a medical bracelet (made of stainless steel) that is permanently on her left wrist. I snuck it on her wrist one night when she was 24 months old and asleep. She just woke up with it and couldn't get it off.

"The bracelet says her full name and identifies her as 'nonverbal, autism.' It also has her address and my cell phone number. We taught her to point at the bracelet when people ask her, 'What's your name?' That way, she can interact with them and knows where the information is should she need to tell someone."

—Amy, Exton, PA

Afraid of Transitions

"FOR THE LONGEST TIME, our son would have a fit every time we went on a walk and turned around to come home. We had no idea what was making him so upset. He even hated it if I had to turn the car around in the driveway and go back the way I came. His tantrums could go on long after we came home. Finally, one day, he said, 'Other way.' That's when we figured it out.

"He wasn't being bratty or a baby. He was really scared. I offered to hold his hand or carry him. He wanted to be held. Now we know to announce that we are turning around before we do. By acknowledging his tantrum and then comforting him, we were able to calm him down and go on. We make several announcements now with every transition from having dinner to getting a bath."

—Ronny, Cincinnati, OH

Tapping Into Technology

"WE BOUGHT AN IPAD, and my daughter Rory took it over. She loves it! It has become a major teaching tool. We have gotten a lot of apps for her and most of them aren't so-called autism apps.

"One that has really helped is called *Shape Builder*, where you can see the outlines of shapes and drag shapes over into a puzzle. I am convinced this is why she is now writing. She had very poor fine motor skills, and they are significantly improved. *ABC Tracer* is another app good for learning to write letters.

"She also loves *Kid Calculator* and has learned a lot about numbers. She can identify numbers up to 100. She uses a drawing app called *Starfall ABCs* to write words. She also likes the flash card apps and has had fun pronouncing all the different kinds of dog breeds, car types, and lots of other categories. They are called *Baby Flash Cards*. There are also *ABA Flash Cards* and applied behavior analysis receptive card apps. Rory has absorbed so much from the different apps, gained motor strength, and figured things out on her own. It's incredible."

—Nora, Gaithersburg, MD

🐿 🐿 🐿 🐿 🐿

You may find some of these ideas helpful and some not as helpful. Whatever you try, don't get frustrated too quickly or give up too soon. Change can be met with resistance, and you and your child are making a change together. So you may need to try something new several times before you get a positive response, or you may need to give a highly desired item or activity to reward the behavior. You may also want to make sure that other people in your home are helping you make this change and that you and your partner are on the same page and both agree to try the change.

Dealing With Your Child's Maladaptive Behaviors

Maladaptive behaviors are behaviors that are inappropriate, disruptive, and not beneficial. In children who have ASD, they may be behaviors that are stereotypic, ritualistic, self-injurious, or aggressive. Sometimes they may be tantrums. In a classroom, your child may run around the room, talk loudly, or disrupt the lesson. It's important to note that although these behaviors can appear "bad" to you, they may be serving an important function for your child.

Children with ASD may engage in maladaptive behaviors when they are anxious, afraid, or confused. Many don't know how to communicate effectively, so they resort to behaviors that are counterproductive and often downright annoying in order to escape a stressful situation or get access to an item or activity they want. The problem is, these behaviors may interfere with your child's ability to learn and may make it difficult to participate in group settings.

Putting an end to maladaptive behaviors isn't easily done, but limiting your child's outbursts can be done, especially if you know the function of your child's behavior. As we have said, many children with ASD become anxious when routines change without warning or when they are in an unfamiliar situation or frustrated with a new task. Parents can help lessen maladaptive behaviors by trying to reduce their child's anxiety whenever possible. Here are some ways to do that.

- *Be clear and precise when you speak to your child about the behavior you expect from her.* Children with ASD may have difficulty reading between the lines and may have a hard time discerning facial expressions. When communicating with your child, say what you mean and mean what you say. Avoid the use of metaphors, idioms, and sarcasm to make your point.

- *Give any direction in simple one-step sentences.* Allow up to 30 seconds (sometimes longer) for your child to take in your verbal direction, process it, formulate a response, and respond. This may feel like a long time, but children with ASD process and respond slower than a typically developing child.

- *Give your child time to do what needs to be done.* It often takes children with ASD longer to complete a task, so patience is critical. If you know your child needs more time, build it into the task. This means adding "get ready" time to your schedule when you are leaving to go somewhere or transitioning from one activity to the next. Some parents find it helpful to set a kitchen or microwave timer to help with time management.

- *Be consistent with your response.* For example, if tantrums occur, it is important that your response be consistent. This way, your child will not be confused about what is appropriate.

- *Use positive reinforcement.* Give your child a reason to behave appropriately, not just a reason to avoid an undesirable behavior. Remember to tell your child what she did right, not just what she did wrong.

- *Develop rapport.* Make sure that you spend some fun time each day with your child doing an activity you both enjoy. This "investment" of time will "fill up the bank," allowing you to "cash in" when you make a request of your child. Think of developing rapport as a necessary step in preventing maladaptive behavior.

- *Stay on a predictable schedule as much as possible.* Children with ASD often become highly anxious when routines change unexpectedly. Let your child know whether something out of the ordinary is happening that day. You can do this verbally or by using visual cards or telling a social story.

- *Remain as calm as you can.* Understandably, it can be hard to remain cool and collected during stressful situations. One suggestion is to use a gentle tone of voice, presenting facts without any emotion and providing information in a logical sequence.

- *Use a visual schedule as much as possible.* Many classrooms use one. This is because children with ASD are generally visual learners, rather than auditory (verbal) learners. Some parents also find it helpful to ask a teacher or therapist to make a visual schedule, especially if they do not have a computer or printer.

Before the Behavior Begins

Of course, it helps if you can anticipate and prevent maladaptive behaviors. That's why it's important to be on the lookout for what Brenda Smith Myles, PhD, calls the "rage cycle." According to Dr Myles, an expert on autism, rage occurs for a reason and typically runs through 3 stages: rumbling, meltdown/rage, and recovery.

Common behaviors during the rumbling stage, which occurs before your child has a complete tantrum or meltdown, include biting of the nails or lips, lowering the voice, tensing muscles, tapping the foot, grimacing, and other indications of discontent. Here are some ways to stop the meltdown in the rumbling stage. Keep in mind, they may be used at home or in the classroom.

- *Use gentle touch.* Assume a child is tapping his foot loudly. By you gently touching his leg or foot, he may stop the behavior.

- *Show interest in your child's interests.* If your child doesn't want to do the task before him, tell him you know he prefers doing something else. By acknowledging his interests, you may deflect inappropriate behavior.

- *Take your child on a walk.* Allow him to break away from the situation, and go on a walk with him instead. While you're walking, let your child say what's on his mind without punishment.

- *Remove your child from the situation completely.* Send him on an errand such as getting something from his bedroom, fetching the mail, or dropping off something at a neighbor's.

- *Send your child to a safe place where he can regain his composure.*

- *Be sensitive to your child's sensory issues.* Whether it's loud noises, noxious smells, or strange textures, many children with ASD have strong preferences or dislikes for certain things that affect their senses. Try to figure out which ones your child likes, and accommodate those. For instance, if he doesn't like hugs, don't insist that he accept one from an adoring relative. If he dislikes loud noises, avoid driving past the fire station. If he's sensitive to smells, skip the perfumed shampoos, soaps, and lotions.

- *Give your child a saying he can use in difficult moments.* You might suggest he repeat the phrase "This will go away" or "Take a deep breath."

- *Look your child in the eye when reaffirming a rule that has been broken.* Avoid engaging in long discussions about who's right and who's wrong. Simply tell him what's expected of him, and move on.

- *Analyze meltdowns.* Consider what was happening in the hours before your child began showing problem behaviors, and try to avoid similar circumstances in the future. Come up with strategies to help yourself stay calm during an episode. Devise ways that you can try to soothe your child next time. Doing an ABCs of behavior (*antecedent, behavior,* and *consequence*) observation form, as discussed in Chapter 5, can help too.

- *Try a little humor.* Whether it's deflecting your child's anxiety or taming the irate glare of an onlooker, a funny comment can sometimes turn the situation into a laughable moment. Make sure your child understands the humor, however, so he doesn't think you're making fun of him. With onlookers, it can help to simply say something like, "I guess he's having a bad day."

For information on the complete rage cycle and other helpful strategies, see Chapter 5, pages 113 through 117.

Using Social Stories

Social stories help improve a child's understanding of certain events while teaching appropriate social skills and behaviors. They often take the form of a storybook that you make about a challenging activity for your child (such as getting a haircut). Sentences may be factual, descriptive, or affirmative, or they may acknowledge a feeling or an opinion by the writer or others. The situation is described in detail and focuses on important social cues, events, and reactions that your child might expect to occur in the situation. They may also include the actions and reactions that might be expected of your child and why. For examples, visit https://carolgraysocialstories.com.

Encouraging Your Child's Social Skills

Most children—and adults too—take their social skills for granted. Early on, they learn how to enter a playgroup and join in with other children. Over time, they learn to read body language and facial expressions and can sense when someone is losing interest in the topic of conversation. They also learn how to safely leave an interaction without offending the other person. For a child who has ASD, such basic social skills can be a challenge and may seem like impossible tasks. Many children with ASD may have difficulty engaging in one-on-one interactions, reading body language, and initiating play. Often they struggle with empathy and have trouble understanding the emotions of others.

For children with ASD, social skills may need to be taught, explicitly and regularly. It's important to know that just because a child doesn't interact with her peers doesn't mean the desire isn't there. She may simply lack the skills that allow for social engagement. Here are some ways that you can help your child develop and hone those skills.

- *Play games that teach social skills, body language, and facial expressions.* Games such as charades may be especially effective. Or you can try watching a television show with the volume turned off. Pause the show and ask your child what the person is feeling and might say.

Then turn the volume back on and play the show. See whether your child is correct.

● *Provide direct instructions on what your child could say or do.* Children with ASD need clear information. While demonstrating specific skills, state out loud what she could do and say in different situations.

● *Mind-reading games can be used to teach children with ASD to understand the perspective of others.* Looking at pictures of various situations, ask your child to describe the thoughts and feelings of the people in the picture.

● *Watch movies and television shows for teaching facial expressions, body language, and good manners.* Encourage your child to pay attention to how emotions are revealed in these expressions. Talk about what the expressions mean, so your child can better understand how others are feeling or thinking.

● *Act out difficult social interactions.* Start by role-playing situations using scripts. As your child's skills improve, let your child improvise what she would say or do.

● *Use social stories to teach your child how to socialize.*

● *Let your child spend time with typically developing peers.*

● *Enlist teachers, teaching assistants, and recess aides in helping to promote your child's social skills.* Ask the teacher to pair up your child with a classroom "buddy" who shares your child's interests. Ask a recess aide to find a child who can interact with your child when your child is on the playground. Suggest that teachers and teaching assistants create group activities that give your child the chance to display her special talents.

● *Teach your child conversational listening skills.* Children with ASD may be listening to someone but not understand why it's important to let that other person know that she's listening. Encourage your child to nod her head or make an acknowledging comment as simple as "Wow!" or "Really?"

● *Look for ways to get your child involved in extracurricular activities.* Whether it's sports, a club, or a group that is focused on a specific hobby or interest, the key is exposing your child to a wide range of opportunities to build friendships and have social interactions. It is important to note, though, that a child with ASD in an extracurricular sport may need some extra support. Team sports may be more demanding and harder to navigate socially. If your child needs this extra support, your local parks and recreation department may offer adaptive recreational activities that your child will enjoy. Some families find that individual sports (for example, swimming, martial arts, running) foster their child's self-esteem and make recreation more accessible. The main thing is, choose something that is fun for your child! For example, my son (Dr Carbone) Ben has a love of sports and has participated in adaptive recreation such as skiing, baseball, basketball, horseback riding, indoor climbing, soccer, swimming, and fitness classes. Through these activities, he has made many friends, has experienced the joy of participating, and all the while is improving his social skills, communication, attention span, and motor skills. In addition, my wife and I have fun watching and meeting other parents. Ask your pediatrician or local ASD support group about adaptive recreation opportunities in your community.

My child has trouble finding solutions to simple problems. What can I do to help?

Try narrating your actions to him, or *living out loud,* as Brenda Smith Myles, PhD, calls it. Living out loud helps your child better understand his environment and what he can do when he's confronted with a problem. For instance, let's say you lock your keys inside the car. You might want to say, "I'm going to stay calm. Now I will call Daddy at work. He's not there. I will call our neighbor Mrs Smith, who has a key. She is home. She will bring me the key." Narrating your actions teaches your child the step-by-step process of solving a problem and reassures him that most problems can be managed without a meltdown.

When Your Child Goes to School

Once your child enters school, his daily routine is no longer entirely in your hands. At this point, it becomes important to communicate your child's unique needs to teachers, administrators, therapists, and support staff at school. Some people may know very little about ASD, while others may be highly skilled and trained to work with children who have ASD. As the parent, you can help teachers better understand what will help them teach your child. Here are some things you can do.

- *Ask about creating a visual schedule.* Children with ASD like predictability, and being able to see what's in store for them can make life at school less stressful. But always remind your child that changes can and will occur, so he is not completely caught off guard by the unexpected fire drill or special event.

- *Teach your child to listen for instructions to other children.* If a teacher tells one student to stop talking, it's a good idea for your child to stay quiet too.

- *Ask the teacher to organize a circle of friends for your child.* Being accepted by peers is important to school-aged children. Ask the teacher if there are students who might make good buddies for your child. These students should be socially astute and open to allowing your child to spend time with them.

- *Share your child's interests with his teachers.* Knowing what your child likes will allow teachers to use that topic when they want to engage your child while delivering a lesson.

- *Ask the teacher to provide your child with a safe space, or cooling-off, area.* A space in the classroom, such as a table or special chair, may be tried first. If that is unsuccessful, a calming area outside the classroom, perhaps an office, should be designated. The idea is to give your child a place to go when he becomes overwhelmed and needs to calm down.

- *Find out whether your child can have some downtime during the day.* Spending a day at school can be stressful for some children. Giving them the opportunity to relax can be reassuring to them and make new activities less stressful.

- *Encourage teachers to be specific and precise when giving instructions.* Children with ASD need clear instructions about what to do and what's expected of them. Simply telling them to clean their desks is often not enough. It's important to tell them exactly what that means. To be clearer, it's better to ask students to put away their notebooks.

- *Praise often.* A compliment stated simply, clearly, and specifically can make a world of difference for a child who has ASD and can give him the confidence he needs to do well. Urge your child's teachers to find moments when your child has done something well and to point those out to him.

- *Break down tasks into smaller components.* Give students a step-by-step description of each mini-task that needs to be done to complete an assignment.

- *Make yourself available to the teacher.* Don't just outline a list of demands. Offer to assist the teacher with understanding your child, and provide strategies for dealing with problems. Be patient and realize that teachers will have different levels of experience and comfort in working with a child with ASD.

- *Reinforce school activities at home.* At home, try using some of the teacher's tools, such as a Picture Exchange Communication System book, a visual schedule, or math manipulatives such as pattern blocks or interlocking cubes. This can help your child be less anxious in class and generalize the skills he is learning at school.

Taking Care of You

You might wonder why a chapter on helping your child has a section about helping you, the child's primary caregiver. It's the classic "oxygen mask" scenario. When you're on an airplane, you're always told to put the oxygen mask on yourself first, before you put it on your child. Only by helping yourself are you better able to take care of your child—any child, for that matter.

- *Keep a list of friends and professional resources you can call to discuss problems.* Enlist their help for practical assistance if you need it.

- *Exercise regularly.* Regular activity releases stress, helps you sleep, and improves your mood. Make time to hit the gym, take a walk, or do some gentle stretching. Do it with a friend and you'll build in some social time too.

- *Consider joining a support group.* Spending time with others who are on the same journey as you are can lessen your stress, give you new coping strategies, and provide you with much-needed information.

- *Find ways to reduce stress.* Whether it's a monthly massage or a weekly lunch with a friend, look for ways to lower your stress. Raising a child who has ASD can be extremely stressful. A recent study of parents of children with ASD who participated in a Mindfulness-Based Stress Reduction program showed that the parents experienced less stress, anxiety, and depression and better sleep and life satisfaction. Taking time for self-care can help you be a better parent and will have beneficial effects on relationships with your child and other family members.

- *Try to get your own sleep.* Easier said than done, perhaps, but a good night's rest can give you the stamina it takes to raise all children. Make sleep a priority in your schedule.

- *Respite care.* Parents of children with ASD occasionally need a short break from the pressures they experience. Respite care, that is, having another trusted person temporarily care for your child, gives your family a chance to rest, refresh, relax, refocus, regroup, and recharge. Researchers have found that receiving respite care is linked with lower parental stress, better marital quality, and fewer child maladaptive behaviors. Perhaps you can rely on a family member for this support or you can ask your pediatrician about opportunities to obtain respite care services through a state or local agency. You can find out more about respite services by visiting the ARCH National Respite Network and Resource Center at https://archrespite.org.

🐌 🐌 🐌 🐌 🐌

Autism Champion: Cathy Purple Cherry

"MY OLDEST SON, MATTHEW CHERRY, 26 years old, was born Igor Sklyarov in Russia on October 23, 1991. We adopted him at the age of 3. He was diagnosed with autism and other special needs. After adopting Matthew, my husband and I had 2 more children, Jason, 21, and Samantha, 18. For the past 20 years, we've been on a pretty intense journey, one I like to call 'raising autism.'

"When we adopted Matthew from Russia, we did not expect to bring home a child with intense complexities. Initially, we did not understand why our son's behaviors were so extreme. Being new parents, we had no basis of comparison to what were age-appropriate activities and responses. Over the next 5 years, our son was tagged with multiple diagnoses including attention-deficit/hyperactivity disorder, obsessive-compulsive disorder, bipolar disorder, reactive attachment disorder, anxiety disorder, fetal alcohol syndrome, and finally autism. During these 5 years, I learned that one of us (between my husband and me) had to become the voice for our son's services. The other took the role of support. Being the more vocal and a staunch advocate, I took the lead. The success to our journey, ultimately, was that my husband was completely supportive in my being the lead. Prior to any meetings, I would read anything I could to prepare myself for the discussions. We created a single voice and presented a united front.

"Having learned successful advocacy through our autism journey, I have the top 3 lessons.

"**Lesson 1:** No one knows your child like you. Never forget it. During the journey of advocacy, many will comment on the successes with your child. Those successes only represent a fraction of a day of involvement. Not until someone steps into your shoes and lives a year in your home could he or she truly begin to understand what raising autism fully entails. Don't let anyone have a more important voice than you. You control all outcomes. And if you don't hear what you expect, ask and ask again.

"**Lesson 2:** Expose everything. You only harm your child's opportunity for appropriate supports when you don't disclose all activities and behaviors to the entire team involved with your family. You must be willing to expose the good, the bad, and the ugly. This is a difficult lesson. Most of us are private about our home life.

"**Lesson 3:** Don't start at the bottom. Begin at the top. You will discover that individuals supporting your children may want the best for them, but they can't make massive change happen—especially when the services are funded through state agencies. If you need critical change for your child, go to the top. That can be the head of service providers, the head of the school system agency, the county executive, the state governor, or even the White House. Don't limit your reach or voice.

"Autism is a family affair. As parents, we do not raise a child on the autism spectrum; we raise a family impacted by the joys and challenges of autism. Raising autism has the potential to be transformative through the evolution, development, growth, and ultimate empowerment of the entire family unit. Through raising a child with autism, we develop exceptional endurance, patience, compassion, perseverance, flexibility, and passion.

"Today, I serve on the national board for the Autism Society of America and I am a Certified Autism Specialist. I have published several journal articles on the topic of special needs design and have presented at conferences throughout the nation. But first and foremost, I am a mother.

"I have written a book that I hope one day to publish. The book is not meant to be scientific or exhaustive. It doesn't discuss therapies, treatments, or a cure (in any traditional sense). Through several true-to-life vignettes, it offers insight into my family's journey through raising a child with autism. It shares the challenges, the love, the horrors, and the humor. It is real. It is honest. It is life with autism."

CHAPTER 13

Autism Spectrum Disorder and Your Family

ASHER'S MOTHER, CARLY, loves her son and celebrates his accomplishments, no matter how small. But accepting his diagnosis of autism and adjusting to the changes that Asher brings to her and her family has been a journey. As you will see, she has made sacrifices and adjustments to accommodate Asher's disability, but the joys that her children bring are worth it. Before Asher, she had what she considered an idyllic life. After Asher, she still has a great life. On some levels, her dreams have changed, but her journey has taught her that new dreams can be just as sweet.

Right from the start, Asher, who is now 7 years old, presented his family with several challenges. He was a "runner" who, without close supervision, could disappear from the house. Because of his sensory needs, he sometimes played rough with his sisters, broke their toys, and jumped on their beds. Perhaps the biggest obstacle was his difficulty in communicating his wants and needs. As any mother would, Carly worked tirelessly to help her son communicate more effectively. She researched strategies to make sure she was using good methods. All the while, she worried—about Asher and his future, about his younger sister who was at higher risk for developing autism spectrum disorder (ASD), and about how all this would affect her family. All the stress began to take its toll, and Carly began showing signs of depression and anxiety. Luckily, through the support of her family and community, she is doing better.

Asher's autism has affected everyone in the family. Carly and her husband do their best to work as a team, but like all parents, she sometimes takes out her frustrations on her spouse. Asher's younger sister has trouble understanding why Asher can leave the dinner table without eating all his food but she can't. Asher's disability sometimes means that going out as a family to a restaurant or traveling for a vacation can present unique challenges and has at times led the family to feel isolated.

Still, Carly has worked hard to include Asher in as much as he can do. She has encouraged her daughters to do the same. "Because he doesn't talk, they forget that he can be talked to," Carly says. Even though there are times when she gets discouraged, she continues to support Asher by making the adjustments he needs to be successful. They've fenced in the yard, installed the proper locks, and adjusted their expectations. "You just learn to celebrate the small things," she says. "With my girls, it might be winning a race. With Asher, it's when he learns to use a fork."

❧ ❧ ❧ ❧ ❧

As this story demonstrates, the diagnosis of ASD can have a tremendous effect on a family. It can cause stress on a marriage and create turmoil for siblings. It can limit activities and social outings. It can burden finances and employment opportunities. For primary caregivers, caring for a child with ASD may even result in mental health issues.

At the same time, families say that having a child with autism can bring unspeakable joy and incredible rewards. Small milestones that may go unnoticed in children with typical development are celebrated at every turn in children who have ASD. And many parents speak of the deep appreciation they feel for their child.

Just as every child with ASD is different, so, too, is every family. While all families go through stressful times, studies have shown that families of children who have ASD often experience higher levels of stress than families who do not. In this chapter, we look at the effect of ASD on loved ones, what families can do to buffer themselves from stressors, and ways that everyone in the family can embrace this new challenge, even gaining strength from the experience.

How Autism Spectrum Disorder Affects Marriages

The effect of ASD on your relationship with your spouse is as varied as marriages themselves. Some couples come together and share the dream of raising a child who attains his full potential. Others become divided in how to raise the child, and one partner may even deny the diagnosis. Still others may struggle but remain committed to keeping their partnership together. Like with any union, whether a marriage affected by ASD survives depends on numerous factors.

For years, people thought that many marriages involving a child with ASD ended in divorce. But a study released in 2010 by researchers at the Kennedy Krieger Institute showed that 64% of children with ASD remain with both parents, a percentage that is no different than for children without ASD.

Another study done at the University of Wisconsin–Madison Waisman Center was less optimistic; that study showed that parents of grown children with autism were more likely to divorce than couples whose children did not have autism. So while the divorce rate between the 2 groups of parents was the same when the child was younger than 8 years, the rate went up after that for parents of children with ASD and down for parents of children without disabilities. According to the study, the prolonged needs of a child with ASD last longer for these couples, causing greater strain on the marriage. The study showed that the rate of divorce was higher for moms who were younger at the time they gave birth to the child with ASD and when the child with ASD was born later in the birth order. Other studies have linked higher rates of divorce in families with a child with other disabilities, such as attention-deficit/hyperactivity disorder.

Despite these findings, experts say that the key to a good marriage involving a child with ASD is the same as it is for other marriages: communicating honestly and openly, spending time together, and providing support to each other. Studies have shown that mothers in particular stress the importance of spousal support, of having a partner who knows the routine, and of splitting the responsibilities. Working together, being flexible, and having someone who is willing to share feelings and concerns is also important.

Family Matters

My husband doesn't provide much help when it comes to caring for our son. How do I get him more involved?

It's not unusual for one parent—often the mother—to become the lead caregiver for a child with autism spectrum disorder (ASD). Men tend to have a more difficult time dealing with situations that do not have a straightforward solution and may instead put their energies into other things. In reality, however, both parents should be sharing in the day-to-day responsibilities. Let your husband know not only how you would value his participation but specific ways he can help. If he is trying, make sure you are thankful even if he is helping in a different way than you would have. You might also suggest he talk with a therapist if he's having trouble accepting the diagnosis. Invite him to your child's appointments so he can learn more about ASD and how he can be more involved. Some fathers may struggle in learning how to connect with children with ASD, so you might try to find an activity just for them that will help them create a stronger bond.

My husband and I want to go out once in a while, but we worry about finding a babysitter who can manage our daughter who has autism. Where can we look for sitters?

Try looking for someone in the ARCH National Respite Network and Resource Center Respite Locator at http://archrespite.org/home. You might find babysitters through a local college or university, especially if it has a special education program. Summer camp counselors who care for children with ASD make great babysitters during the school year. You might also find help through Family Voices (www.familyvoices.org) or the National Center for Family/Professional Partnerships (www.fv-ncfpp.org). If you belong to a church or synagogue, you may find help from fellow members. Local chapters of autism organizations may help you locate a sitter too.

Family Matters (*continued*)

My grandson was just diagnosed as having autism. What does this mean for me as the grandparent?

For most grandparents, having a grandchild with ASD means having another grandchild to love and cherish. But a recent survey showed that having a grandchild with ASD can have a profound effect on grandparents and may shape where they live and how they spend their retirement savings. Some grandparents move to be near their grandchild with autism, while others contribute money to treatments. An amazing 70% even become involved with treatment decisions. Not surprisingly, many worry a great deal about their adult sons and daughters and the stressors they face. Like parents, grandparents may want to learn as much as they can about ASD. Understanding ASD can help him or her become a more effective and compassionate grandparent.

Challenges for Siblings

Most siblings of children who have ASD fare well. Many even become quite helpful in the day-to-day functioning of the household. Some become great advocates for their siblings and even go on to choose professions that assist people with disabilities. But others may experience tremendous stress and resentment. Many siblings experience a mix of emotions, feeling loving and supportive one minute, angry and bitter the next. Exactly how the typically developing children in a household respond to having a sibling with ASD depends on the ages of the children and their maturity levels. It also depends on family dynamics.

Different children will have different concerns. Very young children are often worried about strange behaviors that scare or confuse them. Some children may be afraid of being the target of their sibling's anger and aggression. Others may try to compensate for the things that their siblings can't do. Some children are jealous over the attention that their sibling receives from their parents. Others may be frustrated at not being able to engage in a relationship with their sibling.

Teenagers may be concerned about what the future holds for their sibling with ASD. They may worry about the role they'll need to play in caring for their sibling. Other children may wonder how to explain ASD to their friends and may feel embarrassed by their sibling's unusual behaviors and social challenges. Still others may become worried about their parents' stress and grief, or they may feel the need to take on parental caregiving responsibilities for their sibling with ASD. Whatever emotions your typically developing child expresses, respect those feelings, however uncomfortable they may be to you.

Having open and honest discussions about autism at a level and in a way that your children can understand is critical to helping the siblings of a child with ASD. If you do not tell your other children about their sibling's ASD, they may feel increasingly isolated or confused. But don't offer just one conversation or discussion about autism. Keep talking about it with your children as they grow up. When they are younger, they might not understand the term *ASD*, but you can start by talking about the differences that other children may have and about what it means to have a disability. You could even read books with them that have some characters with disabilities. As they start to inquire about their own responsibilities in caring for their sibling with ASD, it is important to reassure them that you have a plan in place should you (the parents) no longer be able to provide that care. Listen carefully to their concerns, which will certainly change over time. For further information on sibling support organizations, see Appendix A.

It's also important to foster a relationship among siblings. Children who have ASD typically have challenges with social skills. Siblings may give up when they can't engage them in interactions. But siblings can be taught simple ways to engage a child with ASD and with time can provide a natural way for children with ASD to work on their social skills.

Promoting Sibling Harmony

Parents can ease the burden on siblings by trying to set aside some time to be alone with each of their children. It may be as little as a few minutes before bedtime or as much as a weekly afternoon outing. And

A Sister's Story: Shay

"Being a sibling of someone with autism has been a great experience for me. My little brother, who was diagnosed with autism when he was 22 months old, is 9 years younger than me. I am the closest sibling to his age. I have taken on a caregiver role of my own accord since he was born. I have always felt a special bond with him despite his lack of communication through words. From a young age, he would come to me and guide me to what he wanted. I considered him a best friend, not a chore.

"Having a brother with autism has opened my eyes to the challenges and blessings of the families in the world of special needs people. He has been a source of joy for me as I have watched him make great strides in his communication skills. I cried with my mom when I came back from my first year in college and heard him count to 10 on his own at the age of 9. He has made me laugh with his excellent singing skills, belting out 'Reflection' from *Mulan* with such passion and exuberance. Although it has been hard to watch him struggle to communicate his complicated feelings, and I sometimes feel helpless trying to find him the help he needs, I would never trade the lessons I have learned from him. In his simple way, he has taught me what is important in life over the years by being my brother and friend."

remember the important events in all your children's lives. If your child with ASD can't attend another child's graduation, find someone to be with him so you can still go.

Do the best you can to try and set reasonable expectations of your child with ASD as you do with your other children for chores and personal responsibilities. Doing so will not only help your child with ASD develop the skills he needs to live as independently as possible but also help dispel any notions of unfair treatment by siblings. Of course, being fair does not always mean equal responsibilities for all children. You will need to have ongoing talks with siblings about the challenges that autism brings for their sibling with ASD and how they need to be understanding.

Finally, try to model a healthy perspective. How you view your child's ASD can be a source of strength for other family members. By seeking out information and support, you are showing your other children how to be strong and resilient in the face of a challenging circumstance. Also, by dwelling on the positive aspects of parenting your child with

A Parent's Story: Jennifer

For years, Jennifer was a single mother of 3 boys, all with autism. After a difficult divorce and having little support, she did the best she could to navigate the system of services for children with autism spectrum disorder alone. "I drove them to 17 therapies a week, cut the tags out of all their clothes, and confronted all their issues. I worried all the time. When would my oldest son talk and make friends? Why was my middle son biting himself? When would my youngest finally sleep through the night?

"Everything changed when I met and married my second husband. He has 4 children of his own. All are high achievers, athletically gifted, and socially successful. I wondered how the 7 were going to get along under one roof.

"Turns out, they get along great. Some of the issues are mine. For instance, having my stepchildren around accentuates for me all the challenges that my children still face. My step-kids get to do all kinds of stuff that my kids don't get to do, like going to birthday parties and having endless playdates. My kids see what life is like every day for 'normal' kids. I can't really give that to them because we are still trying to learn stuff like how to talk and how to try a new food once in a while. It really breaks my heart.

"On the other hand, having 4 new older siblings who are super-functional has been outstanding for my kids. They have social peer models and language models now. They have extra help doing stuff that Mommy doesn't have extra time for, like learning to ride a bike and tie their shoes. It's awesome. In the few short months since we have moved in together, my kids have made the most gains ever in all areas of development. My stepchildren are the greatest gift in the world to me and to my sons."

ASD, you model the behavior that you want your other children to show toward those with disabilities.

Dealing With Your Own Stress

Raising a child with ASD creates challenges on many levels. For many parents, there is stress in confronting their early concerns about behavior and development and then trying to find answers as to why their child is developing differently than other children. Some parents may have suspected autism all along but had no idea of the implications until they started doing research. Either way, most parents go through a lot of emotions as they come to terms with their child's diagnosis. In fact, a study at Eastern Michigan University showed that families generally view a diagnosis of autism as a life-altering event that may initially lead to feelings of guilt and sadness, along with worry, for their child's future. These emotions can lead many parents to feel overwhelmed.

After the diagnosis, the day-to-day challenges of autism can be stressful too. Successfully confronting the difficult moments that come with raising a child with a disability can tax even the most patient parents. Many of the challenges that affect children with ASD can also affect caregivers. If your child struggles with sleep, for example, you will likely lose sleep in your effort to help your child.

Staying positive in the face of ASD can be difficult, especially in the beginning when there is so much uncertainty about the future. In the face of this stress, you may find that you see less of your friends, spend less time with your spouse or other children, and do less of the things you enjoy. In some cases, you may even have to reduce your work hours or leave your job. The emotional and financial effects of these changes in your life can compound your stress. Some people have been known to develop mental health issues such as anxiety and depression.

While it may seem easy for outsiders to say and harder for you to do, try to find support from friends, other family members, and other families who are raising a child with ASD. Studies have found that parents who seek support from other parents and community organizations generally have less stress. While all parents are different, many find support, understanding, and friendship when they join a parent support group in the community. Meetings with other families can be a major source of comfort and an excellent opportunity for networking. You can find some of these organizations in Chapter 9 and in Appendix A. Likewise, enrolling your child in a recreational program that is appropriate for those with special needs (also known as *adaptive recreation*) allows you to meet other parents of children with disabilities and to share in the joys of watching your child participate.

Taking a break from your caregiving duties can go a long way toward reducing your stress. If family members aren't available, you may consider looking for respite services. Respite services provide care to your child while you take a break from those duties to attend to other family responsibilities or take some time off. While large cities may have respite services readily available, it may be harder to find respite services in small communities. Some respite services can be funded with help from Home and Community-Based Services Waiver programs (see Chapter 10). If there is any possibility you think you'll need respite services in the future, apply for the waiver as soon as possible. Many of these waivers have waiting periods.

Asking for Help for Stress and Emotions

It's OK to ask for help. For some people, the stress, anxiety, or depression can become overwhelming. If that happens to you, you may want to consider talking with a therapist. With a therapist, you should be able to talk honestly about everything you're feeling and experiencing—the good, the bad, and the ugly. Marriage or family therapy can also help work out challenges. To find a good therapist, talk to other parents or look for mental health organizations in your community for a referral.

A Good Read for Parents of Children With Disabilities

The book *You Will Dream New Dreams* by Stanley D. Klein, PhD, and Kim Schive is a collection of essays written by parents of children with disabilities and conveys 4 key messages.

- You are not alone on this journey.
- The range of difficult feelings you have—and will continue to have—are a normal part of the human experience. We, too, have survived, and our lives have continued. You can go on and grow.
- Although there are no easy answers, you will find ways to cope. You are likely to discover inner resources that you did not know existed.
- There is sadness; some dreams are lost. You will mourn, but you can heal. You will be happy again and you will dream new dreams.

Taking Care of You

Mothers, in particular, are vulnerable to the stress of raising a child with ASD. It often results from social isolation, financial burdens, and difficulties in obtaining services. That's why it's so important to take care of yourself as well as your family. Here are some things you can do to guard against stress.

- *Build exercise into your life.* The time involved in raising a child with ASD can be emotionally intense and all-consuming. One of the best ways to take care of yourself is to exercise. Regular physical activity gives you the energy, both physical and mental, that can help you cope. Exercise is also critical to good health, maintaining a healthy weight, and keeping depression at bay. Of course, squeezing in a lengthy workout isn't always easy. Try to build movement into your day instead by taking short walks and exercising in front of the television.

- *Schedule time for self-care.* Several studies have examined the effects of mindfulness-based interventions, such as the program Mindfulness-Based Stress Reduction (MBSR), on the well-being of caregivers of children with ASD. One such study, published in *Pediatrics* in 2014, showed that mothers of children who participated in MBSR or another positive psychology practice reported less stress, depression, and anxiety and improved sleep and life satisfaction. While taking a few minutes for yourself may at first seem counterintuitive, making this investment in yourself may prove beneficial in many aspects of your life as a parent.

- *Devote time to being with friends.* One of the most important ways to reduce your stress is to spend time with friends. A weekly lunch or quick coffee break can nourish, energize, and revitalize you. It's also helpful to spend time with people in the autism community, especially other parents who can know exactly what you are experiencing.

- *Get educated about autism.* As a parent of a child with ASD, knowing not only the medical facts but also the laws, resources, and services surrounding autism is critical. Having this information gives you a distinct advantage when it comes time to advocate for your child. It also gives you the knowledge and confidence you need to cope with challenging situations. As the saying goes, "Knowledge is power."

- *Become a planner.* Being a parent often means playing a variety of roles. One minute, you're a cook; the next, you're a driver. When you have a child with ASD, your responsibilities multiply considerably. Often you're also a therapist, an advocate, and a researcher. To better manage these roles, it helps to become skilled at planning. Knowing what's coming up in your schedule allows you to better maintain the routine and structure that most children with ASD crave, which will lessen their anxiety—and yours.

- *Be on the lookout for depression.* Look for it in your spouse too. Depression isn't just feeling sad or unhappy. It's a serious mood disorder that alters your ability to function and makes it hard to enjoy everyday activities. Depression is common among people caring for children with ASD. In fact, a study from the June 2010 issue of the *American Journal of Psychiatry* showed that 26% of caregivers of children with autism develop depression. If you're having a hard time and think you have depression, talk with your doctor.

A Parent's Story: Cheryl

"We are finally going to see our older son, who lives in San Diego with his wife and little boy. We decide to take our younger son, who has autism. He might like to swim and go to SeaWorld. The only time he has flown was to go to Disneyland a couple of times, and it went OK.

"I make the mistake of telling him we are going on the airplane a week or so before we are leaving. He says, 'Airplane, airplane,' every 15 minutes for a couple of days, then starts adding, 'Disneyland, airplane,' the rest of the week. I say, 'No, we aren't going to Disneyland this time.' Perhaps he thinks if he says it enough times, it will be true.

"We make the usual accommodations for the airplane ride: a backpack full of DVDs, the player charged up, the iPod and the Disney music, books, candy, and Benadryl. I sit next to my son and my husband sits in front of him so that when he kicks the back of the seat the whole way there, it doesn't annoy a stranger. We put the T-shirt on my son that says, 'I have autism, be nice to my mom,' so that we can hopefully avoid the 'stink eye' and get a small amount of compassion.

"We make it to San Diego without a huge amount of distress, still hearing 'Disneyland' every so often. At SeaWorld, he is so afraid that we really might not be going to Disneyland that he can barely enjoy it. He does like the rides and the whales, but we have to buy him a new shirt when his gets wet because he cannot be wearing a wet shirt. The next day, he throws in a couple 'SeaWorlds' with the 'Disneyland' to break up the monotony.

"The ride home is priceless. Disneyland does not happen, so getting through the airport is distressing. He is ticked. We find the airport waiting area for our flight. He tries to get out the emergency exit door at the airport, setting off the alarm. The police come. The alarm goes off for a long, long time. Talk about sensory overload. We get in line to board, the long, long, very slowly moving line. It's like trying to contain a rabid cat inside 2 painted lines. People are getting as agitated as we are.

A Parent's Story: Cheryl (*continued*)

"'Why do they board first class first?' I wonder as the passengers are getting smacked by this flailing boy, their preflight martinis spilling everywhere. He starts to say, '14, 14, 14,' which was the row we were on when leaving for San Diego. I say, 'No, we are in 13 this time. Look, 13, 13, 13.' We get into row 13, finally, and he climbs over row 13 to get into row 14.

"'Hmmm,' I say, 'Maybe we should trade seats with these people?' He is biting me now and crying. The stewardess says, 'Oh, don't bite!' That was like telling a newborn not to cry or a dog not to shed. I pull out the DVD player, my pinch hitter, and to my dismay, the battery is dead. Now I'm questioning if there really is a God. So just to be sure, my husband and I both start praying, 'Please, please, make him go to sleep...' and then a miracle happens. He falls asleep.

"Next time we are going to Disneyland."

- *Get your sleep.* One of the best buffers against depression, stress, and fatigue is a good night's sleep. Do what you can to get your rest, even if it means taking a brief nap during the day. Try to go to bed and get up at the same time every day. Don't go overboard with caffeine late in the day. And try to relax before you crawl into bed.

- *Learn to accept help.* When a friend offers to help you out, tell her what you need. Maybe it's spending an hour with your child so you can take a walk or driving your other child to a soccer game. Whatever it is, don't be afraid to tap your family or friends for some assistance. And make sure to enlist your spouse's help. Studies have shown that most mothers derive a lot of emotional support and practical help from a spouse who is an equal partner.

- *Look for the joys in raising your child.* In spite of all the challenges, many parents say that raising a child with ASD can be thrilling and exciting, especially when your child strives and reaches his potential. To truly appreciate any progress, however, often requires reframing your situation and changing your perspective. Altering your outlook can go a long way in helping you cope with the challenges of autism. Look for ways to define your experiences more positively. Doing so may give you greater confidence and strength.

Recognizing Depression

Depression is a common mood disorder that strikes 9% of all adults in the United States, most of them women. Depression is usually treated with medications, therapy, or a combination of both. According to the National Institute of Mental Health, the signs and symptoms are

- Persistent sad, anxious, or empty feelings
- Feelings of hopelessness or pessimism
- Feelings of guilt, worthlessness, or helplessness
- Irritability and/or restlessness
- Loss of interest in activities or hobbies that were once pleasurable, including sex
- Fatigue and decreased energy
- Difficulty in concentrating, remembering details, and making decisions
- Insomnia, early-morning wakefulness, or excessive sleeping
- Overeating or appetite loss
- Thoughts of suicide or suicide attempts
- Persistent aches or pains, headaches, cramps, or digestive problems that do not ease even with treatment

Resilience

The standard assumption until the 1980s was that having a child with a disability would result in ongoing family suffering. This premise was challenged as researchers began to focus on family strengths, coping skills, and families' positive views of their children and themselves. Families, it was found, could be highly resilient. They are able to respond with strengths that transform them from merely surviving to actually thriving as they face the challenges of raising a child with special needs.

Research studies have identified the following characteristics in parents who successfully adapt to raising a child with a disability:

- Pleasure in providing care for their child
- Seeing their child as a source of joy
- Accomplishment in having done their best for their child
- Strengthened family relationships because of collective response to their child's condition
- A new sense of purpose in life
- Increased spirituality
- New perspective on what is important in life

According to researchers from the Interactive Autism Network (IAN), "Parents told us they had come through the distress and grief of the initial diagnosis to adjust, celebrate their child and thrive." One parent told IAN, "He has taught us a lot about what's important in life." Another parent commented, "We decided not to let ASD be all our family was about."

Families who have successfully navigated the journey of raising a child with ASD have redefined their circumstances, they celebrate their child's specialness and gains, they embrace a new outlook on life, and they appreciate their daily pursuits in new ways.

The scientific literature on family resiliency training shows benefits from structured programs that combine group sessions with individual sessions. Successful programs have been implemented for families in the military who deal with the stress of separation and for families who have undergone specific traumas. Research is currently being conducted on resiliency training for families of children with ASD. We hope to present outcomes of this research in future editions of this book.

Final Word

Learning your child has ASD can certainly change your perception of what you thought your life might be. You may have to restructure your priorities and develop new coping skills. And you may have to change some of your plans for the future. But in their place will be new dreams, new goals, and new priorities. The key is finding ways to adapt and adjust that suit your family, your needs, and your circumstances. It likely won't be easy. But people often find strength from within and from those around them to succeed. By loving your child dearly, you will be inspired to do what you can to learn as much as possible about ASD so that you, too, will be rewarded as you discover what works for your family.

Autism Champion: Jennifer Wood

JENNIFER WOOD OF PLAINFIELD, IL, can still remember the first time she "went to bat" for her son Tripp, who is now 16 years old. "The public special education preschool program would not furnish my 3-year-old with a car seat on the bus," she says. "I searched online until I found applicable statutes, codes, and case law, and I presented these to the school administration, along with a not-empty threat that I would hire a lawyer to ensure my son's safety."

The school listened. "Not only did he have a proper safety harness, but there was one ready and waiting on the first day of school 2 years later for my middle son and another after that for my third son," she says. "My advocacy for my son in the first case solved the problem for all 3 of my sons."

For Jennifer, who spent years as a single mother raising 3 boys with ASD, the incident marked the beginning of her work as a parent advocate. She began speaking at support group meetings for parents of children with special needs and became a volunteer mediator at Individualized Education Program meetings for other families. She also joined the Run for Autism program of the Organization for Autism Research (OAR) and began raising money by running marathons. She spent a year as the OAR national spokesperson while working as a volunteer mediator. She ended her volunteer work to pursue a law degree with a focus on ASD and the law. Today, she is a successful lawyer advocating for many families by helping them get the services that will help their children make the most progress through the educational system and protecting their rights in the legal system.

For someone well versed in the challenges of raising children with ASD, Jennifer says getting a child into therapy is the key—along with a healthy dose of patience. "Therapy is a marathon, not a sprint," she says. She also recommends that parents talk to each other for support. "This journey is lonely enough," she says. "Do not travel it alone if you don't have to."

CHAPTER 14

The Future of Autism Spectrum Disorder

THESE DAYS, WE KNOW A LOT MORE about autism spectrum disorder (ASD) than we ever have before. The rapid surge in the number of people who have been diagnosed as having ASD has made autism a critical area of research. At the same time, it has generated an awareness that we need to improve our understanding of the underlying causes of ASD and improve services for people with ASD and their families. It has also given rise to federal and state laws and regulations designed to empower and protect people with autism, including the right to early intervention services, an appropriate education, and job training. People who have ASD and their families have even become a political force. Clearly, autism has become a topic of intense focus and research in our society, which bodes well for creating opportunities for people who have the condition.

In spite of all these strides, there is still far to go in understanding ASD—why it occurs, genetic and environmental risk factors, and what can be done to treat the individual and support the family. There are still many gaps in services, particularly for underrepresented segments of our population and for adults with ASD. That these disorders vary so widely also warrants more attention if we are to provide children and adults with the best treatment. Keep in mind that autism spans a large spectrum and includes people who are nonverbal and rely on supports to help them meet the demands of their daily routines, as well as those who eventually secure full-time jobs and live independently.

In this chapter, we talk about the gains we've made in improving our understanding of ASD, securing more protections for people with ASD, and providing more services. We also examine what still needs to be done. Where do we go from here? What kinds of research are we looking at? How do we do a better job of supporting the autism community?

Federal Leadership

In 2006, Congress passed the Combating Autism Act (CAA), which was intended to speed up ASD research and improve services for people with ASD and their families. The legislation authorized the federal government to intensify the work it was doing on ASD research, surveillance, prevention, treatment, and education. It also resulted in appropriations of $924 million during the subsequent 5 fiscal years and increased federal spending on autism by at least 50%. In 2014, President Barack Obama signed into law reauthorization of the CAA, which was renamed the Autism Collaboration, Accountability, Research, Education, and Support (CARES) Act. This law allocated more than $1.3 billion in federal ASD funding over 5 years for the National Institutes of Health, the US Centers for Disease Control and Prevention (CDC), and the Human Resources and Services Administration.

The CAA led to the creation of the Interagency Autism Coordinating Committee (IACC), which is made up of representatives from several agencies within the US Department of Health and Human Services, members of the public affected by autism, and participants in the autism advocacy and research community. The IACC reports to Congress on progress being made on ASD. Every year, the IACC publishes a strategic plan that outlines autism research that is being conducted, creates a summary of advances in ASD research, and monitors federal activities related to ASD. The latest strategic plan from the IACC calls for a doubling of the ASD research budget by 2020.

The Autism CARES Act helps fund surveillance and awareness programs under the CDC. Surveillance helps experts understand the *prevalence* of ASD, or how many cases there are at any given time within the United States. The CDC Autism and Developmental Disabilities Monitoring Network has been tracking the prevalence of ASD in children throughout the United States since 2000. Gathering information about ASD prevalence helps identify trends in ASD over time and may eventually help us understand who is at risk for ASD. Let's look at some of the other key areas of interest.

Presidential Proclamation: World Autism Awareness Day

"Every person deserves the chance to reach for their highest hopes and fulfill their greatest potential. On World Autism Awareness Day, we reaffirm our dedication to ensuring that belief is a reality for all those who live on the autism spectrum.... And we uphold our obligation to help make sure every man, woman, and child, regardless of ability or background, is accepted for who they are and able to lead a life free from discrimination and filled with opportunity.

"From home to school and in businesses and communities around the world, people living with autism spectrum disorder contribute in immeasurable ways to our society. They remind us each day that every person is born with unique talents and should be treated with respect, play an active role in planning for their futures, and feel empowered to fully participate in and contribute to their communities. When those with autism have access to equal opportunities, we all do better, and that begins with making sure our country lives up to its commitment to ensure all things are possible for all people.

"Americans with autism play an important role in our national story, and in their daily lives they embody the belief at the heart of our founding: that in America, with hard work and equal access, all people can realize their aspirations. Today, and every day, let us reach for a future in which no person living on the autism spectrum is limited by anything but the size of their dreams—one in which all people have the opportunity to live a life filled with a sense of identity, purpose, and self-determination...."

—President Barack Obama,
April 2, 2016

Earlier and Better Diagnosis

One of the most important changes in recent history has been the emphasis on early diagnosis. Experts now know that the symptoms of ASD can often be reliably detected by the time a child is 24 months old, and even as early as 12 months of age. Yet according to the CDC, the average age of ASD diagnosis is around 4½ years old. Detecting autism early can make a significant difference in child outcomes by facilitating earlier access to treatment and interventions. To emphasize the importance of early diagnosis, the CDC has been promoting its "Learn the Signs. Act Early." campaign since 2004 to bolster autism awareness and encourage developmental monitoring by parents, child care providers, and other professionals who interact with young children, with the goal of achieving an early diagnosis for all children with ASD (and other developmental disabilities). Since 2007, the American Academy of Pediatrics has recommended screening all children for ASD at 18 and 24 months of age, and a 2016 survey showed that 81% of US pediatricians are routinely performing ASD-specific screening.

While these efforts have made an enormous difference, much still needs to be done. Identifying the early signs of ASD continues to be difficult because typical development varies widely in young children, and even children with ASD will often display typical behaviors much of the time. For instance, some children speak at an early age, while others do not speak until much later and yet are still within the range of what's considered typical and appropriate.

Another challenge is the under-identification of children in certain socioeconomic groups. Children who come from disadvantaged backgrounds or live in rural communities may have more difficulty accessing quality health care or services. As a result, many of these children go undiagnosed or are diagnosed at a later age. Even those who are diagnosed may face prolonged waits until therapists are available to provide treatment. Efforts to build public awareness and improve early diagnosis and access to treatment services in these communities will require a better understanding of these socioeconomic disparities.

In addition, there are disparities in diagnosis among certain racial and ethnic groups. According to the CDC 2018 report on ASD prevalence, black and Hispanic children are less likely to be identified with ASD compared with white children. To address these differences, experts want to develop better, more reliable screening tools that are easy to administer to large populations and yet are effective for different groups, including girls, older children, and children who come from different ethnic and racial backgrounds.

Researchers are also hoping to find a reliable biomarker—a distinct biochemical, genetic, or molecular characteristic or substance or a behavioral feature—that identifies young children at risk for ASD or who have ASD. Ideally, the biomarker will be obvious before birth or shortly after. A reliable biomarker will allow for more accurate diagnosis. Without a biomarker, health care experts will continue to rely on observing behaviors that are often not apparent until well after birth, which creates a significant time lag. The delay in diagnosis is a missed opportunity for early intervention. There is currently active research to identify biomarkers in the blood, urine, or brain tissue of children with ASD as well as to identify biomarkers from functional types of brain scans or electrophysiological measures, including looking at patterns of brain signaling for sensory processing, for language processing, and for social activities. Visual tracking patterns in the first months after birth have been studied. Additional work is being done to identify potential biomarkers of ASD within the placenta of pregnant mothers or by examining maternal autoantibodies (immune proteins that target and react with a person's own tissues or organs). At this time, however, this research has not progressed to the point that biomarker testing is done in clinical settings.

Addressing the Entire Spectrum

Some people with ASD have a disability that significantly challenges their ability to communicate wants and needs, so they rely more heavily on caregivers to help with activities of daily living. For others, their disability poses fewer challenges and they achieve a higher level of functioning.

The broadness of the autism spectrum—often referred to as its *heterogeneity*—represents not only the wide range of abilities and needs of those with the diagnosis but also the multiple underlying causes of ASD, as discussed in Chapter 2. Such variability in function, associated medical conditions, and types of underlying brain differences has made it difficult for researchers to identify specific treatments that will lead to the best possible outcome in all individuals with ASD. The diversity of symptoms and causes suggests that different people will respond differently to available interventions, be they behavioral, developmental, medical, or other. The key is knowing which intervention or combination of interventions will work best for whom and how to establish reasonable expectations for future functioning.

Addressing the needs of the entire spectrum also means looking at the needs of adolescents and adults with ASD. Until recently, many people viewed ASD for the challenges it presented during childhood. We are now in the midst of a large group of individuals with ASD who are transitioning to adulthood, and this is increasing the awareness that supports are needed across the life span. The symptoms and needs of individuals with ASD may change over time, and currently, the needs of many adults are not being well addressed.

In the IACC 2016-2017 *Strategic Plan for Autism Spectrum Disorder,* the needs of adults were identified as an area that required more services and research, in particular practical strategies for improving quality of life and functioning among adolescents and adults. This means addressing issues related to secondary education, work opportunities, housing, social participation, and community integration. Adults with ASD also have unique health care needs that will require an increase in adult medical providers' knowledge about ASD and the co-occurring physical and mental health conditions we discuss in earlier chapters (such as epilepsy, gastrointestinal conditions, insomnia, attention-deficit/hyperactivity disorder [ADHD], and anxiety). The goal is to help adolescents transition into adulthood with the opportunity to lead meaningful and self-determined lives in the communities of their choice with access to services they need and desire.

Yet another gap is the relative lack of understanding of ASD in girls and women. Until now, boys have outnumbered girls in prevalence studies by a ratio of 4 to 1, in large part because the disorder is more commonly identified in boys than girls. Newer research, however, now indicates that ASD may be more common in girls than previously thought, and there are concerns that the current screening and diagnostic tools used may be less effective in identifying girls with ASD. The IACC has called for more research on the underlying biology of ASD in girls and women, the development of better screening and diagnostic instruments to detect ASD in girls, and better services and supports for girls and women with ASD.

For more information about the IACC and to review the latest strategic plan, visit https://iacc.hhs.gov.

The Push for Insurance Coverage of Autism

As any parent can tell you, the cost of autism can be significant. To help families financially, advocacy groups—including the American Academy of Pediatrics and its state chapters—have been pushing hard for insurance coverage. To date, 48 states have enacted legislation that requires some form of insurance coverage for evaluation and treatment of children with autism. Details of the laws vary by state. Families, pediatricians, and other advocates continue to work with state lawmakers to improve existing laws and enact new policies to improve insurance coverage for children with autism. To learn more about your state's laws regarding autism insurance, visit Autism Speaks at www.autismspeaks.org/advocacy/insurancereform.

Fast Fact

In recent years, the amount of funding dedicated to autism research has surged. Back in 2000, the National Institutes of Health allocated about $50 million toward autism research. By 2017, that figure had jumped to $245 million. Interest in autism research is also reflected in the rising number of medical journals dedicated specifically to autism, including *Autism, Autism Research and Treatment,* and the *Journal of Autism and Developmental Disorders.*

Improving Treatment

Finding the best treatment for someone with ASD remains a significant challenge, largely because the biology of autism continues to be so incompletely understood. We currently know that there are many different causes of ASD. That may mean that certain people with ASD will respond better to specific treatments. Efforts are underway, for example, in people with conditions such as fragile X syndrome and neurofibromatosis type 1 to test specific medications in order to look for a disease-specific response to treatment. As the specific genetic cause is identified in more and more people with ASD, this type of approach may expand considerably in the future.

Behavioral and developmental interventions continue to be treatments that are backed by solid scientific evidence. While methods such as applied behavior analysis have been studied in young children with ASD, more research is needed to know how to best implement these treatments in older children, in schools, and in resource-limited settings such as rural communities. At the same time, more studies are needed on pharmacological treatments and dietary supplements for those with ASD. So far, the US Food and Drug Administration has approved only risperidone and aripiprazole for treating irritability and aggression in some children with ASD and has approved no medications that treat the core symptoms of ASD. In addition, many parents are giving their children dietary supplements or using special diets to treat ASD, despite a lack of research studies that support their use.

We also need to better understand how to recognize and treat co-occurring medical and mental health conditions that are common in people with ASD, such as epilepsy, gastrointestinal disorders, sleep issues, anxiety, and ADHD. The Autism Treatment Network (ATN), a collection of centers specializing in the care of children with ASD, has been working to improve the medical care of children with ASD. The sites within the ATN care for more than 30,000 children, and by performing pooled research studies of this large group of children, they can identify the best ways to evaluate and treat co-occurring conditions. On the basis of this research, supported through the Autism CARES Act, the ATN has published guidelines on the treatment of insomnia, constipation, ADHD, and anxiety in children with ASD. These guidelines have been shared with pediatricians all over the world. For more information about the ATN, visit www.autismspeaks.org/science/resources-programs/autism-treatment-network.

The Path Forward for Children With Autism

With appropriate support, children with autism spectrum disorder (ASD) can make significant developmental progress. Our scientific understanding of ASD is increasing but far from complete. The American Academy of Pediatrics strongly supports ongoing studies funded through federal agencies such as the Centers for Disease Control and Prevention, the National Institutes of Health, and the Health Resources and Services Administration to determine the underlying biology of ASD and identify interventions and services that support children with ASD and their families.

Support for Research

Extensive research on ASD still needs to be done, and it will require significant collaboration, money, and manpower. For it to be successful, the field will require researchers to share more data, which will improve their analyses of the information gathered. Collecting this information will help researchers determine whether early diagnosis and services, as well as the types of services, affect the course of an individual's ASD.

To enhance research efforts, scientists also need more human tissue. These tissues and samples will need to come not only from people with ASD but also from people who do not have the disorder for comparison. Developing methods and procedures for storing and accessing these specimens will be critical to the process too.

In addition, research will require more surveillance. Closely observing autism over time will help experts track the numbers of children with ASD and prevalence trends. It will also help identify potential risk factors and protective factors. Information gleaned from this surveillance may be used to improve early diagnosis, education, and health services, as well as community programs.

Future research must also examine the most cost-effective way to deliver needed services for the growing population of people with ASD. For instance, researchers of a study published in 2014 estimated that the cost of supporting an individual with ASD across his or her lifetime was between $1.4 million and $2.4 million. The largest components of this cost were special education services and lost productivity in parents. During adulthood, residential care and loss of work productivity contributed the most. Studies such as this one raise questions about how investments in treatments of children with ASD can potentially produce long-term societal savings by enabling individuals to become more functionally independent. The initial research in this area favors investment in the treatment of young children with ASD. For example, a 2017 study showed that the cost of treating young children with the Early Start Denver Model (see Chapter 4) were fully offset within just a few years after the intervention because of reductions in need for later services.

At the same time, we need to look to the future and assess whether we have the workforce required to meet the needs of the growing numbers of children with ASD. Currently, families are having difficulty accessing ASD diagnostic evaluations and behavioral and developmental therapies because of a lack of trained professionals. The number of training programs is increasing, but producing enough new professionals for the future will require a sustained commitment to support training efforts. One such training program is the Leadership Education in Neurodevelopmental and Related Disabilities (LEND) Program. Funded through the Autism CARES Act of 2014, LEND programs promote education, early detection, and intervention in infants, children, and adolescents with ASD. LEND program trainees participate in academic, clinical, leadership, and community opportunities and receive training in cultural and linguistic competence using a family-centered approach in caring for children with ASD. In 2015 alone, 683 LEND faculty members from 43 LEND programs across the United States mentored trainees to increase the pipeline of professionals ready to work with children with ASD and other developmental disabilities. In that same year, more than 100,000 ASD diagnostic evaluations were conducted by LEND faculty or trainees.

There are ways that you can help support the research efforts to learn more about ASD. If you have a child with ASD or have autism yourself, you may want to consider participating in research studies. (Go to https://clinicaltrials.gov to participate in or learn about federally and privately funded clinical trials.) The information you provide may be critical to building our understanding of this complex condition and ultimately may lead to improvements in the care of individuals with ASD. Several other large-scale research project opportunities are summarized here and in Chapter 2.

- SPARK is an online autism study with the goal of speeding up research and advancing the understanding of autism. The study aims to recruit 50,000 people with autism and their families. It is open to anyone with a diagnosis of autism in the United States. SPARK provides summary and individual results as well as monthly webinars on related topics, presented by clinicians and researchers. Learn more at www.sparkforautism.org.

- Interactive Autism Network, or IAN, is an innovative online project designed to accelerate the pace of autism research by allowing parents to report information about their child's diagnosis, behavior, environment, services received, and progress over time. More information is available at https://iancommunity.org.

ɛ؏ ɛ؏ ɛ؏ ɛ؏ ɛ؏

Autism Champion: Geraldine Dawson, PhD

"MY INTEREST IN AUTISM BEGAN in graduate school when I was training as a clinical psychologist. My first client was a child with autism. What struck me was our lack of understanding of autism: How is it that a child has difficulty forming social relationships? By understanding this, I believed we would not only be able to help individuals with autism; we would also learn how we all form relationships. Intellectually, this was a compelling topic, but it also captured my heart. At that time, there was little to offer to help this little boy or support his parents. I felt this was an area where I could devote myself and hopefully make a difference.

"Over the past few decades, it's been gratifying to see how much we have learned. Now we have many more tools to help a child and family. We now understand that autism is not one condition but many different conditions with many different causes and variable expression. This requires individualized treatments to address the needs of each person. Our research is identifying biomarkers that can help us to better recognize the subtypes of autism and provide the right treatment for each person.

"During this same time period, the prevalence of autism increased by more than 1,000%. One of the most enjoyable parts of my job is training young people so we can build capacity to better meet the needs of people with autism. There is still a huge gap between our knowledge about effective treatments and delivering them to communities, locally and globally. Sally Rogers and I developed an effective early intervention for young children with autism. The challenge is how to deliver treatments to communities that don't have trained professionals. We hope that technologies, such as telehealth, will be part of the solution. We can now identify infants at risk for autism and provide intervention before the full syndrome is present so that disabling symptoms can be reduced or prevented. We have shown that when a child is provided with early behavioral intervention, this not only has a significant impact on the child's cognitive ability, social skills, and language skills, but it also improves brain function and long-term outcomes.

"My goal as a researcher and clinician has been to help reduce the disabilities associated with autism while promoting the unique talents and special abilities associated with it. In this regard, we are learning much from adults with autism who have become effective self-advocates and are shaping policy and research priorities. At the national and international levels, I also have advocated for services, insurance benefits, and research funding so we can continue to develop more effective treatments of people with autism. Throughout my career, my inspiration has been the individuals with autism and their families I have met along the way. It's been an honor to be part of their lives and to partner with them to make the world a better place for people with autism and other disabilities."

Editors' note: Dr Dawson is one of the foremost researchers internationally in the field of autism; the recipient of many awards; the inaugural chief science officer for Autism Speaks, serving in multiple leadership positions nationally and internationally; and currently director of the Duke Center for Autism and Brain Development.

CHAPTER 15

Advocating for Children With Autism Spectrum Disorder

ALL PARENTS ARE ADVOCATES whenever they speak out on behalf of their children. But for parents of children who have autism spectrum disorder (ASD) like you, advocacy can often go beyond your child to become a personal crusade in a world still struggling to understand this complex neurological condition and how to accommodate people who have needs associated with it.

The dictionary defines *advocate* as someone who strongly and publicly supports someone or something. You'd be hard-pressed to find people with stronger opinions about autism than parents of children who have ASD. These days, parents are at the forefront of autism advocacy. Many become impassioned about autism after they struggle to meet the needs of their own children. Others find themselves doing endless amounts of research into autism and then becoming committed to sharing that knowledge and putting it to good use. Still others want to promote a particular message about an aspect of autism. The good news is, autism organizations are more than eager to tap into the energy and drive that these advocate parents bring to the cause.

Throughout this book, you've read profiles of people who are advocates for autism. But you can make a difference, too, by getting involved in your local school, your hometown community, or nonprofit groups. In this chapter, we look at what it takes to be an advocate and the many ways you can get involved. Maybe you will find inspiration in these pages to become an advocate yourself.

What Advocates Do

Advocates, first and foremost, are educators. They're in the public teaching people about ASD, what it is, and how it affects lives. Advocates may be teaching lawmakers about the importance of autism-related legislation, helping parents understand their rights under special education law, or educating the community about ASD. Advocates aren't shy about taking a position and persuading others to understand the value of their stance, whether they're trying to convince the school board that a new special education teacher is needed or asking politicians for more money to fund autism research.

Choosing to Advocate for Children

Advocacy at the community, state, or federal level can make a meaningful and lasting difference to children in your community and state and nationwide. Community, state, and federal advocacy allows you to become part of a broader network of advocates that works systemically to raise awareness, educate, and create policies that can help keep children safe and healthy.

For many people, becoming an advocate starts with identifying an unmet need and having the desire to make changes to improve the situation. For others, advocacy grows out of genuine concern and kindness for those less fortunate. Others may see advocacy as a way to show appreciation for the opportunities they have received, a chance for them to "pay it forward."

And advocacy, on any level, doesn't need to be done on a grand scale or performed over the course of an entire lifetime. Plenty of people have found smaller causes in their own communities and have turned them into worthwhile pursuits. The key to finding your cause is to tap into your passion, that is, to find what matters most to you. For many people, that passion rests with their children and other loved ones.

> **Fast Fact**
>
> Parents aren't the only ones advocating on behalf of children with autism spectrum disorder. Pediatricians and other physicians, teachers, administrators, therapists, and special education providers also get involved in doing advocacy work.

One of the most important things to do before you get "out there" is to have a clear goal in mind. What exactly do you want? What is your role as the advocate? How will you get there? Sometimes it takes time to figure out what your immediate goal is. But if you have a long-term plan, it may help shape what you do now.

Required Skills for Advocacy

Anyone can sound off with her views in a meeting, on a blog, or in a letter. But effective advocates possess skills that allow them to make their points clearly and precisely, with the goal of persuading others— and getting the results they seek. Here are some of the skills that these effective advocates display.

- *They know how to do research and gather facts.* Advocates gather facts and information. As they gather information and organize documents and records, they learn about a child's disability and educational history. Advocates use facts and independent documentation to work with schools and education officials to achieve appropriate services and outcomes for their children.

- *They become familiar with the players in their school, community, or organization.* Advocates know how decisions are made, and they know who makes them.

- *They know about their legal rights.* Advocates stay on top of special education laws, regulations, and cases involving children with special needs. They also know the procedures to follow to protect their rights and children's rights.

Eunice Kennedy Shriver, A Well-known Advocate

Among the most well-known advocates for individuals with disabilities was Eunice Kennedy Shriver, who launched Special Olympics. Mrs Shriver was the sister of President John F. Kennedy and Senator Edward M. "Ted" Kennedy of Massachusetts. Her passion for advocating for individuals with disabilities grew out of her love for her sister Rosemary, the eldest daughter of Joseph Kennedy and his wife, Rose.

As a child, Rosemary was slow to crawl, walk, and speak. Once she was in school, it was apparent she had an intellectual disability, and as a young woman, she grew increasingly agitated and had violent mood swings. Unable to care for herself, Rosemary spent the rest of her life in an institution, where she received the daily care she needed, until her death at the age of 86.

Mrs Shriver had deep compassion for her older sister and the challenges that Rosemary faced throughout her life. In 1962, she started a day camp for young people with intellectual disabilities that was in her backyard and that she called *Camp Shriver.* She wanted to see the children use their skills in a variety of sports and physical activities. The camp grew in popularity. Six years later, the first International Special Olympics Summer Games were held in Chicago, IL. Mrs Shriver promised that this new organization would give children with intellectual disabilities the chance to play, compete, and grow. Today, the Special Olympics are held in 172 countries and serve nearly 5 million people.

But Mrs Shriver did not stop there. She also took over leadership of the Joseph P. Kennedy Jr. Foundation, an organization founded to honor her oldest brother, Joseph, who was killed in World War II. Mrs Shriver worked tirelessly on behalf of people with intellectual disabilities. She helped launch the National Institute of Child Health and Human Development in 1962. She also helped establish the Eunice Kennedy Shriver Intellectual and Developmental Disabilities Research Centers and the University Affiliated Facilities, now known as *University Centers for Excellence in Developmental Disabilities Education, Research, and Service.* Her efforts to develop clinical

> **Eunice Kennedy Shriver, A Well-known Advocate (*continued*)**
>
> training programs for professionals who were working with children with disabilities and special health care needs have evolved into the Leadership Education in Neurodevelopmental and Related Disabilities programs.
>
> Mrs Shriver died in 2009, leaving behind a legacy of work on behalf of those who are disabled.

- *They always arrive prepared.* Advocates are planners who go to meetings, presentations, and other events with all the key information they need. They prepare ahead of time and know their objectives before they go. They also know whom they need to approach and influence.

- *They ask questions and are good listeners.* Advocates know they sometimes have to probe for answers and aren't afraid to ask questions, even if the answer seems obvious.

- *They are record keepers.* Information is critical in the world of advocacy work, so smart advocates always keep documents on hand. They also take extensive notes and write follow-up letters if they have lingering questions or to confirm what happened at a meeting.

- *They put their energy into finding solutions, not assigning blame.* Looking for someone to blame accomplishes nothing. Advocates prefer instead to spend their precious time seeking solutions to their problems. They do it using the knowledge they acquire.

- *They aren't afraid to tell their stories.* Putting a face on a policy issue or while seeking a solution to a challenge taps into the hope and potential of an advocate's personal experience and can help bring about meaningful change.

- *They know how to get their point across without being confrontational.* They are good communicators who have learned the art of negotiation and mastered understanding when it's important to talk and to listen. They realize the importance of making everyone feel as if they "win" in some way, if possible.

"For all those whose cares have been our concern, the work goes on, the cause endures, the hope still lives, and the dream shall never die."

—**Senator Edward M. "Ted" Kennedy, August 12, 1980**

Types of Advocacy Work

The word *advocate* is broad for a simple reason: there's a lot you can do. It can be as basic as writing a check to support autism research or as involved as creating an autism support group in your community. It can be lobbying state legislators for reforms to help people with ASD, writing articles about autism in your local newspaper, or volunteering for an organization to stuff envelopes. The possibilities for involvement are endless but always start from the same place: love for your child and concern for her well-being.

As we've already noted, most people who become advocates discover their passion while working on behalf of their own children. If they're successful, they may feel empowered and want to get involved so they can help improve the lives of other children. The next thing they know, they are involved in the local chapter of an autism organization, participating in a walk to raise money, or writing letters to their Congressional representatives on behalf of people who have ASD. Others become involved when a friend encourages them to take up the cause.

If you think you'd like to advocate in the field of autism, consider your passion, talents, and interests. Consult the resources in Appendix A and talk to others in your community. You'll be amazed at all the ways you can help out.

You Can Do It!

Anyone can be an advocate. The most important thing to do as an advocate is to become well versed in the topic. Knowledge is power. So read about ASD and special education laws and stay informed about related legislation. Find out how other organizations raise money or create awareness. Talk to others who know what you need to learn.

Subscribe to appropriate magazines and journals. Keep up-to-date on ongoing developments, and network and share information with other individuals and groups.

At this point, you might be saying you're too shy, too easily intimidated, or too scared to be an advocate. No doubt, being an advocate takes a degree of confidence and courage. For some people, that can come naturally. With others, it might take more effort and time. No matter where you stand right now, your confidence in advocating will grow over time. Each time you get results, no matter how small or big, you'll feel that much more empowered to speak out. Just remember, no one knows your story better than you.

If you do decide to pursue advocacy work, don't overlook your own needs in the process. Raising children with ASD takes an excessive amount of time, energy, and patience. Add jobs, home maintenance, and advocacy into the mix and you'll probably feel a bit overwhelmed. If you become an advocate, make sure to take time for yourself to recharge and renew. For many parents, advocating allows them to feel as if they are able to take some control of a situation and diagnosis for which there is very little.

The Road Ahead

By reading this book, you have gained a solid base of information on how to raise a child with ASD. But acquiring knowledge shouldn't stop here. Autism has become a major public health concern, and as a result, the field is constantly evolving. Staying on top of the latest research and developments will help you be the best possible parent and advocate.

Parenting a child with ASD isn't easy. There will be days when you want to cry, scream, and throw your own tantrum. There will be many moments when you are tired and worn out. But there will also be many days when you celebrate and rejoice in all that your child has accomplished and how far you and your family have come. We hope this book, while helping you understand and face the challenges, above all helps provide more opportunity for you to acknowledge and embrace the joyous moments and unique gifts that appear along your journey.

༄ ༄ ༄ ༄ ༄

Autism Champion: Cheryl C. Smith, BS

As THE MOTHER of a young child with severe autism, Cheryl C. Smith, BS, was unsure of how she could afford to send her son Carson to a special school. "His kindergarten tuition at the Carmen B. Pingree Center for Children with Autism was more than my son's tuition in medical school at the University of Utah," she recalls. (The center was recently renamed to the Carmen B. Pingree Autism Center of Learning.)

Cheryl met with her state representative, J. Morgan Philpot, and he agreed to sponsor a bill. "I spent the next months doing interviews, sending letters and e-mails, making calls, talking to parents, taking tours, and going up to the capitol," Cheryl recalls. "I worked on it for more than 50 hours a week while the session was in."

Her efforts paid off. In 2005, Utah became the first state in the United States to offer private school scholarships to children with special needs. It was named the Carson Smith Scholarship. "People approach me all the time teary-eyed and tell me thanks for the work I did, that they could not have had their child in the place their child needed to be without the scholarship," Cheryl says. "Some were able to stay home with their other children; some, to pay off that second mortgage they took out for their disabled child; some, to reinstate their phone. But I didn't do it alone."

Cheryl is past president/founder of the Autism Council of Utah. Carson started talking around age 9 years; his first heartwarming word, *Mom*. Cheryl's advice on raising a child with ASD: "Give yourself a break. We can't fix everything. Most things don't change, no matter how long we cry or how much cookie dough we eat. The things that we deal with may or may not change, but we can always dig down to find the joy in ourselves."

🐿 🐿 🐿 🐿 🐿

Afterword

Shana's Special Wish

Written by Nicole Ashley Herzog

Age 9

This story is dedicated to all the Shanas and Freddys of the world and to my brother Eli who doesn't understand how much I love and accept him just the way he is.

❦ ❦ ❦ ❦ ❦

ON A SWEET LITTLE STREET lived a sweet little family: Mommy, Daddy, and Shana (that's me). We were as happy as could be, but I knew we would be even happier if I had a little brother or sister. Pretty much that's all I ever talked about. And whenever I made a wish, I always wished for the same thing. Like when we were at the mall, and I threw the 5 pennies and one quarter that were at the bottom of my purse into the fountain, or the time when I blew out the candles on my birthday cake. I wished and wished. And do you know what happened? A miracle! After all my wishing, finally, a baby was on the way!

When the baby arrived, he was so cute—at least that's what everyone said. I thought he looked weird. He had plenty of wrinkles, just like my grandpa. But just the same, I loved my new little brother to pieces. He smiled at me and he was chubby, and he followed me with his eyes and became very excited whenever I came into the room. It was great. I loved to make him laugh by tickling him and playing peekaboo.

Our life went on as usual. We were a sweet little family: Mommy, Daddy, Shana, and Freddy. We were as happy as could be, except lately, Mommy and Daddy had worried looks on their faces, and sometimes I saw Mommy crying.

"What's wrong, Mommy?" I asked. "Oh, Mommy's just a little sad, Shana. Nothing for you to worry about. Hey, how about some hot chocolate?" Mommy knows I love hot chocolate. Hot chocolate and coconut jelly beans always make me happy. "Yay! I'll get the mugs!"

One night as Freddy wobbly walked around in his "Here comes trouble" T-shirt and puffy diaper, he carried a little set of wooden numbers from my puzzle box. "Aw, isn't that cute, Mommy? Freddy likes my number puzzle." He walked around saying, "Eight! Seven!" And he held up the number 6 and turned it upside down and said, "Nine!" It was so wonderfully funny because Freddy hadn't really said any words up until that moment.

The thing is, Freddy started carrying those numbers around with him everywhere he went. And once when I pointed to a guitar and asked him, "Hey, Freddy, what do you see?" he said, "Eight!" And do you know what? That guitar really did look like an 8. Suddenly, I realized Freddy didn't just like numbers. Freddy LOVED numbers. He especially loved the number 8. He even took Daddy's glasses off one day at the park and held them sideways. And guess what he said? That's right…8!

I caught myself starting to get annoyed with the kid. Eight this, 8 that. "Yeah, OK, Freddy. We get it!" Because you see, I wanted to read to Freddy and be silly with Freddy and play school with Freddy. But all he cared about were those stinkin' numbers. Seventeen also seemed to make quite an impression on him. Hmm. One plus 7 equals…8. Ahhh!

Still, Freddy is as cute as a button. He has a little chubby face with big pink cheeks and a huge smile. But something is different about him. Mommy told me he has something called *autism*. "Autism? What's that Mommy? Is Freddy sick?" I asked. "No, Shana. He's not sick. But his little brain works very differently than other people's brains." I asked, "And is that why he loves numbers so much?" Mommy nodded yes, and her eyes became watery as she turned and smiled at Freddy who had just walked into the room with 2 straws, proudly showing us how he had bent one of them to make a 7.

At that moment, we both laughed. I hugged and kissed Freddy and made him play ring-around-the-rosy. And do you know what? Freddy laughed and giggled, and he loved ring-around-the-rosy.

Like most kids, Freddy loves to play in the water and go down the waterslide at the pool. But I notice Freddy never has any little friends who want to play with him. Sometimes that makes me sad because I wish Freddy did have friends, friends that would look past the funny noises he makes or the way he flaps his little hands when he's really excited. But that's OK, because Freddy has me, and I will always be his friend.

Recently, Freddy has discovered other interests. He loves classical music, especially Mozart and Bach. Oh, and how could I forget his fascination with Christmas music. I remember one summer when it was a scorching 100 degrees outside and we had the air conditioner on full blast as "Jingle Bells" blared from Mommy's car radio. Luckily, that's the summer I got my iPod.

Even though Freddy isn't perfect, and he may not be the little brother I had wished for, I wouldn't trade him for all the coconut jelly beans in the world. Because I love Freddy, and he loves me…almost as much as he loves the number 8.

Appendixes

A. Resources 303

B. Emergency Information Form for Children
   With Autism Spectrum Disorder 317

C. Early Intervention Program Referral Form 319

D. Medication Flowchart 321

Appendix A

Resources

This is not an all-inclusive list; however, the following suggestions will help you get started in your search for information. Make sure your pediatrician knows about your questions and concerns; share the information you find in your research. Remember, you and your pediatrician are partners in your child's health.

Please note: Listing here does not imply an endorsement by the American Academy of Pediatrics (AAP). The AAP is not responsible for the content of the resources. Phone numbers and Web sites are as current as possible but may change at any time.

American Academy of Pediatrics Resources

American Academy of Pediatrics
800/433-9016

www.AAP.org
The American Academy of Pediatrics is an organization of 67,000 primary care pediatricians, pediatric medical subspecialists, and pediatric surgical specialists dedicated to the health, safety, and well-being of infants, children, adolescents, and young adults.

www.HealthyChildren.org
The official AAP Web site for parents.

www.AAP.org/autism
The AAP Council on Children With Disabilities (COCWD) is dedicated to the optimal care and development of children with disabilities and to the support of their families within a medical home. The COCWD Autism Subcommittee serves as the main point of contact for the AAP on issues related to autism spectrum disorder (ASD).

www.medicalhomeinfo.org

The National Center for Medical Home Implementation is a cooperative agreement between the Maternal and Child Health Bureau and the AAP that provides medical home resources and advocacy materials, technical assistance, and tools to physicians, families, and other medical and nonmedical providers who care for children, including children with special needs.

Government Web Sites

Center for Parent Information and Resources
973/642-8100

www.parentcenterhub.org

Information about laws, services, and research that affect children with disabilities, including autism.

Centers for Disease Control and Prevention
800/CDC-INFO (232-4636)

www.cdc.gov/ncbddd/autism

www.cdc.gov/ncbddd/actearly

Offers information about the prevalence of autism and trends in autism as well as the "Learn the Signs. Act Early." campaign.

Early Childhood Technical Assistance Center
http://ectacenter.org

Supported by the US Department of Education Office of Special Education Programs under the provisions of the Individuals with Disabilities Education Act.

Interagency Autism Coordinating Committee
https://iacc.hhs.gov

Coordinates and seeks community input on all federally funded autism research.

Maternal and Child Health Digital Library at Georgetown University

877/624-1935

www.mchlibrary.org/families/frb-autism.php

A selection of current, high-quality resources about ASD identification and intervention; separate sections identify resources about ASD and environmental health research and concerns about vaccines.

National Center for Complementary and Integrative Health

888/644-6226

https://nccih.nih.gov

https://nccih.nih.gov/health/autism

Lead agency for scientific research on complementary and integrative medicine.

National Institute of Mental Health

866/615-6464

www.nimh.nih.gov

Information about ASD, including news, clinical trials, and access to other Web sites.

National Institute of Neurological Disorders and Stroke

800/352-9424

www.ninds.nih.gov/disorders/autism/autism.htm

Provides information about autism as well as organizations focused on autism.

US Department of Education Individuals with Disabilities Education Act

http://idea.ed.gov

www2.ed.gov/policy/speced/guid/idea/monitor/state-contact-list.html

Provides information about the federal laws that ensure services for children with disabilities.

Educational and Therapeutic Organizations

Association for Behavioral Analysis International
269/492-9310

www.abainternational.org

Membership organization that develops, supports, and enhances the field of applied behavior analysis.

Epilepsy Foundation of America
800/332-1000

www.epilepsy.com

A foundation dedicated to improving and saving lives through public education, access to care campaigns, research initiatives, therapy funding, and community services.

ICDL (Interdisciplinary Council on Development and Learning) (Home of DIR and DIRFloortime)
301/304-8834

www.icdl.com

Among its objectives, the Developmental, Individual Difference, Relationship-based (DIR) approach (also called *Greenspan Floortime* or *DIRFloortime*) includes building healthy foundations for social, emotional, and intellectual capacities rather than focusing on skills and isolated behaviors.

Medical Home Portal
www.medicalhomeportal.org

The Medical Home Portal is a unique source of reliable information about children and youths with special health care needs, offering a one-stop shop for families, physicians, medical home teams, and other professionals and caregivers.

The portal has the following module that covers ASD: www.medicalhomeportal.org/diagnoses-and-conditions/autism-spectrum-disorder

Parent to Parent USA

518/637-9441

www.p2pusa.org

Parent to Parent USA is a national organization that connects parents with other families and provides emotional and informational support for families of children who have special needs.

Responsive Classroom

216/368-1707

www.responsiveclassroom.org

A parent-mediated program of instruction for children younger than 6 years that focuses on cognition, communication, and social-emotional functioning.

The SCERTS Model

http://scerts.com

Focuses on children with challenges in social communication and emotional regulation.

Social Thinking

www.socialthinking.com

A curriculum for parents and clinicians that provides practical frameworks, strategies, activities, and vocabulary to help people aged 4 years through adulthood improve their social thinking and related social skills and build stronger relationships.

TEACCH Autism Program

919/966-2174

www.teacch.com

Evidence-based program at the University of North Carolina School of Medicine that uses structured teaching to work with people who have ASD in building life skills.

Other Associations and Resources

Academic Consortium for Integrative Medicine and Health

703/556-9222

www.imconsortium.org

Aims to advance the principles and practices of integrative health care within academic institutions; includes 51 academic medical centers and affiliate institutions and provides membership with a community of support for its academic missions and a collective voice for influencing change.

American Academy of Child and Adolescent Psychiatry

202/966-7300

www.aacap.org

Professional medical organization focused on the health and treatment of children affected by mental, behavioral, and developmental disorders.

The Arc

www.thearc.org

The Arc is a community resource for people with developmental and intellectual disabilities. They have the following companion site that is specifically for ASD:

Autism NOW

https://autismNOW.org

The Autism NOW Center is a source for resources and information on community-based solutions for individuals with autism, for individuals with other developmental disabilities, and for their families. A national initiative of The Arc.

Association for Science in Autism Treatment

www.asatonline.org

Organization that promotes the use of effective, science-based treatments of people with autism, regardless of age, severity of condition, income, or place of residence.

Association of University Centers on Disabilities

301/588-8252

www.aucd.org

A resource for local, state, national, and international agencies, organizations, and policy makers concerned about people living with developmental and other disabilities and their families.

Autism Science Foundation

914/810-9100

www.autismsciencefoundation.org

Helps support autism research and provides information about autism to the general public.

Autism Society of America

800/3AUTISM (328-8476) × 9620

www.autism-society.org

Organization that strives to improve the lives of people affected by autism by providing information about services and the latest in treatment, education, research, and advocacy.

Autism Speaks

888/288-4762

www.autismspeaks.org

Supports research into the causes, prevention, and treatments of, and a cure for, autism; raising awareness of autism; and advocating for the needs of individuals with autism and their families. Also offers a toolkit for families: www.autismspeaks.org/family-services/tool-kits.

Autism Speaks Autism Treatment Network

www.autismspeaks.org/science/resources-programs/autism-treatment-network

The Autism Treatment Network is a collaboration of Autism Speaks and some of the finest children's hospitals and academic institutions in North America, specializing in multidisciplinary medical care for children with autism. Together, they work to develop evidence-based protocols and standards of care for many of the most challenging medical conditions surrounding autism today. Autism Treatment Network best practices are shared with physicians and medical facilities nationwide to improve outcomes for all children with autism.

Autism Wandering Awareness Alerts Response and Education (AWAARE) Collaboration

http://awaare.nationalautismassociation.org

Initiative by the National Autism Association to prevent wandering incidents and deaths within the autism community.

Autistic Self Advocacy Network

http://autisticadvocacy.org

The Autistic Self Advocacy Network is a good resource for young adults interested in advocating for their rights.

Best Buddies

305/374-2233

www.bestbuddies.org

The world's largest organization dedicated to ending the social, physical, and economic isolation of the 200 million people with intellectual and developmental disabilities.

Disability Scoop

www.disabilityscoop.com

This site provides up-to-date news on autism and other disabilities.

Easterseals

800/221-6827

www.easterseals.com

Provides services for individuals with autism, developmental disabilities, physical disabilities, and other special needs, as well as their families.

Family Voices

888/835-5669

www.familyvoices.org

Aims to achieve family-centered care for all children and youths with special health care needs or disabilities (or both).

National Center for Family/Professional Partnerships

888/835-5669

www.fv-ncfpp.org

A project of Family Voices, promotes families as partners in the decision-making of health care for children and youths with special health care needs at all levels of care.

Got Transition/Center for Health Care Transition Improvement

202/223-1500

www.gottransition.org

National resource that supports optimal transitions from pediatric to adult models of health care for youths with and without special health care needs.

Interactive Autism Network

www.iancommunity.org

Online project that brings together people affected by ASD and researchers; goal is to facilitate research that will lead to advancements in understanding and treating ASD.

Organization for Autism Research

866/366-9710

www.researchautism.org

Focuses on applied research and how it provides tangible and practical benefits to people with autism and their families.

Sibling Support Project

www.siblingsupport.org

The Sibling Support Project is the first national program dedicated to the lifelong and ever-changing concerns of millions of brothers and sisters of people with special health, developmental, and mental health concerns.

Siblings of Autism

https://siblingsofautism.org

This organization is dedicated to supporting the siblings of individuals who have ASD through scholarships, respite funds, and outreach programs.

SPARK

https://sparkforautism.org

SPARK, which stands for Simons Foundation Powering Autism Research for Knowledge, seeks to speed up research and better understand autism in order to help improve lives. SPARK is a large autism research project with the goal of understanding the genetic and environmental factors that influence autism.

Special Needs Alliance

www.specialneedsalliance.com

National not-for-profit organization of attorneys dedicated to the practice of disability and public benefits law; connects individuals with disabilities, their families, and their advisors with nearby attorneys who focus their practices in the disability law arena.

Special Olympics

800/700-8585

www.specialolympics.org

Provides children and adults with intellectual disabilities year-round sports training and athletic competition in a variety of Olympic-type sports to develop physical fitness, demonstrate courage, experience joy, and participate in a sharing of gifts, skills, and friendship with their families, other Special Olympics athletes, and the community.

Spectrum News

www.spectrumnews.org

This site provides layperson updates on the latest research and policy news related to autism.

Books

General

Autism Women's Network. *What Every Autistic Girl Wishes Her Parents Knew.* Lincoln, NE: DragonBee; 2017

Bashe PR. *Asperger Syndrome: The OASIS Guide; Advice, Inspiration, Insight, and Hope From Early Intervention to Adulthood.* 3rd rev ed. New York, NY: Harmony Books; 2014

Grandin T, Panek R. *The Autistic Brain: Thinking Across the Spectrum.* New York, NY: First Mariner Books; 2013

Notbohm E. *Ten Things Every Child With Autism Wishes You Knew.* 1st rev ed. Arlington, TX: Future Horizons; 2012

Ozonoff S, Dawson G, McPartland JC. *A Parent's Guide to High-Functioning Autism Spectrum Disorder: How to Meet the Challenges and Help Your Child Thrive.* 2nd ed. New York, NY: Guilford; 2015

Prizant BM. *Uniquely Human: A Different Way of Seeing Autism.* New York, NY: Simon & Schuster Paperbacks; 2015

Reber D. *Differently Wired: Raising an Exceptional Child in a Conventional World.* New York, NY: Workman; 2018

Silberman S. *Neurotribes: The Legacy of Autism and the Future of Neurodiversity.* New York, NY: Avery; 2016

Verdick E, Reeve E. *The Survival Guide for Kids With Autism Spectrum Disorders (and Their Parents).* Minneapolis, MN: Free Spirit Publishing; 2012

Behavior Management, Social Skills, and Health

Bondy A, Frost L. *A Picture's Worth: PECS and Other Visual Communication Strategies in Autism.* 2nd ed. Bethesda, MD: Woodbine House; 2011

Cicero F. *Toilet Training Success: A Guide for Teaching Individuals With Developmental Disabilities.* New York, NY: DRL Books; 2012

Durand VM. *Sleep Better! A Guide to Improving Sleep for Children With Special Needs.* Rev ed. Baltimore, MD: Paul H. Brookes; 2014

Gibbs VD. *Self-regulation and Mindfulness: Over 82 Exercises & Worksheets for Sensory Processing Disorder, ADHD, & Autism Spectrum Disorder.* Eau Claire, WI: PESI Publishing & Media; 2017

Gray C. *The New Social Story Book.* 15th anniv ed. Arlington, TX: Future Horizons; 2015

Greene RW. *The Explosive Child: A New Approach for Understanding and Parenting Easily Frustrated, Chronically Inflexible Children.* New York, NY: HarperCollins Publishers; 2014

Harris G, Shea E. *Food Refusal and Avoidant Eating in Children, Including Those With Autism Spectrum Conditions: A Practical Guide for Parents and Professionals.* London, England: Jessica Kingsley Publishers; 2018

Kemper KJ. *Mental Health, Naturally: The Family Guide to Holistic Care for a Healthy Mind and Body.* Elk Grove Village, IL: American Academy of Pediatrics; 2010

Kluth P, Shouse J. *The Autism Checklist: A Practical Reference for Parents and Teachers.* San Francisco, CA: Jossey-Bass; 2009

McClannahan LE, Krantz PJ. *Activity Schedules for Children With Autism: Teaching Independent Behavior.* 2nd ed. Bethesda, MD: Woodbine House; 2010

Moor J. *Playing, Laughing, and Learning With Children on the Autism Spectrum: A Practical Resource of Play Ideas for Parents and Carers.* 2nd ed. London, England: Jessica Kingsley Publishers; 2008

Notbohm E, Zysk V. *1001 Great Ideas for Teaching and Raising Children With Autism or Asperger's.* 2nd rev ed. Arlington, TX: Future Horizons; 2010

Rogers SJ, Dawson G, Vismara LA. *An Early Start for Your Child With Autism: Using Everyday Activities to Help Kids Connect, Communicate, and Learn.* New York, NY: Guilford; 2012

Tarbox J, Bermudez TL. *Treating Feeding Challenges in Autism: Turning the Tables on Mealtime.* London, England: Academic Press; 2017

Wilde KC. *Autistic Logistics: A Parent's Guide to Tackling Bedtime, Toilet Training, Tantrums, Hitting, and Other Everyday Challenges.* London, England: Jessica Kingsley Publishers; 2015

Wilens TE. Hammerness PG. *Straight Talk About Psychiatric Medications for Kids.* 4th ed. New York, NY: Guilford; 2016

Winner MG, Crooke P. *You Are a Social Detective: Explaining Social Thinking to Kids.* Great Barrington, MA: North River Press; 2010

Winner MG, Murphy LK. *Social Thinking and Me.* Santa Clara, CA: Think Social Publishing; 2016

Adolescence and Adulthood

Glasberg BA, LaRue RH. *Functional Behavior Assessment for People With Autism: Making Sense of Seemingly Senseless Behavior.* 2nd ed. Bethesda, MD: Woodbine House; 2015

Koegel LK, LaZebnik C. *Growing Up on the Spectrum: A Guide to Life, Love, and Learning for Teens and Young Adults With Autism and Asperger's.* New York, NY: Penguin Group; 2009

Mahler KJ. *Hygiene and Related Behaviors for Children and Adolescents With Autism Spectrum and Related Disorders: A Fun Curriculum With a Focus on Social Understanding.* Shawnee Mission, KS: AAPC; 2009

McHenry I, Moog C. *The Autism Playbook for Teens: Imagination-Based Mindfulness Activities to Calm Yourself, Build Independence, and Connect With Others.* Oakland, CA: Instant Help Books; 2014

Organization for Autism Research. *Life Journey Through Autism: A Guide for Transition to Adulthood.* Arlington, VA: Organization for Autism Research; 2006. Reaffirmed 2017

O'Toole JC, Bojanowski B. *The Asperkid's (Secret) Book of Social Rules: The Handbook of Not-So-Obvious Social Guidelines for Tweens and Teens With Asperger Syndrome.* London, England: Jessica Kingsley Publishers; 2013

Winner MG, Crooke P. *Socially Curious and Curiously Social: A Social Thinking Guidebook for Bright Teens and Young Adults.* Great Barrington, MA: North River Press; 2011

Magazines and Newsletters

Autism Asperger's Digest
800/674-3771
www.autismdigest.com

Magazine with current research, practical tips, and informative discussions on topics of concern to families with children and adults on the spectrum.

Autism Spectrum News
978/733-4481
www.mhnews-autism.org

Quarterly publication that provides news, information, and resources about scientific research, evidence-based clinical treatments, and family issues.

Appendix B

Emergency Information Form for Children With Autism Spectrum Disorder

Today's date	
Your name	
Do you CONSENT to the release of this form to health care professionals?	● Yes ○ No
Is this a new form or an update?	

Information About the Child

Child's name		Primary address	
Birth date		City, state, zip	
Patient's nickname		Primary language	
Primary means of communication		Does he/she wear a medical ID bracelet?	
Parent/guardian #1		Parent/guardian #2	
Phone number		Phone number	
Emergency contact		Emergency contact	

Providers & Facilities

Care Provider	Provider's Name	Specialties	Office Number, Fax, and E-mail
Primary care			
Specialist 1			
Specialist 2			
Specialist 3			
Specialist 4			
Specialist 5			
Others			
Primary pharmacy (branch, phone, other)			
Anticipated primary emergency department (name, phone, other)			
Anticipated tertiary care center (name, phone, other)			

Clinical Information/Management Data

Diagnoses/past procedures (list all), starting with most important		1
		2
		3
		4
Baseline physical findings		
Baseline vital signs		
Most recent height and weight (including date)		
Baseline neurologic status		
Description of cognitive/developmental age for		
	Receptive language	
	Expressive language	
Description of cognitive skills		
Description of gross motor skills		
Description of fine motor skills		
Comfort items		
Does he/she wander off? If so, to where? Describe.		

Medications		Significant Laboratory Results (eg, blood tests, x-ray, ECG)
1		1
2		2
3		Technology Devices (eg, communication aids)
4		1
5		2
Allergies: Medications/Food to Be Avoided & Why		Procedures to Be Avoided & Why
1		1
2		2
3		3
4		4

Immunizations (mo/y)

DPT dates		Varicella status	
DTaP dates		Hep B dates	
OPV or IPV dates		Hep A dates	
MMR dates		Meningococcal	specify which one if possible
Hib dates		TB status	
Pneumococcal-7		HP virus	
Pneumococcal-13		Influenza	
Rotavirus		Tdap	
Other		Other	

Comments on child, family, or other specific medical issues	

Physician/Provider Signature	Printed Name

American Academy
of Pediatrics

DEDICATED TO THE HEALTH OF ALL CHILDREN™

Appendix C

Early Intervention Program Referral Form

Please complete this form for referring a child to Early Intervention (Part C) if you prefer to do so in writing. Also please indicate the feedback that you want to receive from the Early Intervention Program in response to your referral. Diagnosis of a specific condition or disorder is not necessary for a referral.

Parent/Child Contact Information

Child Name:

Date of Birth: / /   Child Age: (Months)   Gender: ☐ M ☐ F

Home Address:

Parent/Guardian: Relationship to Child:

Primary Language: Home Phone: Other Phone:

Reason(s) for Referral to Early Intervention

(Please check all that apply)

☐ Identified condition or diagnosis (e.g., spina bifida, Down syndrome):

☐ Suspected developmental delay or concern (Please check areas of concern):

  ☐ Motor/Physical ☐ Cognitive ☐ Social/Emotional ☐ Speech/Language ☐ Behavior Other

☐ At Risk (Describe risk factors):

☐ Other (Describe):

Referral Source Contact Information

Person Making Referral: Date of Referral: / /

Address:

Office Phone: Office Fax: E-mail:

Early Intervention Program Contact Information

Program Name:

Address: City: State: Zip:

Office Phone: Office Fax: E-mail:

Feedback Requested by the Referral Source

Date Referral Received: / /   Date of Initial Appointment with Child/Family: / /

Name of Assigned Service Coordinator:

Office Phone: Office Fax: E-mail:

After initial appointment, please send the following information:

☐ Status of Initial Family Contact   ☐ Changes in Services Being Provided

☐ Developmental Evaluation Results   ☐ Periodic Progress Reports/Summaries

☐ Services Being Provided to Child/Family   ☐ Other (Describe):
(Including: names of providers and frequency of services)

Release of Information Consent

I,   (Print name of parent or guardian), give my permission for my pediatric health care provider,

(print provider's name), to share any and all pertinent information regarding my child,

(print child's name), with the early intervention program.

Parent/Legal Guardian Signature: Date: / /

This form is available on the National Center of Medical Home Initiatives for Children with Special Needs website. Go to http://pediatrics.aappublications.org/content/pediatrics/suppl/2007/11/21/120.5.1153.DC1/EI_Referral_Form.pdf to download this form and learn more about Early Intervention.

This form was developed as part of a collaboration between the American Academy of Pediatrics and the Tracking, Referral and Assessment Center for Excellence, Orelena Hawks Puckett Institute, Inc. The development of this form was supported, in part, by funding from the US Department of Education, Office of Special Education Programs, Research to Practice Division (H324G020002).

Reprinted from American Academy of Pediatrics Council on Children with Disabilities. Role of the medical home in family-centered early intervention services.

Appendix D

Medication Flowchart

Patient:			
Medication	**Date Started/ Target Symptom(s)**	**Dosage Changes/ Benefits/Side Effects**	**Date Discontinued/ Reason**

Adapted with permission from Alan Rosenblatt, MD, SC.

Index

A

AAP. *See* American Academy of Pediatrics (AAP)

ABA. *See* Applied behavior analysis (ABA)

ABA Flash Cards (app), 244

ABCs of behavior, 74–75, 123, 248

ABC Tracer (app), 244

Abdominal pain, 58

ABLE accounts, 208–209, 236

Accessible pediatric practices, 171–173

Achieving a Better Life Experience (ABLE) Act, 208–209, 236

Acid reflux and sleep disorders, 128

Adaptive sports and recreation, 199, 251, 266

ADHD. *See* Attention-deficit/hyperactivity disorder (ADHD)

Administration on Intellectual and Developmental Disabilities, 190

Adolescence, 215–216. *See also* Young adults with autism

behavioral concerns during, 225–226

and being out in the world with autism, 227

budding sexuality in, 226–228

encouraging child's daily living skills in, 222

entering adulthood from, 231–233

issues experienced in, 216–217

job options and, 233–235

lingering questions about autism and, 232

medical concerns during, 222–225

postsecondary education and, 231–233

privacy and health examination during, 224

puberty during, 105–106, 223, 226–228

self-advocacy in, 220–222

strengthening community connections in, 230–231

strengthening social skills in, 228–230

transition plan in, 217–220

travel safety during, 225

Adult day program services, 235

Adulthood, entering of, 231–233

Advocacy, autism, 16–17

activities in, 290–291

all parents as, 289

Autistic Self Advocacy Network (ASAN) and, 71

by Eunice Kennedy Shriver, 292–293

getting involved in, 294–295

required skills for, 291–293

road ahead for, 295

self-advocacy in, 220–222

types of, 294

Age at diagnosis of ASD, 42, 43

Age of parents, 21, 35

Aggression and self-injury, 60–61, 73

during adolescence, 225

medications for, 136–137

Air pollutants, 32–33

Alcohol use during pregnancy, 34

α_2-adrenergic agonists, 126, 132, 139

Alternative medicine, 144

American Academy of Ophthalmology, 160

American Academy of Pediatrics (AAP)
  on behavioral optometry, 160
  on chaperones during health
      examinations of adolescents, 224
  emergency information form for children
      with autism, 317–318
  National Center for Medical Home
      Implementation Web site, 225
  resources on autism, 303–304
  Section on Integrative Medicine, 166
  support for ongoing studies on autism,
      283
  on transition planning and long-term
      goals, 223
  universal screening recommendations,
      72
American Association for Pediatric
      Ophthalmology and Strabismus,
      160
American College of Medical Genetics and
      Genomics, 25
American Journal of Psychiatry, 268
American Psychiatric Association, 8
Americans with Disabilities Act, 173
Amino acids, 157
Angelman syndrome, 26, 29
Antecedent in ABCs of behavior, 74–75, 123
Antibiotics, 158
Anticonvulsants, 33
Antiepileptic medications, 125, 126
Antipsychotic medications, 126, 140
Antiviral agents, 158
Anti-yeast treatments, 158–159
Anxiety, 61
  asking for help with, 266
  generalized anxiety disorder, 134
  homework, 175
  medications for, 137
  nonbiological interventions for, 161
  sleep disorders and, 128
  weighted vests for, 88
Applied behavior analysis (ABA), 74–78,
      96, 101
  discrete trial training, 76–77

incidental teaching, 77
  pivotal response training, 78
  verbal behavior, 78
ARCH National Respite Network and
      Resource Center, 254, 260
Aripiprazole (Abilify), 140
ASAN. *See* Autistic Self Advocacy Network
      (ASAN)
ASD. *See* Autism spectrum disorder (ASD)
ASD Video Glossary, 72
Asperger syndrome, 11, 20
Asperger Syndrome and Difficult Moments:
      Practical Solutions for Tantrums,
      Rage, and Meltdowns (Myles), 118
Association of University Centers on
      Disabilities (AUCD), 190
Atlantic, The (journal), 6
ATN. *See* Autism Treatment Network (ATN)
Atomoxetine (Strattera), 140
Attention, joint, 50–51
Attention-deficit/hyperactivity disorder
      (ADHD), 3, 135, 184
  as common associated health problem
      with autism, 60
  medications for, 136
  neurofeedback for, 165
  omega-3 fatty acids and, 151
  yoga for, 164
Atypical antipsychotics, 140
Atypical neuroleptics, 140
Audiologists as members of interdisciplinary
      teams, 65
Auditory integration therapy, 159
Autism
  early diagnoses of, 5–6
  first child diagnosed with, by Leo Kanner, 6
  Freudian psychoanalysts on, 6
  genetic influence and, 8–9
  history of, 5–10
  infantile, 8, 9, 20
  originally classified as form of
      schizophrenia in *DSM*, 8
  public awareness of, 277
  regressive, 48

Autism (journal), 281

Autism and Developmental Disabilities Monitoring (ADDM) Network, 19

Autism champions

Alison Singer, 39

Brenda Smith Myles, 114, 118–119

Carmen Pingree, 16–17

Catherine Lord, 68

Cathy Purple Cherry, 255–256

Cheryl C. Smith, 296

Denise D. Resnik, 201–202

Geraldine Dawson, 286

Jason Cherry, 184–185

Jennifer Wood, 274

Kirsten Sneid, 91–92

Lorri Shealy Unumb, 214

Tim Page, 237–238

Autism Collaboration, Accountability, Research, Education, and Support (CARES) Act, 276

Autism Council of Utah, 296

Autism Diagnostic Interview, Revised (ADI-R), 68

Autism Diagnostic Observation Schedule (ADOS), 68

Autism Hangout, 193

Autism Research and Treatment (journal), 281

Autism Science Foundation, 39, 188

Autism Society of America, 189, 256

Autism Society of the Heartland, 91

Autism Society of Utah, 17

Autism Speaks, 39, 88, 126, 189

Autism spectrum disorder (ASD)

during adolescence (*See* Adolescence)

brain structure differences and, 23–24

causes of (*See* Causes of autism)

challenges of, 21–22, 55–56

cognitive challenges and, 55

common health problems associated with, 56–62

community support for (*See* Community services)

cost of caring for someone with, 203

definitions of, 4, 10

new, 11

diagnosis of (*See* Diagnosis of autism)

early signs of, 7–8

educational services for (*See* Educational services)

effects on families (*See* Family of child who has autism)

everyday strategies for (*See* Everyday strategies)

future of (*See* Future of autism spectrum disorder)

genetics and (*See* Genetic disorders and autism; Genetic factors of autism)

help with understanding, 3–4

in identical twins, 9, 22

interdisciplinary teams and, 62–66

interventions for (*See* Interventions)

language differences and, 46

main deficits of, 80–81

outgrowing of, 4, 5, 92

prevalence of, 4, 19 20

recognizing, 9

research on, 37–38, 281, 283–285

resilience in children with, 271–272

resources on, 303–316

sensory-motor symptoms of, 55–56

sex, biological, and, 4, 24, 42–43, 124–125, 280–281

as urgent public health concern, 20

variance in severity of, 42

what we know and don't know about, 12–13

Autism Spectrum Quotient (AQ)—Adolescent Version, 66

Autism Spectrum Screening Questionnaire (ASSQ), 66

Autism Support Network, 193

Autism Treatment Network (ATN), 282

Autism Wandering Awareness Alerts Response and Education Collaboration, 198

Autistic Self Advocacy Network (ASAN), 71, 221, 222

Autoimmune conditions, 57

B

Babbling, 45
Baby Flash Cards (app), 244
Back pain, 164
BCBAs. *See* Board certified behavior analysts (BCBAs)
Behavioral concerns during adolescence, 225–226
Behavioral intervention plan (BIP), 113
Behavioral optometry, 160
Behavioral therapy, 2
    for sleep problems, 130–134
Behavior in ABCs of behavior, 74–75, 123
Behaviors in school
    challenging, 108, 112–113
    stress and the "rage cycle" and, 113–117
Being away from home, strategies for handling, 242
Being on time strategy, 241
Best Buddies, 105, 230–231
Bettelheim, Bruno, 6, 12
Bifidobacterium, 152
BIP. *See* Behavioral intervention plan (BIP)
Bipolar disorder, 33, 135
    medications for, 137–138
Birth trauma, 36
Blood cancer, 33
Board certified behavior analysts (BCBAs), 76
Body language, 249–250
Bone marrow cancer, 33
Brainstem, 23
Brain structure differences and autism, 23–24
Brief Infant-Toddler Social Emotional Assessment (BITSEA), 66
Broad autism phenotype, 38
Brushing of teeth, 241–242
Bullying, 106

C

Calcium, 148
    alternative sources of, 149
Calm, remaining, 247
Camp Shriver, 292

Cancer, 33, 184–185
Candida infections, 158–159
Cannabidiol, 155–156
Carbone, Paul, 2, 4, 143, 251
Cardiovascular health during adolescence, 223
Care notebooks, 178–179
Carmen B. Pingree Autism Center of Learning, 17, 296
Carnitine, 157
Carnosine, 157
Carson Smith Scholarship, 296
Casein, 13, 14
Causes of autism
    air pollutants, 32–33
    drug exposures, 33
    environmental exposures, 13–14, 29–34
    epigenetic, 29
    gastrointestinal tract abnormalities as, 14, 58
    genetic (*See* Genetic disorders and autism; Genetic factors of autism)
    gluten and casein as possible (*See* Gluten-free/casein-free [GFCF] diet)
    ongoing research into, 37–38
    thimerosal as, 14
    vaccines as possible, 13–14, 30–32
CDC. *See* Centers for Disease Control and Prevention (CDC)
Celiac disease, 57, 147
Center for Parent Information and Resources (CPIR), 189–190
Centers for Autism and Developmental Disabilities Research and Epidemiology, 37
Centers for Disease Control and Prevention (CDC), 4, 12, 19–20, 24, 276
    on age at diagnosis, 43
    Centers for Autism and Developmental Disabilities Research and Epidemiology, 37
    future of diagnosis and, 277–278
    on intellectual disability and autism, 55
    on teen suicide rates, 139
    vaccine schedule created by, 31

Centers for Medicare & Medicaid Services
(CMS), 211
Certified Autism Specialists, 256
Challenges of autism, 21–22
cognitive, 55
Challenging behaviors in schools, 108, 112–113
decision to use medication for, 122–124
stress and the "rage cycle" in, 113–117
Chaperones, medical, 224
CHARGE (Childhood Autism Risks from
Genetics and the Environment), 37
Chelation therapy, 33, 162–163
Cherry, Cathy Purple, 255–256
Cherry, Jason, 184–185, 255
Cherry, Matthew, 184–185, 255–256
Cherry, Samantha, 184, 255
Childhood Autism Syndrome Test (CAST), 66
Child neurologists as members of
interdisciplinary teams, 65
Children's Health Insurance Program
(CHIP), 211–212
Children's Hospital of Philadelphia, 37
CHIP. *See* Children's Health Insurance
Program (CHIP)
Chromosome microarray analysis, 27
Chromosomes, 22, 25
and fragile X syndrome, 21, 25, 282
Churches and synagogues, 195
Classroom options, 102–103
Clear directions, giving, 250, 253
Clonidine (Catapres or Kapvay), 126, 132, 139
CMS. *See* Centers for Medicare & Medicaid
Services (CMS)
Cognitive challenges and autism, 55
Colleges and universities, community
services from, 190–191
Combating Autism Act (CAA), 276
Communication and Symbolic Behavior
Scales Developmental Profile
Infant-Toddler Checklist (CSBS
DP ITC), 66
Community connections, strengthening
adolescents', 230–231

Community services, 187–188
accessing, 196–199
adaptive sports and recreation, 199
Autism Science Foundation, 39, 188
Autism Society of America, 189
Autism Speaks, 39, 88, 126, 189
and businesses that cater to autism,
194–195
Center for Parent Information and
Resources (CPIR), 189–190
colleges and universities, 190–191
final word on, 200
many forms of, 188–191
online support, 192–194
power of support groups and, 191–192
Compassion in pediatric care, 176
Complementary medicine, 144
Comprehensive evaluation, 63
Congenital rubella syndrome, 21, 33
Consequence in ABCs of behavior, 74–75, 123
Consistent responses to behavior, parents',
246
Constipation, 126–127, 152
Constructive play, 53
Continuous and comprehensive care in
medical homes, 173–174
Conventional medicine, 144
Conversational listening skills, 250
Cooling-off area, 252
Coordinated care, 174
Copy number variants, 24
Craniosacral therapy, 160
Cultural competence, 176

D

Daily living skills, encouragement of, 222
Dairy products, 148
Dating, 232
Dawson, Geraldine, 286
DDS. *See* Disability Determination Services
(DDS)
Declarative language, 81
Delayed sleep-phase syndrome, 128, 129

Depression, 61–62
major, 134–135
medications for, 137
in parents, 268, 271
recognizing, 271
sleep disorders and, 128
Developmental, Individual Difference,
Relationship-based (DIR)
approach, 78–79
Developmental pediatricians as members of
interdisciplinary teams, 65
Developmental relationship interventions,
78–83
naturalistic developmental behavioral
interventions (NDBIs), 81–83
Relationship Development Intervention
(RDI), 80–81
Developmental screening, 63
questionnaires for, 66
Developmental surveillance, 63
Dextroamphetamine (Dexedrine), 139
Diabetes, gestational, 36
Diagnosis of autism, 1, 3, 41
age at, 42, 43
based on observations and parental
input, 41, 43
as challenging, 64
in children with intellectual disability or
global developmental delay, 42
common features of autism and, 55–56
common health problems and, 56–62
difficulty of, 5, 41–42
discussed with child, 109–111, 221
early monitoring of infants for, 43–45
early signs and, 7–8, 45–54
effects on family, 258
future of, 277–279
grieving with, 1, 66–67, 267
increase in, 4–5, 13, 19–21
interdisciplinary assessment team in, 65
professionals involved in, 62–66
screening questionnaires in, 66
sex, biological, and, 42–43
unnecessary tests for, 163

unusual language development and,
45–48
*Diagnostic and Statistical Manual of Mental
Disorders* (DSM)
first and second editions of, 8
third edition of, 9, 20
fourth edition of, 10
pervasive developmental disorders
in, 11
fifth edition of, 10, 11, 20
on sensory challenges with ASD, 87
Diagnostic substitution, 20
Diarrhea, 127, 152
caused by nystatin, 159
Dietary changes
for anxiety, 161
gluten-free/casein-free (GFCF) diet, 2, 13,
14, 147–149
for lactose intolerance, 128
Dietary supplements
amino acids, 157
cannabidiol, 155–156
daily recommended and tolerable upper
intake levels, 154
GFCF diet and, 149
melatonin, 131–132, 154, 155
multivitamins, 152–153
omega-3 fatty acids, 151
for oxidative stress, 156
probiotics, 151–152
vitamin B_6 and magnesium, 150–151
vitamin C, 153
Dimethylglycine, 156
Diphenhydramine (Benadryl), 132
DIR. *See* Developmental, Individual
Difference, Relationship-based
(DIR) approach
DIRFloortime, 79
Disability Determination Services (DDS), 204
Discover Theatre, 194
Discrete trial training (DTT), 76–77
Discriminative stimulus in discrete trial
training, 76

Discussing autism diagnosis with children, 109–111

Disruptive mood dysregulation disorder (DMDD), 135
medications for, 137–138

DMDD. *See* Disruptive mood dysregulation disorder (DMDD)

DNA, 22
Early Autism Risk Longitudinal Investigation (EARLI) and, 37
epigenetics and, 29
and fragile X syndrome, 21
genetic testing of, 27–28
and Rett syndrome, 26

Docosahexaenoic acid, 151

Doctor visits, 179–182. *See also* Pediatricians

Dogs, service, 193

Dopamine, 153

Downtime at school, 252

Dressing, self-, 243

Driving, 232

Driving different routes, strategies for handling, 243

Drug exposures during pregnancy as risk factor, 33–34

DSM. *See Diagnostic and Statistical Manual of Mental Disorders (DSM)*

DTT. *See* Discrete trial training (DTT)

Dynamic education program, 81

E

Early Autism Risk Longitudinal Investigation (EARLI), 37

Early childhood special education (ECSE) programs, 93, 100

Early Intervention (EI) Program, 88–89
accessing, 196–197
referral form, 319

Early intervention programs, 93

Early monitoring for autism, 43–45

Early signs of autism, 7–8, 45–54

Early Start Denver Model (ESDM), 82–83

Eastern Michigan University, 265

Echoic words, 78

Echolalia, 47
tics and, 59

Eczema, 152

Educational services, 93–94. *See also* School(s)
accessing, 197, 199
after high school, 231–233
difficulties in school for children with autism, 108–117
elementary school, 102–104
guidelines for teaching children with autism, 99–108
high school, 107–108
Individualized Education Program (IEP) and, 94–97
Individuals with Disabilities Education Act (IDEA) and, 20, 89, 94
middle school, 104–106
National Professional Development Center (NPDC) on Autism Spectrum Disorder, 99
preschool, 91, 100–101
TEACCH (Treatment and Education of Autistic and related Communication-handicapped CHildren) method and, 97–99

EI. *See* Early Intervention (EI) Program

Eicosapentaenoic acid, 151

Electroencephalogram (EEG), 124–126

Elementary school education, 102–104

Elopement, 198

Emergency information form, 317–318

Emily Post's Etiquette, 237

Emotional referencing, 80

Encephalopathy, 36

Encopresis, 127

Environmental exposures and risk for autism, 13–14, 29–34

Environmental Influences on Child Health Outcomes program, 38

Epidiolex, 155

Epigenetics, 29

Epilepsy, 57
medications for, 33, 124–126
sleep disorders and, 128

Epilepsy Foundation of America, 126

Equine-assisted therapy, 165

Escitalopram (Lexapro), 138

ESDM. *See* Early Start Denver Model (ESDM)

Everyday strategies, 239–240

    being away from home, 242

    being on time, 241

    for dealing with child's maladaptive
        behaviors, 245–249

    driving different routes, 243

    fear of transitions, 244

    for getting through the day, 240–245

    helping child identify self, 243

    routines, 240–241

    self-dressing, 243

    shoe tying, 242

    technology use, 244–245

    teeth brushing, 241–242

Exercise, importance of, 254, 267

Exfoliative dermatitis, 159

Expanding College for Exceptional Learners,
    92

Extinction burst, 131

Extracurricular activities, 199, 251

Eye contact, 248

F

Facial expressions, 249–250

Family-centered medical homes, 173

Family health factors and risk for autism,
    35–36

Family of child who has autism, 257–258

    challenges for siblings in, 261–262

    dealing with stress in, 265–267

    final word on, 273

    grandparents in, 261

    marriage health in, 259–260

    promoting sibling harmony in, 262–265

    resilience in, 271–272

    self-care in, 253–254, 267–271

Family Voices, 88, 260

FBA. *See* Functional behavioral analysis (FBA)

Fear of transitions, 244

Federal Insurance Contributions Act (FICA),
    205, 206

Fetal alcohol syndrome, 34, 184

Fetal distress, 36

Fiber, alternative sources of, 149

FICA. *See* Federal Insurance Contributions
    Act (FICA)

15q duplication syndromes, 27

Financial assistance, 203

    government health insurance, 210–212

    government programs for, 204–210

    from private organizations, 213

    special needs trust (SNT), 208

    Stephen Beck Jr., Achieving a Better
        Life Experience (ABLE) Act and,
        208–209, 236

    Tax Equity and Financial Responsibility
        Act (TEFRA) of 1982, 210

Flexible thinking, 81

"Floortime" model, 79

Flowchart, medication, 321

Fluoxetine (Prozac), 138

Focused interventions to develop specific
    skills, 83–88

Folate, 156

Folic acid, 156

Folinic acid, 156

Food and Drug Administration (FDA), US,
    155–156, 282

Foresight and hindsight, 81

4 Paws for Ability, 193

Fragile X syndrome (FXS), 21, 25, 282

Freudian psychoanalysis, 6

Friendships, 52–53

    in middle school, 105

Full mainstreaming

    with support, 103

    without support, 103

Functional behavioral analysis (FBA), 76,
    108, 112

Future of autism spectrum disorder, 275–276

    addressing the entire spectrum, 279–281

    advocacy and, 295

    earlier and better diagnosis in, 277–279

federal leadership in, 276–277

improving treatment in, 281–283

support for research and, 283–285

FXS. *See* Fragile X syndrome (FXS)

G

Games, 249–250

Gastroenterologists, 183

Gastroesophageal reflux and sleep disorders, 128

Gastrointestinal problems

gastrointestinal tract abnormalities, 14, 57–58

medications for, 126–128

probiotics and, 151–152

sleep disorders and, 128

Gene mutations, 22

epigenetics and, 29

Generalization, 70

Generalized anxiety disorder, 134

Generalizing new skills, 73

Genetic counselors as members of interdisciplinary teams, 65

Genetic disorders and autism

Angelman syndrome, 26

15q duplication syndromes, 27

fragile X syndrome, 25

phenylketonuria, 26

Rett syndrome, 26

seizures and epilepsy and, 125

16p11.2 deletion syndrome, 27

16p11.2 duplication syndrome, 27

tuberous sclerosis complex, 26

Genetic factors of autism, 8–9, 21, 22–25, 38

epigenetics and, 29

future of, 282

Geneticists, 182

as members of interdisciplinary teams, 65

Genetic testing, 27–28

medications and, 140

German measles, 33

Gestational diabetes, 36

Getting through the day, strategies for, 240–245

GFCF diet. *See* Gluten-free/casein-free (GFCF) diet

Giant words, 48

Gluten-free/casein-free (GFCF) diet, 2, 13, 14, 147–148

alternative sources of key nutrients and, 149

anxiety and, 161

deciding whether to try, 148–149

Goals, development of, 70–71

Got Transition/Center for Health Care Transition Improvement Web site, 236

Government health insurance, 210–212. *See also* Medicaid

Government programs

applying for, 206–207

home and community-based service waivers, 207–210

Social Security Disability Insurance (SSDI), 205–206

Supplemental Security Income (SSI), 204–205

Government Web sites, 304–305

Graduated extinction, 130

Grandparents, 261

Greater Kansas City Autism Initiative, 91

Greenspan, Stanley, 79

Greenspan Floortime, 79–80

Grieving with autism diagnosis, 1, 66–67

Guanfacine (Tenex or Intuniv), 126, 132, 139

Gutstein, Steven, 80

H

Having an Electroencephalogram: A Guide for Parents (Autism Speaks), 126

HBOT. *See* Hyperbaric oxygen therapy (HBOT)

HCBS. *See* Home and Community-Based Services (HCBS) Waiver program

Health care teams, 65, 182–183

interdisciplinary assessment team, 65

Health insurance
  coverage for ICAM under, 166–167
  government, 210–212
  private, 212–213
  push for coverage of autism in, 281
Health problems common with autism, 56–62
  during adolescence, 222–225
  aggression and self-injury, 60–61, 73
  anxiety disorders, 61
  attention-deficit/hyperactivity disorder, 60
  depression, 61–62
  gastrointestinal disorders, 14, 57–58
  obesity, 59–60
  seizures and epilepsy, 57
  sleep disorders, 59
  tics, 59
Health supervision visits, 72, 172
  during adolescence, 223
Healthy Bodies toolkit, 228
Heart of Sailing, 194
Heavy metals, 33
Herzog, Nicole Ashley, 297–299
Heterogeneity, 279
High school education, 107–108
Hodgkin lymphoma, 184
Home and Community-Based Services
      (HCBS) Waiver program, 207–210
Home base, 116
Horses, therapy with, 165
Housing options for people with autism, 232
Human Resources and Services
      Administration, 276
Humor, 248
Hydroxyzine (Atarax or Vistaril), 133
Hyperbaric oxygen therapy (HBOT), 163
Hypersensitivity, 55–56
Hyposensitivity, 55

I

IAN. *See* Interactive Autism Network (IAN)
ICAM. *See* Integrative, complementary, and
      alternative medicine (ICAM)
IDEA. *See* Individuals with Disabilities
      Education Act (IDEA)

Identical twins, 9, 22
IEP. *See* Individualized Education Program
      (IEP)
Incidental teaching, 77
Inclusion, 102
Inclusive individual support model, 231
Individualized Education Program (IEP),
      94–97, 197, 199, 217, 274
Individualized Education Program (IEP):
      Summary, Process and Practical Tips
      (Autism Speaks), 97
Individualized Family Service Plan (IFSP), 89
Individualized Plan for Employment (IPE),
      234–235
Individuals with Disabilities Education Act
      (IDEA), 20, 89, 94, 197, 217
Infantile autism, 8, 9, 20
Infants, early monitoring for autism in, 43–45
Infections
  interventions that eliminate, 157–159
  during pregnancy as risk factor, 33–34
Inorganic mercury, 33
Integration, 102
Integrative, complementary, and alternative
      medicine (ICAM), 142, 143–144
  defining, 144–146
  dietary supplements in, 150–156
  final word on, 167–168
  finding practitioners of, 165–166
  insurance coverage for, 166–167
  interventions that eliminate infections,
      157–159
  mind-body therapies, 164–165
  nonbiological interventions, 159–162
  supplements for oxidative stress in, 156
  therapies that are too good to be true
      in, 167
  therapies to avoid in, 162–164
Integrative medicine, 144–145
Intellectual and Developmental Disabilities
      Research Centers, 191
Intellectual disability, 42, 55
  adolescence and, 216–217
  seizures and epilepsy and, 125

Interactive Autism Network (IAN), 272, 285

Interagency Autism Coordinating Committee (IACC), 276, 280–281

Interdisciplinary assessment team, 65

Interests of child
acknowledgment of, 247
restricted, 54
shared with teachers, 252

Inter-pregnancy interval, 35

Interventions, 69. *See also* Medications
applied behavior analysis (ABA), 74–78, 96, 101
components of good plan in, 72–74
developing goals and treatment plan for, 70–71
Developmental, Individual Difference, Relationship-based (DIR) approach, 78–79
developmental relationship, 78–83
discrete trial training (DTT), 76–77
focused to develop specific skills, 83–88
future of, 281–283
how to access autism, 88–90
incidental teaching in, 77
naturalistic developmental behavioral interventions (NDBIs), 81–83
occupational therapy, 86–87
pivotal response training (PRT), 78
Relationship Development Intervention (RDI), 80–81
sensory integration therapy, 87–88
for sleep problems, behavioral, 130–134
social skills, 84–85
speech-language therapy, 83–87
symbolic (or pretend) play skills, 85–86
verbal behavior (VB), 78
when to begin, 71–74

Intravenous immunoglobulin (IVIG), 157–158

Intra-verbal language, 78

IPE. *See* Individualized Plan for Employment (IPE)

Iron, alternative sources of, 149

Irritability and severe disruptive behavior, medications for, 136–137

Irritable bowel syndrome, 152

IVIG. *See* Intravenous immunoglobulin (IVIG)

J

Jaundice, 36

Jewish Social Service Agency, 213

Job options for young adults with autism, 233–235

Johns Hopkins University, 5, 37

Joint attention, 50–51

Joseph P. Kennedy Jr. Foundation, 292

Journal of Autism and Developmental Disorders, 281

Journal of Child Psychology and Psychiatry, 8

Journal of Developmental and Behavioral Pediatrics, 64

K

Kaiser Permanente, 37

Kanner, Leo, 5–6, 19

Kansas Center for Autism Research and Training (K-CART), 91

Kansas Coalition for Autism Legislation, 91

Kennedy, Edward M., 292, 294

Kennedy, John F., 292

Kennedy, Joseph, 292

Kennedy, Rose, 292

Kennedy, Rosemary, 292

Kennedy Krieger Institute, 259

Kid Calculator (app), 244

Klein, Stanley, 267

Krug Asperger's Disorder Index (KADI), 66

L

Lactobacillus, 152

Lactose intolerance, 128

Lamotrigine (Lamictal), 125

Language development, unusual, 45–46, 67
developmental milestones and, 43–45, 49–50
echolalia, 47
giant words, 48
pop-up words, 47–48

Leadership Education in
    Neurodevelopmental and Related
    Disabilities (LEND) Program, 284
Leadership Education in
    Neurodevelopmental and Related
    Disabilities (LEND) programs,
    190–191
Lead exposure, 33
"Leaky gut," 58, 147
"Learn the Signs. Act Early" campaign, 12
Least restrictive environments, 102
*Let Me Hear Your Voice: A Family's Triumph Over
    Autism* (Maurice), 201
Levetiracetam (Keppra), 125
Limbic system, 23
Listening skills for school, 252
Living out loud, 251
Long-term planning for people with autism,
    235–236
Lord, Catherine, 68
Lovaas, O. Ivar, 68, 75–76
Lovaas Model, 75
Low birth weight, 36
Low Intensity Support Services (LISS)
    program, 213

M

Macrocephaly, 23
Magnesium, 150–151
Mainstreaming, 102
    partial, 102
    with support, full, 103
    without support, full, 103
Major depression, 134–135
Maladaptive behaviors
    actions to take before start of, 247–248
    during adolescence, 225–226
    behavioral intervention plan (BIP) for, 113
    behavioral therapy for, 2, 130–134
    "rage cycle" and, 113–117, 247
    in school, 108, 112–113
    strategies for dealing with, 245–249
Mand words, 78

Manic depression. *See* Bipolar disorder
Marijuana, 155
Marriage health, 259–260
Massage, 161, 165
Maternal and Child Health Bureau, 20, 190
Maurice, Catherine, 201
Measles-mumps-rubella (MMR) vaccine, 14,
    30, 34
Medicaid, 90, 207, 211
    Home and Community-Based Services
        (HCBS) Waiver program and,
        209–210
    special needs trust (SNT) and, 208
    Tax Equity and Financial Responsibility
        Act (TEFRA) of 1982 and, 210
Medical bracelets, 243
Medical chaperones, 224
Medical conditions, treatment of associated
    during adolescence, 222–225
    gastrointestinal problems, 126–128
    seizures/epilepsy, 124–126
    sleep disturbances, 128–130
    tics, 126
Medical Home Portal, 126
Medical homes
    accessible, 171–173
    compassion in, 176
    continuous and comprehensive care in,
        173–174
    coordinated care by, 174
    cultural competence in, 176
    family-centered, 173
Medical insurance, 90
Medications, 121–122. *See also* Interventions
    α_2-adrenergic agonists, 126, 132, 139
    for associated medical conditions,
        124–130
    atypical antipsychotics, 140
    decision to start, 122–124
    flowchart, 321
    gastrointestinal, 126–128
    genetic testing and, 140
    guidelines for using, 141–142
    melatonin, 131–132, 154, 155, 162

precautions with, 138, 141
for psychiatric conditions, 135–140
psychotropic, 122
seizure/epilepsy, 33, 124–126
selective norepinephrine reuptake
    inhibitors (SNRIs), 140
selective serotonin reuptake inhibitors
    (SSRIs), 34, 138–139
sleep, 131–134
stimulant, 139
tics, 126
trial period for, 141
Melatonin, 131–132, 154, 155, 162
Meltdown/rage in "rage cycle," 116–117, 247
analyzing, 248
medications for, 136–137
Methylation, 156
Methylcobalamin, 156
Methyl groups, 29
Methylphenidate (Ritalin), 139
Middle school education, 104–106
Mild autism
    language development and, 46
    treatment needs and, 74
Milestones, developmental, 43–45, 49–50
DIR approach and, 79
Mind-body therapies, 164–165
Mindfulness-Based Stress Reduction
    program, 254, 267
MIND Institute, 37
Mind-reading games, 250
Mini-tasks, 253
MiraLax, 127
Mirtazapine (Remeron), 133
Mixed/hybrid model of postsecondary
    education, 231
MMR vaccine. *See* Measles-mumps-rubella
    (MMR) vaccine
Modified Checklist for Autism in Toddlers,
    Revised, with Follow-Up
    (M-CHAT-R/F), 66
Monitoring, early autism, 43–45
Motor skill differences with autism, 56
tics and, 59

Multiple myeloma, 33
Multivitamins, 152–153
Music therapy, 165
Myles, Brenda Smith, 114, 118–119, 247, 251

N

Name, response to, 51–52
National Center for Complementary and
    Integrative Health, 146
National Center for Family/Professional
    Partnerships, 260
National Council for Accreditation of Teacher
    Education, 119
National Institute of Child Health and
    Human Development, 191, 292
National Institutes of Health, 146, 276
    on neurofeedback therapy, 164–165
National Professional Development Center
    (NPDC) on Autism Spectrum
    Disorder, 99
National Survey of Children's Health, 19–20
Naturalistic developmental behavioral
    interventions (NDBIs), 81–83
Natural language paradigm, 78
NDBIs. *See* Naturalistic developmental
    behavioral interventions (NDBIs)
Necrotizing enterocolitis, 152
Neocortex, 24
Neurodevelopmental pediatricians, 182
Neurodiversity movement, 71
Neurofeedback therapy (NFT), 164–165
Neurofibromatosis type 1, 282
Neurologists, child, 182
    as members of interdisciplinary teams, 65
Neurotransmitters, 153
New England Journal of Medicine, 30
NFT. *See* Neurofeedback therapy (NFT)
Nonbiological interventions
    auditory integration therapy, 159
    behavioral optometry, 160
    craniosacral therapy, 160
    sensory integration therapy, 87–88,
        159–162
Norepinephrine, 153

NPDC. *See* National Professional
    Development Center (NPDC) on
    Autism Spectrum Disorder
Nursing care coordinators, 183
Nutritionists, 183
Nystatin, 159

O

OAR. *See* Organization for Autism Research
    (OAR)
Obama, Barack, 276, 277
Obesity, 59–60
    during adolescence, 223
Obsessive-compulsive disorder (OCD), 59, 135
    medications for, 136
Obstructive sleep apnea, 128, 129
Occupational therapists (OTs), 87
    as members of interdisciplinary teams, 65
Occupational therapy, 86–87
OCD. *See* Obsessive-compulsive disorder
    (OCD)
Omega-3 fatty acids, 151
Omeprazole (Prilosec), 128
One-step directions, 246
Online support, 192–194
*Opening Doors to Self-determination Skills:
    Planning for Life After High School*
    (Wisconsin Department of Public
    Instruction), 221
Operants, 78
Optometry, behavioral, 160
Organization for Autism Research (OAR), 274
Orthogenic School, 6
OTs. *See* Occupational therapists (OTs)
Outgrowing of autism, 4, 5, 92
Oxcarbazepine (Trileptal), 125
Oxidative stress, 156
Oxytocin, 29

P

Page, Tim, 237–238
Pain, abdominal, 58

Parents, 1, 143
    as advocates, 289
    age of, as factor in increased risk of
        autism, 21, 35
    becoming educated about autism, 268
    becoming good at planning, 268
    being a good partner to pediatricians,
        176–177
    bottom line for, 15
    consistent responses by, 246
    dealing with maladaptive behaviors in
        children, 245–249
    depression in, 268, 271
    grieving with autism diagnosis, 1, 66–67,
        267
    importance of exercise for, 254, 267
    importance of sleep for, 254, 270
    keeping care notebooks, 178–179
    learning to accept help, 270
    looking for the joy in raising their child,
        270–271
    marriage health of, 259–260
    resilience in, 271–272
    self-care for, 253–254, 267–271
    spending time with friends, 268
    taking children to doctor visits, 179–182
    working with interdisciplinary teams,
        62–66
    working with teachers, 252–253
Parent's Observations of Social Interactions
    (POSI), 66
Partial mainstreaming, 102
Patient Protection and Affordable Care Act,
    212
Pediatricians, 169–170
    being a good parent partner to, 176–177
    developmental, 65, 182
    final word on partnering with, 183
    in health care teams, 65, 182–183
    as parents of children with autism, 1–2,
        143, 251
    parents taking concerns over autism to,
        62–66

practice of, as child's medical home,
171–176
privacy for adolescents' examinations
by, 224
transition planning and, 223–225
visits with, 179–182
what to expect from, 170–171
Pediatric practices
accessible, 171–173
compassion in, 176
continuous and comprehensive care in,
173–174
coordinated care by, 174
cultural competence in, 176
family-centered, 173
Pediatrics (journal), 267
Peers, circle of, 250, 252
Pervasive developmental disorders, 11
Pesticides, 33, 147
Phenobarbital, 125
Phenylalanine, 26
Phenylketonuria, 26
Picture Exchange Communication System,
84
Pikes Peak Therapeutic Riding Center, 194
Pingree, Carmen, 16–17
Pivotal response training (PRT), 78
Planning skills for parents, 268
Plastic exposure, 33
Play, pretend, 52–53
Play and Language for Autistic Youngsters
(PLAY) Project, 80
Poison Help line, 142
Polychlorinated biphenyls, 33
Polysomnography, 129–130
Pop-up words, 47–48
Positive reinforcement, 246
Post–high school education, 231–233
Postsecondary education, 231–233
Pragmatic communication, 83
Pragmatic language, 46
Praise, frequent, 253
Precision medicine, 140

Pregnancy
alcohol use during, 34
amount of time between, 35
complications, newborn's health and, 36
exposure to drugs during, 33–34
gestational diabetes, 36
infections during, 33–34
Preschool programs, 91, 100–101
Pretend play skills, 52–53
interventions for, 85–86
Preterm birth, 36
Priapism, 134
Private health insurance, 212–213
Private organizations, assistance from, 213
Probiotics, 151–152
Program for Infants and Toddlers with
Disabilities, 89
Program for the Education and Enrichment
of Relationship Skills, 86, 229
Prompts in discrete trial training, 77
Protein, 148
alternative sources of, 149
PRT. *See* Pivotal response training (PRT)
Psychiatric conditions
common, 134–135
common medications for, 135–140
Psychiatrists, 183
as members of interdisciplinary teams,
65
Psychologists, 183
as members of interdisciplinary teams,
65
Psychotropic medications, 122
Puberty, 105–106, 223
Public awareness of autism, 277
Purkinje cells, 23
Pyridoxine, 150–151

Q

Questionnaires, autism screening, 66

R

Race as risk factor for autism, 4
Radiographs, 41
"Rage cycle" and stress, 113–117, 247, 248
Rain Man (movie), 55
Ramelteon (Rozerem), 132
Randomized, controlled clinical trials (RCTs),
    145, 146
    on cannabidiols, 155
Ranitidin (Zantac), 127–128
Rapport with child, 246
RCT. *See* Randomized, controlled clinical
    trials (RCTs)
RDI. *See* Relationship Development
    Intervention (RDI)
Recovery in "rage cycle," 117, 247
Recreation opportunities, 199, 251, 266
Redirecting, 115
Registered dieticians, 183
Regressive autism, 48
Relational information processing, 81
Relationship Development Intervention
    (RDI), 80–81
Religious services, 195
Removal of child from stressful situations,
    247–248
Repetitive and unusual behaviors, 53–54
Research, autism, 37–38, 281, 283–285
Resilience, 271–272
Resnik, Denise D., 201–202
Resources
    AAP, 303–304
    book, 313–316
    educational and therapeutic
        organizations, 306–307
    government Web sites, 304–305
    magazine and newsletter, 316
    other associations and, 308–313
Respite care, 254, 260
Response to name, 51–52
Restless legs syndrome, 128, 129
Restricted interests, 54
Rett syndrome, 26
Rimland, Bernard, 8

Risk factors
    drugs during pregnancy, 33
    environmental exposures, 13–14, 29–34
    family health factors and, 35–36
    infections during pregnancy, 33–34
    parental age, 21, 35
    race, 4
    sex, biological, 4, 24
Risperidone (Risperdal), 140
Ritualistic play, 53
Routines
    driving different routes and, 243
    for getting through the day, 240–241, 246
    supporting, 115
    visual schedules for, 247, 252
Rubella, 33
Rumbling in the "rage cycle," 114–116, 247
Run for Autism, 274
Rush University Medical Center Autism
        Resource Directory, 187
Ryan's Law, 214

S

Saccharomyces, 152
S-adenosylhomocysteine (SAM-e), 156
Safe space, 252
Safety
    travel, for adolescents with autism, 225
    wandering and, 198
Savants, 55
Scheduled awakenings, 131
Schedules, visual, 247, 252
Schive, Kim, 267
Schizophrenia, 5, 8
    wheat in diets of patients with, 147
School(s). *See also* Educational services
    accessing services provided by, 197–199
    challenging behaviors in, 108–113
    circle of peers in, 250, 252
    downtime at, 252
    elementary, 102–104
    high, 107–108
    home reinforcement of activities
        from, 253

middle, 104–106

mini-tasks in, 253

postsecondary, 231–233

preschool(s), 91, 100–101

safe space/cooling-off area in, 252

tips for when child goes to, 252–253

Schopler, Eric, 97

Scientific American (magazine), 6

Screening, developmental, 63

questionnaires for, 66

Secretin, 163–164

Section 1915(c), Social Security Act, 207

Seizures and epilepsy, 57

medications for, 33, 124–126

Selective norepinephrine reuptake inhibitors (SNRIs), 140

Selective serotonin reuptake inhibitors (SSRIs), 34, 138–139

Self-advocacy, 220–222

Self-awareness, 106

Self-care by parents, 253–254, 267–271

Self-contained classrooms, 102

Self-dressing, 243

Self-injury, 60–61

during adolescence, 225

medications for, 136–137

Self-soothing techniques, 128

Sensory integration therapy, 87–88, 159

Sensory issues, 248

Sensory-motor stage, 52

Sensory-motor symptoms of autism, 55–56

Serotonin, 153

Sertraline (Zoloft), 138

Service dogs, 193

Severity of ASD, 42

Sex, biological, and autism, 4, 24, 280–281

diagnosis and, 42–43

seizures and epilepsy and, 125

Sexuality, emerging, 105–106, 223, 226–228

Shape Builder (app), 244

Shealy, Ryan, 214

Sheely, Rachelle, 80

Shoe tying, 242

Shriver, Eunice Kennedy, 292–293

Siblings, 38, 184–185

challenges for, 261–262

promoting harmony among, 262–265

Siblings of Autism, 184, 185

Signs of ASD, early, 7–8

Simon's Foundation Autism Research Initiative, 38

Singer, Alison, 39

16p11.2 deletion syndrome, 27

16p11.2 duplication syndrome, 27

Skinner, B.F., 74, 78

Sleep diaries, 129

Sleep disturbances, 59

causes of, 128–130

medications for, 131–132, 131–134, 137, 154, 155, 162

in middle school children, 105

in parents, 254, 270

sleep hygiene and behavioral treatments of, 130–134, 133

yoga for, 164

Sleep hygiene, 130, 133

Smith, Cheryl C., 296

Sneid, Kirsten, 91–92

Social Communication Questionnaire (SCQ), 66

Social coordination, 80

Social orienting, 51–52

Social Security Act, 205, 207

Social Security Administration (SSA), 206–207

Social Security Disability Insurance (SSDI), 205–206

applying for, 206–207

Social skills

in adolescence, 228–230

deficits in, 48

joint attention, 50–51

pretend play skills and friendships, 52–53

repetitive and unusual behaviors, 53–54

restricted interests, 54

social orienting, 51–52

Social skills (*continued*)
  developmental interventions for, 84–85
  encouraging, 249–251
  theory of mind and, 230
Social stories, 249, 250
Social workers, 183
  as members of interdisciplinary teams, 65
Southwest Autism Research & Resource
    Center (SARRC), 201
SPARK Study, 38, 285
Special needs trust (SNT), 208
Special Olympics, 231, 292
Special Playdate, 194
Speech-language pathologists as members
    of interdisciplinary teams, 65
Speech-language therapy, 83–86
Sports, adaptive, 199, 251
SSA. *See* Social Security Administration (SSA)
SSI. *See* Supplemental Security Income (SSI)
SSRIs. *See* Selective serotonin reuptake
    inhibitors (SSRIs)
Starfall ABCs (app), 244
Stephen Beck Jr., Achieving a Better Life
    Experience (ABLE) Act,
    208–209, 236
Stereotypies, 53–54
Stimulants, 139
Strategic Plan for Autism Spectrum Disorder,
    2016-2017 (Interagency Autism
    Coordinating Committee), 280
Stress
  aggression and parental, 73
  asking for help with, 266
  dealing with family, 265–267
  finding ways to reduce parental, 254
  goals for reducing, 70
  "rage cycle" and, 113–117, 247, 248
  remaining calm during, 247
  of travel, 269–270
Study to Explore Early Development, 37
Supplemental care trust, 208

Supplemental Security Income (SSI),
    204–205
  applying for, 206–207
  special needs trust (SNT) and, 208
Support groups
  online, 192–194
  for parents, 254
  power of, 191–192
Surveillance, developmental, 63
Symbolic play skills, 85–86

T

Tactile defensiveness, 56
Tacts, words as, 78
Tantrums
  during adolescence, 225
  medications for, 136–137
Tax Equity and Financial Responsibility Act
    (TEFRA) of 1982, 210
TEACCH (Treatment and *Education*
    of Autistic and related
    Communication-handicapped
    CHildren), 97–99
Teachers and parents working together,
    252–253
Technology use, 244–245
Teeth brushing, 241–242
TEFRA. *See* Tax Equity and Financial
    Responsibility Act (TEFRA) of 1982
Television and movies for teaching social
    skills, 249–250
Temporal lobes, 23
Thalidomide, 33
Theory of mind, 230
Thimerosal, 14, 30–31
Thompson Center for Autism and
    Neurodevelopmental
    Disabilities, 91
Tics, 59
  during adolescence, 223
  medications for, 126
Title V, Social Security Act, 205
Topiramate (Topamax), 125, 126
Touch, gentle, 56, 247

Tourette syndrome, 59
    medications for, 126
Transition plans, 217–220
    long-term, 235–236
    team members for, 219
Transitions, fear of, 244
Travel
    safety for adolescents, 225
    stress of, 269–270
Trazodone (Desyrel), 133–134
Treatment plan, development of, 70–71
Trial period, medication, 141
Triplett, Donald, 6
TSC. *See* Tuberous sclerosis complex (TSC)
Tuberous sclerosis complex (TSC), 26
Twins, identical, 9, 22

Vests, weighted, 88
Visual schedules, 247, 252
Vitamin A, 154
Vitamin B_6 and magnesium, 150–151
Vitamin B_{12}, 156
Vitamin C, 153
Vitamin D
    alternative sources of, 149
    daily recommended and tolerable upper
        intake levels, 154
    role in neurological health, 148
    for strong bones, 148
Vitamin E, 154
Vocal outbursts, medications for, 136–137
Vocational rehabilitation (VR), 233, 234–235
VR. *See* Vocational rehabilitation (VR)

U

University Centers for Excellence in
        Developmental Disabilities
        (UCEDD) Education, Research,
        and Service, 190, 292
University of California, Davis, 37
University of California, Los Angeles
        (UCLA), 229
University of Michigan, 228
University of North Carolina, 97
University of Pennsylvania, 37
University of Wisconsin–Madison Waisman
        Center, 259
Unumb, Lorri Shealy, 214
Unumb, Ryan, 214
US Geological Survey, 199
US National Park Service, 199

W

Walking, talking with child while, 247
Wandering, 198
Washington Post, 237
Weighted vests, 88
Weight gain, 223
Whole exome sequencing, 27
Wieder, Serena, 79
Wood, Jennifer, 274
Words
    giant, 48
    pop-up, 47–48
World Autism Awareness Day, 277

X

X chromosomes, 21, 25, 282

V

Y

Vaccines, 13–14, 30–32
    nonstandard schedules for, 31–32
    thimerosal in, 14, 30–31
Valproate, 33
Valproic acid (Depakote), 125
VB. *See* Verbal behavior (VB)
Verbal behavior (VB), 78

Yoga, 164
Young adults with autism. *See also*
        Adolescence
    adult day program services for, 235
    dating by, 232
    driving by, 232
    job options for, 233–235
    living arrangements for, 232

Young adults with autism (*continued*)
    planning for the future for, 235–236
    postsecondary educational options for,
        231–233
    vocational rehabilitation for, 233, 234–235
You Will Dream New Dreams (Klein and
        Schive), 267

Z

Ziggurat Group, 118–119
Zonisamide (Zonegran), 125